Gray Areas

Publication of the Advanced Seminar Series
is made possible by generous support from
The Brown Foundation, Inc., of Houston, Texas.

**School of American Research
Advanced Seminar Series**

Richard M. Leventhal
General Editor

Gray Areas

Contributors

Philip B. Stafford
The Center on Aging and Community at the Indiana Institute on Disability and Community; the Evergreen Institute on Elder Environments, Inc.; and Department of Anthropology at Indiana University, Bloomington

Paula C. Carder
Kaiser Permanente/Center for Health Research, Portland, Oregon

J. Neil Henderson
Department of Health Promotion Sciences at the University of Oklahoma Health Sciences Center; Department of Anthropology; and the Department of Geriatric Medicine, University of Oklahoma

Dallas M. High
Department of Philosophy, University of Kentucky

Jeanie Kayser-Jones
School of Nursing and the Medical Anthropology Program, School of Medicine, University of California, San Francisco; and the UCSF/John A. Hartford Center of Geriatric Nursing Excellence

Graham D. Rowles
Department of Geography, Behavioral Science, and Nursing; Ph.D. Program in Gerontology; and the Sanders-Brown Center on Aging at the University of Kentucky

Margaret A. Perkinson
Departments of Anthropology and Psychology, Washington University, St. Louis

Joel S. Savishinsky
Department of Anthropology and The Gerontology Institute, Ithaca College

Renee Rose Shield
Center for Gerontology and Health Care, Brown University

Maria D. Vesperi
Department of Anthropology, New College of Florida

Gray Areas

Ethnographic Encounters with Nursing Home Culture

Edited by Philip B. Stafford

School of American Research Press
Santa Fe

James Currey
Oxford

School of American Research Press   **James Currey Ltd**

Post Office Box 2188   73 Botley Road
Santa Fe, New Mexico 87504-2188   Oxford OX2 0BS

Director: James F. Brooks
Executive Editor: Catherine Cocks
Manuscript Editor: Kate Talbot
Design and Production: Cynthia Welch
Indexer: Sylvia Coates
Printer: Maple-Vail Book Group

Library of Congress Cataloging-in-Publication Data:

Gray areas : ethnographic encounters with nursing home culture / edited
by Philip B. Stafford.— 1st ed.
   p. cm. — (School of American Research advanced seminar series)
Includes bibliographical references and index.
   ISBN 1-930618-30-1 (pa : alk. paper) – ISBN 1-930618-31-x (cl : alk.
paper)
   1. Nursing homes—Social aspects. 2. Ethnology. I. Stafford, Philip
B. II. Series.
   RA997.G68 2003
   362.1'6–dc21
                          2003007898

British Library Cataloguing in Publication Data:

Gray areas : ethnographic encounters with nursing home culture — (A School of American
Research advanced seminar)
1. Nursing homes—Anthropological aspects 2. Nursing home patients 3. Nursing home
patients—Family relationships 4. Nursing homes—Administration I. Stafford, Philip B.
II. School of American Research
362.1'6
ISBN 0-85255-938-0 (James Currey cloth) and ISBN 0-85255-937-2 (James Currey paper)

Contents

Figures and Tables

Acknowledgments

The editor would like to express his appreciation for the generous support provided by the School of American Research. This support was initiated with the hosting of the advanced seminar on nursing home ethnography in 1995 and patiently extended through numerous iterations of the manuscript. SAR Press Editor Catherine Cocks and copy editor Kate Talbot have been particularly helpful in the late stages of this project.

On behalf of the authors, the editor would like to also thank Jay Gubrium and Haim Hazan for their original contributions to the advanced seminar in Santa Fe. Their insights into broad questions of anthropological theory and ethnographic practice have certainly helped inform the character and spirit of this manuscript.

Gray Areas

Ethnographic Encounters with Nursing Home Culture

1

Introduction

Philip B. Stafford

I was a child of about seven years when my grandmother came to live with us. I remember her stroke, and I remember my mother referring to the "dropsy" that caused her to take to her bed. I have no recollection of any therapy, nor can I remember clearly whether she became bed-bound in one fell swoop or gradually. I learned a new word, though—*invalid*.

For the next seven years, "Nonny" remained in a sickroom we created for her just off our living room. The experience of caring for her was generally positive, although stressful for her daughter-in-law, my mother. The aggravation of my mother's back injury, from a childhood diving board accident, precipitated Nonny's entry into a nursing home about twenty miles away.

My memory of visiting Nonny in the nursing home is vivid but not extensive. (She resided there only a few months, as I recall.) I can picture a large ward, occupied by six or eight elderly women. I recall my sense that Nonny's bed was in the middle of a large room, with only curtains for privacy. My bodily memory recalls tension, some fear, and awkwardness about what was supposed to happen during visits. I can also recall the feeling that all of us, including Nonny, were trying to maintain our sense of humor through a difficult situation. We all laughed with Nonny as she cursed under her breath at the horrible din made by the dutiful ladies in the visiting kitchen band.

Thinking about that time, more than forty years ago, I realize that I have a good mental picture of the nursing home of the late 1950s and early 1960s. Nonny's residence retained features of an earlier era's old age home but was evolving into a medical-type facility, characterized by wards, hospital beds, and privacy curtains. I think that Nonny might have been satisfied with a definition of the facility as "a place for peaceful recuperation." However, the pandemonium of a visiting kitchen band certainly undercut this definition! Clearly, the ladies of the kitchen band were operating under a different understanding as to the meaning of that space.

Just what these spaces *are* has not been fully resolved to this date, yet they affect a significant number of people and constitute a major modern institution in the fullest sense of the term, comparable to other "total institutions" (Goffman 1961), such as schools, prisons, hospitals, bases, and camps.

Most agree that demographic pressures primarily caused the rapid development of the nursing home industry in the 1960s and 1970s. That a burgeoning number of elderly have been admitted to nursing homes since 1955 is *not* in question. As early as 1979, there was growing recognition that the nursing home population was expanding dramatically. Dunlop (1979:1) was reporting that between the years 1963 and 1973 the number of nursing home beds grew 117 percent, from 510,000 to 1.1 million. Whereas the institutionalization rate of the elderly was 2.9 percent in 1963, by 1973 it had risen to 5.2 percent! By 1985, as Foner (1994:9) reports, the number of nursing home beds had soared to 1.5 million. Although some have argued that the creation of the Medicare and Medicaid systems led to a quantum leap in nursing home admissions, Dunlop provides convincing evidence that the "growth in nursing home bed stock was more rapid before the implementation of Medicaid and Medicare than afterward" (1979:2). Indeed, the primary impetus for the growth of nursing home care was simply an increase in the population of the "oldest old," particularly unmarried females.

The demographic shift alone, however, does not explain the *form* that eldercare took in the final decades of the twentieth century. As early as 1978, these US institutions had evolved as a *medical model* of care, derived from the hospital template, unlike the path followed in some European countries, as noted by the Kanes:

> In the United States...institutional care of the elderly is con-
> ceived and financed as a health service even though institu-
> tional placement provides complete social context for an
> individual and obviously constitutes a rather dramatic inter-
> vention. (1978:913, cited in Johnson and Grant 1985:142)

As Dunlop (1979:100) notes, private, proprietary, *nonmedical* old age homes did well under the original Social Security laws, which gave elders funds to purchase care but prohibited payments to residents of public institutions. In 1940, 41 percent of institutionalized elderly lived in group quarters (boarding homes) rather than in nursing care homes. The 1950 Amendment to the Social Security Act, however, enabled public institutions (such as city and county homes) to receive direct assistance. With the 1954 amendment to the Hill-Burton Act (which originally provided funds for construction of hospitals), nonproprietary facilities providing skilled nursing care became eligible for construction and equipment grants. The term *nursing home* emerged, defined as a "facility for the accommodation of convalescents or other persons who are not acutely ill and not in need of hospital care, but who require skilled nursing care and related services" (cited in Dunlop 1979:104–105). Authorizing $10 million annually in 1954, $35 million annually by 1964, and $85 million by 1974, the federal government played a major role in providing the bricks and mortar for the development of this institution. By 1970, the proportion of institutionalized elderly in group quarters had fallen to 12 percent; the proportion of elderly in nursing homes had risen from 34 percent (in 1940) to 72 percent.

While the nonproprietary nursing home industry was benefiting from the Hill-Burton Act, the proprietary industry, through lobbying efforts of the American Nursing Home Association, began seeking governmental support. The Small Business Administration Loan Program gave guaranteed loans to small businesses, and the Federal Housing Administration (FHA) Section 232 program guaranteed mortgages offered by lenders (under very generous terms) for proprietary developers with a state-authorized certificate of need. The annual congressional appropriation reached $82 million by 1974. By the same year, with the help of Section 232, more than 110,000 nursing home beds were constructed. In 1972, Congress, through Medicaid, defined for reimbursement a level of care called *intermediate,* below the level of skilled care, for the following:

> Care and services to those individuals who do not require
> the care and treatment which a hospital or skilled nursing
> home is designed to provide, but who because of their mental or physical condition require care and services (above
> the level of room and board) which can be made available to
> them only through institutional services (cited in Dunlop
> 1979:119).

With this new definition of care, a critical threshold was crossed, and support for *custodial* care—such as bathing and feeding, care that might otherwise be provided in domestic environments—was relegated to the full-scale, medicalized, increasingly proprietary institutions.

Johnson and Grant, following the Kanes, also note that the medical model of care is dominant in the American nursing home. In this model, the individual patient's "problem" is a health problem (disease) that needs treatment, not a problem requiring a range of services (social, psychological, and physical). Assessment focuses on presence or absence of disease and extent of pathology, rather than on the ability to function or the degree of fitness.[1] Providers of service are arranged in a hierarchy, with the physician at the pinnacle, rather than organized into multidisciplinary teams that include informal supports. Treatment is technical and often specialized, instead of comprehensive and coordinated (Johnson and Grant 1985:141). Johnson and Grant aver that the reality of nursing home care is one in which nurses, not physicians, dominate. Nevertheless, the environment is predominantly medical in design, as well described by Kayser-Jones in this volume (Chapter 2).

MEDICINE AND POWER

We can go a step further and discuss those features of nursing home life that are not derived merely from the medical model but from the more general model of the *total institution,* as Erving Goffman (1961) and Jules Henry (1963) pointed out long ago. They noted that the imperative for *any* institution is to extend control over its "inmates" (a term also used by Carobeth Laird to refer to herself, in her 1979 memoir of nursing home life, discussed later in this introduction). Indeed, the parallels among different forms of institutional control are hard to deny:

> While one might find obvious differences across the categories, each of the institutions has an all-encompassing or totalizing character, creating a world for the inmates. The institutions break down barriers ordinarily separating three spheres of life—sleep, play and work. In normal society, the individual tends to sleep, work and play in different places, with different co-participants, under different authorities, and without an overall, imposed rational plan. Moreover, in the total institution, there is a basic split between the supervisors and the supervised. Information and communication across the boundary is closely monitored and rigidly controlled. (Goffman 1961:4)[2]

Whereas Goffman noted the strong parallels across the range of total institutions, Foucault traced the historical roots of the broader Western concept of disciplinary control, not through raw exercise of power but through more subtle devices of environmental design: "the certain concerted distribution of bodies, surfaces, lights and features" (1979:200). He documents two movements in Western society that culminated in several institutional forms:

1. The "clinical gaze" of the physician, viewing signs of disease at the body's surface, unmediated by the patient and categorized according to increasingly sophisticated taxonomies (Steven Katz 1996)

2. The institutional practices of seeing and categorizing associated with the state's public health response to the killing plagues of Europe in the Middle Ages

Foucault argues that the strategy of control by observation inspired the architect Jeremy Bentham to invent his Panopticon, which was, literally, a "machine for seeing." In Bentham's plan, any large group of people needing to be observed and corrected, whether prisoners, workers, students, or patients, would be housed in an especially suited architectural edifice in which the smallest number of supervisors could maintain a constant surveillance over the much larger group of inmates.

Is "being seen" an ongoing feature of life in the nursing home? There is no doubt. As foyers and vestibules have evolved in private homes to serve as transitional zones protecting private space from public intrusion, so, too, have nursing home lobbies separated patients from the outside world. Such separation could be seen as the benevolent protection of residents' privacy, except that, for individual patients, no such defensible space exists. Beyond the lobby, privacy evaporates. Resident doors cannot be locked and are often left open. Bathrooms are relatively public spaces. Beauty parlors, for shampooing and hair care, are often in full view of the public lobby. The nurses' station, a ubiquitous feature of nursing home design, serves as the modern equivalent of the Panopticon.[3]

The nursing home, in addition to being a medicalized environment, possesses many features that draw from the more fundamental spatial and material pattern of the total institution. By definition, this stands in stark contrast to another fundamental cultural pattern, that of home and the domestic environment. Ironically—and this point is major—although the nursing home has evolved as a medical institution, it strives to maintain a home-like character. Can home and hospital coexist in the same space? *This is, perhaps, the chief problematic of the nursing home—its inherent cultural ambiguity.*

THE NURSING HOME AS A CULTURAL SPACE UPHELD BY SOCIAL PROCESS

As a cultural space, the medical institution of the nursing home establishes codes for understanding and behavior. It is a crucible for the generation of meanings held and acted on by those who move through its halls. In the material sense, it concretizes assumptions about who lives there, works there, and visits there and what they are expected to do and be. Members of the culture—patients, workers, and visitors—see and interpret what's going on through an active process of "reading" the environment and the human interactions within it. The cultural space does not fully determine meaning, however. No single reading is correct, although one may be more powerful than another. Rather, the "text" of the nursing home provides a backdrop for interpretation, always subject to revision and multiple readings.

It is precisely this notion of the nursing home as a cultural space for interpretation that provided the framework for the advanced seminar "Nursing Home Ethnography," held in the fall of 1995 at The School of American Research in Santa Fe, New Mexico. The seminar brought together ten scholars who had conducted extensive ethnographic research in nursing home environments. This research spanned nearly thirty years and was conducted in facilities both large and small, in the United States and abroad. The scholars represented a variety of ethnographically oriented disciplines, including anthropology, nursing, sociology, gerontology, and human geography. Over the course of an intensely stimulating and enjoyable week, each scholar presented a paper for critique by the group. Toward the close of the week, the group attempted to synthesize its findings and derive general conclusions about the "state of the art" of nursing home ethnography, with attention to issues needing further research and issues of public policy and education. This volume provides an overview of the research.

With any interdisciplinary effort, it would be naive to assume that participants are completely consistent or uniform in the use of terms, methods, or a frame of reference. To be sure, these papers contain substantive differences in theoretical and methodological orientation. With respect to a procedural framework, the papers range from the more positivistic approach of Kayser-Jones to the interpretive approach of Vesperi. The former study involves a large, multi-site project and an attempt to understand the contributions of several variables in a kind of causal model of decision making in episodes of acute illness. The latter study focuses on the use of irony as a vehicle for understanding the nursing home experience of one individual, T. D., as voiced in the interaction between that individual and the ethnographer, with whom T. D. had a longstanding relationship. Even though the two papers are poles apart in scope (as research projects), they share an important methodological feature: an ethnographic respect for what people say is going on around them, conjoined with an attempt to understand what is being said in the context of a complex social environment.

Both approaches, although widely different in scope, demonstrate the contributions ethnography can make to our understanding of this major institution. As Vesperi notes in another publication, citing Sanjek (1990:14), ethnography's strong suit is validity, not reliability. The validity of her rendering of T. D.'s life is due, in great part, to the extensive narrative provided to the reader and to her own appearance on the stage as a co-participant in the production of the ethnographic text. In this regard, going beyond an *n of 1* becomes a huge undertaking, and substantiating the validity of the data becomes more difficult with the addition of each "cast member" to the rolls. Kayser-Jones's project and that of Rowles and High are truly ambitious because they attempt to listen carefully to many, many voices. Yet, the large studies of Kayser-Jones and Rowles and High are the "stuff" of which public policy is often made, so their use of ethnography is commendable.

Other features differentiate these papers from one another. Some use speech (narrative) as *representational,* and others, as *constitutive* of social life. When Rowles and High's informant, Eulalah, discusses her belief that her husband, Albert, was being overmedicated for Parkinson's symptoms, she is representing a particular belief about the nursing home pattern of care. When Vesperi's informant, T. D., relates the story of his life to the ethnographer, he is constituting that life in the context of the interaction between informant and ethnographer, with the nursing home as a backdrop for a dramaturgical event. What we conceive of as the truth value of each of these narrative forms varies considerably, depending on this distinction.

Given the range of differences across the papers, is it possible to derive a general model for understanding this institution we call "the nursing home"? I believe that it is and that this book makes a major contribution. Taken together, these papers offer a general picture of the nursing home as *a contested cultural space upheld by social processes.* The diagram in figure 1.1 provides an overview of this model, drawing from the heritage of Herbert Blumer at the micro level of social interaction and the legacy of Michel Foucault at the macro level of cultural epistemes.

In a traditional *normative sociological* model of the nursing home, the relevant domains (medical, home, and economic) would be seen

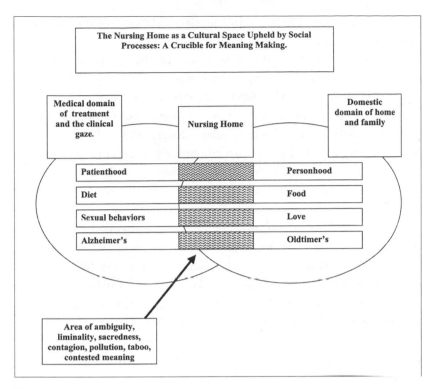

The Nursing Home as a Cultural Space Upheld by Social Processes: A Crucible for Meaning Making.

Medical domain of treatment and the clinical gaze.

Nursing Home

Domestic domain of home and family

Patienthood	Personhood
Diet	Food
Sexual behaviors	Love
Alzheimer's	Oldtimer's

Area of ambiguity, liminality, sacredness, contagion, pollution, taboo, contested meaning

FIGURE 1.1

The nursing home as a cultural space.

as structural influences.[4] The *economic* domain, for example, might be characterized by work patterns, regulatory forces, policies, demography, and so on. The *medical* domain of the "patients" might be traditionally described as age, income, ethnicity, and diagnosis. In a *cultural* model of the nursing home, however, the domains are not described as the concatenation of structural forces, variables, vectors, or influences, but as crucibles for meaning making. External structural notions such as political economy would play a role in a cultural model, but not as a set of structural forces as much as a set of ideologies that inform what people think and do. Economic forces, for example, would become categories of reference and meaning for the actors involved and would manifest themselves in cultural concepts such as units of care (commodification), bosses and workers (bureaucratization), and nurse/patient ratios (the rationalization of work).

Tim Diamond (1992), in *Making Gray Gold,* offers a similar observation, referring to the parallel "narratives" that describe the nursing home world from the inside (the front-line caregiver's perspective) and the outside (the capitalist system of labor and service commodification). Both narratives, however, are systems of meaning and reference for those who employ them and, as such, are cultural phenomena. The contribution of this particular volume is that it shows how daily life (meaning making) in the nursing home is inherently problematic because the participants carry out their existence in the contested cultural domains of hospital/home. The medical domain of treatment and clinical care, as believed in and acted on by the overseers, overlaps with the domestic domain of home and family, which shapes the orientation and mindset of the residents. In this setting, behavior can be, and is, oriented variously to both realms by those who live and work within it. Similarly, interpretation of others' behavior by participants (taking account of others) draws upon the same variety of domains.

As Anthony Wallace (1961) noted some time ago, there is no a priori necessity to assume that culture is a seamless entity, that the cognitive domains of participants are always completely overlapping, or that social life always proceeds in a framework of mutual understanding. He showed convincingly that nonoverlapping cognitive maps are probably the rule, not the exception, in social life. What is perhaps notable for so many of those who live and work within the nursing home is, however, the degree to which ambiguity, anomaly, and ambivalence are painfully ubiquitous in the setting. Basic features of human existence—age, the body, food, possessions, sexuality, sickness, dying, and personhood itself—become, in the nursing home, contested domains of meaning, taking on different valences, depending on which interpretive framework one relies on. When you enter the nursing home as a patient, you experience a loss of self, of personhood. Your walking becomes "ambulation." Your food becomes your "diet." Your eccentricities become your "behaviors." Your life becomes your "record."

Although Kayser-Jones does not discount the interpretive notion of culture, she sees it as but one way of discussing the constellation of forces that, together, influence medical decision making and, ultimately, treatment outcomes in the nursing home. Her discussion of physicians' attitudes towards patients with dementia exemplifies the attention given to cultural phenomena, while relating this to macro-level values celebrating youth and despising the incompetencies of old age. She then places these cultural texts within an analysis of the institution that notes the influence of more traditionally defined structural forces—staffing patterns, demography, and political-economic factors. In the end, she presents a bleak picture, noting how decisions made about acute care in the nursing home are all too often inconsistent with the needs and desires of patients, for whom she speaks as a very credible nurse-advocate.

Vesperi, in her chapter, makes use of ethnography to elucidate the nursing home experience, drawing upon critical theory for its approach (Clifford and Marcus 1986) and literary criticism for its substance (Burke 1969, 1973). This ethnographic text represents neither the simple, so-called objective observations of the anthropologist nor the unadulterated narrative of the informant. Rather, it is the joint construction of the researcher and the informant (Maria and T. D.), a conversation, conjoined with interpretation and commentary by both parties. Even though the text is the product of two interlocutors, its meaning arises from the presence of a third party—an audience. As readers, as external observers, we are the audience, and the meaning of the text becomes dramaturgical. In this sense, T. D.'s way of being in the world is a literary one. His life in the nursing home is constituted through the trope we call *irony*.

Employing Kenneth Burke's definition of *irony*, Vesperi, with T. D., calls out in us the sense of tragedy in which we are sympathetic with T. D.'s victim status yet powerless to prevent its inevitable course. This dramatic tension well describes the ambivalent status of the nursing home as a plane of meaning making in which the promise of medicine is in a constant struggle with fate.

Savishinsky's chapter gives us a direct view of the inevitable tensions and conflicts playing themselves out in the everyday world of the nursing home. As in prison, many tensions erupt into struggles around food. In the nursing home, the differential cultural meanings attached to food (as either medical diet or simply something that should taste good) provide a basis for miscommunication and misinterpretation of behaviors and feelings. Like Vesperi, Savishinsky clearly sees ethnography as the method by which we can document these little dramas of life, and of death. Indeed, the patient's refusal to accept food at the end of life becomes the dramatic vehicle for the final symbolic struggle of patients to define themselves in the context of this institution.

Stafford's work draws upon voices *outside* the nursing home to elucidate meanings within. He suggests that, if we are to know how patients and staff attempt to create *home* within the institution, it is important to look back to the home-based lives of persons living outside, following Gubrium's lead (Gubrium 1993). The meaning of home is, after all, not derived from the institution but from its opposite. For older people living in institutions, there is *always* a prior existence. Forgetting to take this diachronic perspective, we often view older residents only in their existential present.

Henderson's work brings another significant element into play: the creation of meanings useful for the marketing of the nursing home to an audience of consumers. He describes the rapid development of the dementia special care unit, purported to be the solution to the special needs, characteristics, and stresses associated with care for persons with Alzheimer's disease. He asks why these units persist in the face of sparse evidence to support their efficacy and points to the answer: understanding the disease as a cultural and not merely physiological phenomenon. In an argument that echoes Illich's (1978) observations on the "needs-creating" aspect of capitalism, Henderson shows how the outward character of special care has evolved in response to market demand.

In addition to being a domain of meaning making, as addressed by Kayser-Jones, Vesperi, Savishinsky, Stafford, and Henderson, the nursing home is a domain for relationship making, well described by Rowles and High, Shield, and Perkinson. The authors in the second section remind us that it is unfair to stereotype nursing homes as uniformly oppressive of the residents and workers. Indeed, the authors paint a picture of the institution as a diverse constellation of forces, ideologies, and players. There are, to be sure, casualties. There are also lively, spirited human beings who are able to flourish, adapt, and find meaning in new relationships, new hobbies, and new roles. Family members unburdened by exhausting home care responsibilities can find a new freedom to interact with a loved one in a context divorced from awkward dependencies.

Shield reports that family members, after they achieve some clarification of their potential role, can assume important and satisfying advocacy responsibilities on behalf of an institutionalized family member. Likewise, frontline workers positively contribute to the quality of care and the quality of life within the nursing home when given empowerment in their jobs and support for developing enduring relationships with patients and fellow workers. Shield adds an important reflexivity to her work by acknowledging her own role as caregiver for her mother. She incorporates the meanings of this experience into her research and lends an additional layer of validity, akin to that of Vesperi's work with her institutionalized uncle.

Rowles and High used extensive participant-observation research, along with a quantitative analysis of extensive interview material, to demonstrate beyond a doubt that, counter to the myth, family members play a significant role in decision making in nursing homes. This was a consistent finding across several diverse facilities. Moreover, they document that families use various strategies of involvement to exert their influence over the facility or over their institutionalized relative. Some are, of course, more positive than others or provide more or less control for the patient. Nevertheless, family ties remain strong and often consistent with previous lifelong styles. They affirm the often noted fact that a single, nominated, family caregiver mediates family relationships with dependent elders.

Perkinson's chapter represents the movement from basic to applied research in this significant modern institution and extends the focus on family caregiving roles. Indeed, providing support for families to clarify their roles vis-à-vis the nursing home is precisely the focus of Perkinson's work. She uses ethnography to elucidate the understandings and interpretations that family and staff bring to bear on the subject of family roles and then transforms that data into a proposal for applied research. Respecting the multiple perspectives on care, she demonstrates a program in which focus groups assist families in arriving at decisions that preserve the health and promote the autonomy of a loved one who may not retain a decision-making capacity. This multiple perspectives approach echoes the observation of most ethnographers in this collection and reaffirms the value of an ethnography that respects diverse views and voices. One recalls, here, the evocative phrase of Gubrium (1991), who has described these systems as a "mosaic of care." Perkinson adds that redoubling the effort to understand and involve family members may transform the institution and, presumably, diminish the power of the medical model to dominate the bodies of those for whom we care.

With respect to both cultural meanings and relationships, it is the nursing home as contested cultural domain that pulls these papers together into a whole. Savishinsky discusses the implications of viewing food as either diet (medical) or comestible (domestic) and the cultural tension that emerges from contrasting interpretations. Rowles and High, Shield, Perkinson, and Kayser-Jones document the tensions attendant upon differential interpretations of patienthood and professional and family caregiver roles—interpretations derived from alternative cultural models of the institution. Vesperi amply documents the struggle of one individual to define self through narrative, a self cut off from its social and historical moorings.

It is no coincidence that another observer of the nursing home, Carobeth Laird, titled her nursing home memoir *Limbo*. Being betwixt and between, in limbo, in the gray areas of meaning, defines the daily existence of many players in this scene—residents, patients, workers, and visitors. That people, particularly old people (and particularly under-rewarded, hardworking single women) struggle to keep their personhood intact in the face of these challenges is great testimony to the strength and resilience of the human spirit. That those who live and work within this setting are subject to these challenges does not imply that they are uniformly overwhelmed. Most people make the best of a bad situation and find a middle ground of meaning. The tactic of irony, so well described by Vesperi and evoked by T. D., is one significant way to do this. To deal with the ambiguities of this scene, patients, workers, and family members employ other adaptive strategies. They are well described by the scholars in this volume, who have listened closely to the voices of those within. To report that people adapt, however, is not to eschew the goal of reform. Indeed, the concept of contested cultural domains can provide a framework for an entire edifice of public policy and practice recommendations relating to the reward system, worker education, patient advocacy, hierarchies of power, conflict mediation, architectural design, and other aspects of nursing home reform.

THE NURSING HOME AS DOUBLE BURIAL

Robert Hertz (1960, orig. 1928) noted some time ago that death and dying are only partially understood as biological events. An anthropology of death and dying is, as he suggested, a study of rites of passage—the cultural beliefs and practices surrounding the movement of people out of the social world of the living. For Hertz, the practice of double burial was especially interesting, for it draws attention to social death and the means by which customs enable society to reestablish order following the loss of its members. Specifically, *double burial* is the practice of burying a corpse at death and later reburying it, after its flesh has rotted away to reveal a clean skeleton. The time following the "first" death is, for the survivors and the "dead," a period of disruption, mourning, and distress. As such, the mourners *and* the nursing home resident are subject to a host of taboos designed to isolate them and prevent their intrusion into the world of the living. Only after the second burial, which might be weeks, months, or even years after the first, are the mourners and the deceased released from their liminal state and allowed to reenter their respective worlds (of the living and of the dead).

Hertz (1960:85) noted insightfully that rites of passage (into death) sometimes begin while the individual decrepit elder is still (biologically) alive, thus highlighting the insignificance of the biological event in the face of the more important social process.

Is admission to a nursing home the first burial? This question was posed to seminar participants by Neil Henderson, citing Otto von Mering's insights into this concept. Clearly, the dread with which many American elders view the nursing home far outweighs the physical dangers that might be associated with this setting. Many times have I heard elders proclaim that entry is a fate worse than death. Death itself is feared less than a long, lingering stay in the nursing home. Forget that a nursing home stay can, in the end, be meaningful and, for many, preferable to "being a burden on the children." The institution is feared. Those who work within have low status in our society. Those who live within endure a social death, cut off in many ways from the outside world, as Rowles and High demonstrate.

From whence does this dread arise? Perhaps from the very ambivalence and ambiguity pervading this institution so fully. Being neither home nor hospital but claiming to be both, the institution draws meaning from polar spheres of experience. A preface to death yet straining toward life, the institution struggles to define itself within a culture that values a quick death in old age as the "good" death (what gerontologists call "squaring the curve"). Trying to balance domestic ideals and medical mastery, the institution too often succeeds at neither. The nursing home maintains an iffy status as a transitional object mediating life and death, here and there, self and not self, presence and absence. Yet, the nursing home does not play this mediative role well, perhaps because this role is not well understood. The *taboos* associated with the liminal or marginal status of the nursing home are present, but a paucity of liminal *rites*, prescriptions, and proscriptions are assigned to those who move within this state. Absent also from the scene is any intense bond among the "initiates," called *communitas* by Turner and noted for the nursing home by Shield (1988:207–208) and Hornum (1995:153).

The nursing home has the potential to assist people, ceremonially, with movement from life to nonlife. However, it rarely fulfills this mission because it is duty-bound, as well, to fulfill the dictates of the medical model and keep people alive at all costs. In the cultural order, the hospital exists as a clear domain. The home exists as a clear domain. The nursing home, caught in the middle, dwells in an unending no-man's land, a gray area in our society.[5]

THE NURSING HOME AS A REAL-WORLD EXPERIENCE

To anyone who has gone through the trauma of admitting an elderly family member or friend to a nursing home, the preceding argument might sound unnecessarily harsh. Generalizing blithely about the social function of institutionalization in Western society does not acknowledge the intensely personal, often painful and extended struggle of families and patients trying to define the meaning of institutionalization for themselves. Additionally, and this is important, institutionalization of frail elders is not uniformly a negative experience, as these papers show. The exhausted spouse who has cared night and day for a belligerent Alzheimer's patient at home may be grateful that her society has provided a setting for the patient, which relieves her from the literally killing burdens of care. Moreover, as Rowles and High and Perkinson clearly demonstrate, the great majority of family members stay connected with their loved ones and do not abandon their elders, as the stereotypes would suggest. Those family members who resort, in the end, to admitting a loved one to a facility, as well as those dedicated persons who work within such facilities, *must* operate on the premise that some good is being accomplished. Otherwise, such facilities could not exist.

Of course, that is the point. An anthropological perspective on nursing homes is as much about how people define what they are doing as necessary as it is about whether these facilities should exist. This distinction, which clarifies the differences between understanding and judgment, goes to the heart of intellectual discourse today. Postmodernists might argue that judgment is never justified because the so-called objective observer is merely engaging in the same act of self-persuasion as the observed other, legitimated perhaps by the power attributed to scientific knowledge, but delusional nonetheless. Others might argue that, although truth may be contingent, we *must* act to improve the human condition, which echoes Tylor's (1904) notion of anthropology as the reformer's science.

In the seminar, many lively discussions were held about whether the nursing home is an inevitable consequence of Western society and/or whether an anthropology of the institution can be reformist in any sense. Interestingly, as the academy discusses whether this institution we gloss as "the nursing home" is inevitable, rapid changes going on suggest, on the face of it, that the institution may be evolving. Assisted living, residential care, cluster housing, adult foster care—these may be the nursing homes of the future. To address these rapid changes, it was deemed important to include an additional chapter to extend the discussion beyond the framework of the traditional nursing home. In one of the first ethnographic studies of assisted living, Paula Carder reveals that the same struggle for meaning occupies the time and attention of staff and residents of this new form of living. Yet, irony raises its head again as we learn that even though residents (not "patients") find a ready audience for their expressions of domesticity (oppressed in the nursing home), their attempts to define medical needs are, conversely, oppressed in the assisted living environment.

Carder describes a resident who sought the installation of a raised toilet seat for her apartment and was told, "No, we're a social model, not a medical model, so we don't provide things like that because not everyone needs it." Despite the irony of so-called progress, it does appear that certain elements of the assisted living model do reflect a step toward greater agency for individuals and increased efforts to promote critical reflection and interpretation of cultural meanings as an ongoing, deliberative process of care and support, namely, the concept of the Negotiated Service Agreement.

Stepping beyond the walls of the institutions to the rapidly growing area of home care, it should be noted that the issue of contested meanings of care is very real in this environment as well. In an ethnographic study of Taiwanese home care workers, Wang (2002) demonstrates the efforts of home care clients to bend the cultural meanings of care their way by establishing fictive filial relationships with the female caregivers. These attempts to make formal caregivers into daughters, however, undercut the disciplinary rules of professionalism under which the caregivers are pressured to operate, rules that promote distance from, instead of intimacy with, one's clients. Hence, the women who care are engrossed in an ongoing effort to maintain their personal identity and integrity in the face of the competing ideologies of home and hospital. Moreover, although the achievement of filial intimacy might best meet the needs of elderly clients, this gendered asset is debased in the formal economy, where care is commodified.

Another trend worth pointing out, as Rowles and High suggest, is a growing "culture change" movement within the field of long-term care, led by innovators such as William Thomas, Rose Marie Fagan, and other members of the Pioneer Network. This movement seems to be embedded in a fuller understanding of the concept of culture, yet we should caution against the presumption that culture is an imposed, not an emergent, phenomenon. As Carder notes in her chapter on assisted living, it takes more than the imposition of a new lexicon to foster real change. William Thomas would agree (personal communication) and feels that some institutions have taken on the trappings of his Eden Alternative model (pets, plants, and the like) without fundamentally questioning the presumptions of care and basic human needs.

CONCLUSION: THE ROLE OF ETHNOGRAPHY
IN LONG-TERM CARE

The following chapters enable us to enter into the interpretive process by which patients, residents, staff, family members, and volunteers make meaning and build relationships within the context of long-term care. This is a primary contribution of this work. Moreover, the ethnographers reveal themselves to us as partners in that process of meaning making and interpretation. The increasing openness and transparency of ethnography to the reader reminds one of those modern industrial buildings with glass surrounds that reveal to the passerby the inner workings of the machine. The widespread use of quoted speech, as well as the use of first-person interpretation by the authors, enables the reading audience to be convinced, or not, in the fresh air of an open and democratic discourse. In the end, I would argue that interpretation can provide as solid a base as causal explanation for the making of social policy.

This postmodern premise that what we are, what we know, is not a fact but only an argument has chased some scholars from the academy to the Panglossian garden. The premise can certainly leave one immobilized, even stunned. Bryan Green (1993), for example, argues convincingly that the field of gerontology does not simply *study* old age—it *creates* old age. Likewise, many have argued that anthropology could not exist without its "other," produced by its own disciplinary workings. Indeed, in the seminar, Hazan (2002) drew close parallels between anthropology and gerontology with regard to the creation of their respective "others." For anthropology, the "other" is the exotic tribe, the field, the informant. For gerontology, the "other" is the elder, the elderly, the aged.

A critical anthropology, a critical gerontology, would be concerned with the mode by which each discipline creates its object of study. To its credit, anthropology has paid attention to this issue of late, and this volume extends that effort. In addition, this work provides compelling insights into the quotidian workings of an institution that is, in many ways, hidden from view, albeit exposed to bright light from time to time in the guise of scandal and sensationalism.[6] Clearly, another volume is needed, however, and should build on this work to understand its implications for policy, regulation, architectural design, training, personnel supports, and program development—but this is an excellent start.

Notes

1. The point is probably exaggerated. In the United States, national nursing home regulations derived from the Omnibus Budget Reconciliation Act of 1987 now call for extensive admission assessments (the minimum data set) that do address functional and psycho-social health.

2. Renee Rose Shield (1988:101ff.) discusses the limitations of Goffman's model for the understanding of nursing homes. She argues that many elements of the total institution are present in nursing homes but that there are also many differences. The patient population is heterogeneous, and bureaucratic practices and ideologies are based on care motives as opposed to rehabilitation and release. Staff goals are not monolithic but, at times, even in competition with one another.

3. Residents take advantage of these opportunities as well, to extend control over their environment. Sites where they can observe the goings-on are valuable to them, too. However, their desire to loiter at the nurses' station or other centers of power is sometimes seen as obtrusive rather than as an adaptive strategy.

4. Thomas P. Wilson (1970:59ff.) provided an early and very clear definition of normative sociology, with its emphasis on rule-governed behaviors and deductive explanation. He posed this against approaches that view social interaction as an interpretive, meaning-making process wherein rules are emergent, subject to reinterpretation, and meaning is typically context-dependent or indexical (1970:66ff.).

5. In her chapter, Vesperi also cites the Beckettian themes and notes that real humans can transcend these dilemmas and make effective passage from life to death. We are not always trapped in the unresolvable dilemmas that can exist forever in a play.

6. In another article, Vesperi (1987) notes that the public discourse around long-term care reverberates between "no attention" and "scandal, with calls for reform." I might add that this is not unlike what we see with other issues, such as prison conditions and animal rights. There is very little ongoing, serious dialog in the media about long-term care.

2

The Treatment of Acute Illness in Nursing Homes

The Environmental Context of Decision Making

Jeanie Kayser-Jones

It seems not only fitting but also necessary to begin a paper on the cultural context of decision making in nursing homes with an excerpt from a classic ethnography, *Culture Against Man* (Henry 1963). A review published in *The New York Sunday Herald Tribune* states the following about this book:

> Once upon a rare while a book appears that is so cogently conceived and so brilliantly executed as to command that any future work on the subject take this book seriously into account or be diminished by the failure to do so.

It is noteworthy that the circumstances Henry described so vividly in 1963 are similar to conditions in many nursing homes today. He writes powerfully and movingly about the plight of the elderly in three hospitals for the aged—the quiet and stillness of the institutions, the hopefulness of the residents despite inattention to their needs, their constant hunger, and their strategies for coping with an inadequate amount of food.

This paper deals with the treatment of acute illness in nursing homes. Because physicians are the key figures in making treatment decisions, I shall select a few lines about their noticeable absence in nursing homes, illustrating the similarity between conditions in nursing homes in the 1960s and today. In describing Muni San, a large public hospital for the elderly, Henry says this:

> In Muni San there is a sense of responsibility: somewhere among its vast reaches there are doctors who, though never encountered by our researchers, must exist, for patients have seen them, and doctors prescribe for them. Muni San furnishes medicines and dresses injuries; it provides diets for diabetics, and if they become gangrenous, they receive surgery. (1963:406–407)

While conducting research in nursing homes (thirty years after Henry), I, too, have noted the absence of physicians, even when residents become acutely ill and need the on-site attention of a physician. In most nursing homes today, physicians are nearly invisible. I am currently studying two proprietary nursing homes. Each has a medical director. During the past eighteen months of data collection (1994–95), I have not seen the medical directors of these two facilities, despite my being in the nursing homes weekly, during both daytime and evening hours.

This paper is not a condemnation of physicians or nursing staff. Sometimes physicians visit their patients often, even daily, knowing that Medicaid will not reimburse them. Many nurses work extremely hard at substandard salaries, attempting to provide the necessary care. This chapter is a description and analysis of

- how treatment decisions are made in nursing homes when elderly residents become acutely ill; and

- how multiple factors, which I call the *cultural context of decision making,* influence the decision-making process

AN AGING POPULATION AND NURSING HOME CARE

Care of the elderly is one of the most important and perhaps controversial issues in health care today. The increase in the number and proportion of older people throughout the world is a major success story of the latter part of the twentieth century. In 1990, nearly 32 million Americans were sixty-five years and older; it is projected that by the year 2030, this number will double, and 64 million people will be over the age of sixty-five (Zedlewski and McBride 1992).

A relatively recent but very important demographic trend is that more people are living to very old age, eight-five years and older. In 1985, the United Nations estimated that nine countries (China, India, the United States, the Soviet Union, Japan, Brazil, Indonesia, the Federal Republic of Germany, and Italy) had more than 1 million people eighty years of age and older. The country with the most octogenarians was the United States, with 6,198,000 (US Department of Commerce Bureau of the Census 1987).

Not surprisingly, the use of health care services increases with age. There has been growing concern about the rapidly escalating cost of health care, and some believe that a disproportionate amount of health care dollars is being spent on the care of the elderly. Because of the increasing cost of health care, federal and state governments have been experimenting for several years with different approaches to financing health care. In 1983, Congress enacted Title Six of the Social Security Amendment, which provides for prospective payment to general hospitals for Medicare patients. Under this system, patients are placed into categories referred to as Diagnosis-Related Groups (DRGs), and hospitals receive a fixed payment for a given diagnosis (for example, a flat fee for a heart attack without complications) (Kapp 1984). Fixed payment serves as an incentive for hospitals to discharge elderly patients as quickly as possible. In earlier years, nursing homes typically admitted people with chronic conditions, but now they admit elderly people in a sub-acute condition after a short hospital stay. This practice will undoubtedly continue as insurers look for alternatives to high-cost hospital care (Burton 1994). Many nursing homes, however, do not have the professional staff and resources (such as laboratory, X-ray, and pharmacy services) to provide sub-acute care. Residents in a sub-acute or chronic condition can, and often do, become acutely ill. At this time, critical life and death treatment decisions are made, the subject of this paper.

THE STUDY

The treatment of acute illness of nursing home residents is a huge problem that concerns health care providers, the elderly, and their families. A large body of literature on the ethical, legal, and economic issues must be considered. The factors influencing treatment, however, have not been systematically investigated.

The cumulative effect of an aging population, the availability of sophisticated biomedical technology, and the escalating cost of health care present our society with a challenge in the fair distribution of resources. As the demand for health care continues to grow, so does the controversy over what percentage of the gross national product should be spent on health. Some say that choices will have to be made (Callahan 1987). These concerns prompted me to develop a research project to investigate the factors that influence the decision-making process involved when elderly nursing home residents acquire an acute illness.

THE METHOD

The data presented here are part of a larger study that investigated the social-cultural factors and other circumstances influencing the decision-making process in the evaluation and treatment of acute illness in nursing homes (see Kayser-Jones 1990a, 1991, 1995; Kayser-Jones and Kapp 1989; Wiener and Kayser-Jones 1989, 1990). Participant observation, in-depth interviews with physicians, nursing staff, nursing home residents, and family members (100 in each category), and event analysis were used to gather data.

The research was conducted from 1985 to 1990 in three West Coast nursing homes, including a 1,200-bed, government-owned, long-term care facility (Facility A) and two proprietary nursing homes (Facility B, with 135 beds, and Facility C, with 182 beds). About one-third of the data was gathered in each setting. Data were gathered by the author, a project director, and six research assistants (medical and graduate nursing and sociology students), two in each facility. Data collection proceeded in two stages: an intensive, three-month period of participant observation, followed by a twelve-month period during which participant observation continued, but in-depth interviews and event analysis were the primary focus.

The data presented in this paper were obtained primarily through *event analysis,* a data collection strategy used to describe in detail what occurred when a resident became acutely ill. Data on acute-illness episodes were collected at the rate of six per month in each of the three facilities over a twelve-month period for a total of 216 cases. In each of the three nursing homes, we followed seventy to seventy-two residents who became acutely ill. Our goal was to obtain detailed descriptive data of each acute-illness episode to characterize and explain the unique features of the event with an aim toward bringing together diverse information from many cases into a clear and unified interpretation (Pelto 1970). An *acute illness* was defined as a change in the individual's health associated with specific signs and symptoms of recent onset.

Because our goal was to investigate the decision-making process in the evaluation and treatment of acute illness in nursing homes, we did not follow residents to the acute hospital to observe and record the treatment they received there. When they returned to the nursing home, however, data describing their treatment in the hospital were obtained from the hospital discharge summary, which accompanied them on their return to the nursing home.

We obtained much of the data firsthand. When this was not possible, we obtained data retrospectively through informal interviews with doctors, nursing staff, patients, and their family and friends and from written sources, such as doctors' orders and progress notes, nurses' notes, and laboratory and X-ray reports.

Initially, we planned to observe and record physicians' interactions with residents and their families when an acute illness occurred. Unfortunately, this was often impossible. Federal regulations require that physicians visit their nursing home residents only once a month. Reimbursement for additional visits is difficult to obtain and entails extensive paperwork on the part of the physician. We found that often, when residents became acutely ill, physicians were notified and treatment options were discussed by telephone with the family and nursing staff.

Purposive sampling, that is, selecting participants according to the needs of the study (Morse 1989:119), was used to obtain a representative sample of the various types of acute illnesses found in each nursing home. Purposive sampling is characterized by the use of judgment and operates on the belief that the investigator's knowledge and expertise can be used to select the population to be included in the sample. We included residents who varied along significant variables, such as marital, mental, and physical status, age, ethnicity, and diagnosis. For example, residents who were relatively young (65–79 years) and some who were very old (80–112 years), residents who were mentally alert and some who had severe cognitive impairment, and residents who reflected the ethnic composition of the research settings were inducted into the study.

Forty percent of the people who acquired an acute illness were male, and 60 percent were female. Interestingly, 20 percent (forty-two residents) were ninety years of age and over; 53 percent were eighty years and older. The mean age was 78.9 years. As would be expected among people of this age, 50 percent were widowed, 23 percent were married, 12 percent divorced, and 15 percent single (never married). A large proportion (77 percent) had living relatives, that is, a spouse, son, daughter, grandchild, niece, nephew, brother, or sister.

It would have been difficult, and in many cases impossible, to administer a mental status questionnaire to an acutely ill resident, so we asked the nurse in charge for an evaluation of the resident's mental status. The majority, 72 percent, were moderately to severely impaired cognitively.

The Katz Activities of Daily Living (ADL) was used to assess the functional status of residents who became acutely ill (Katz et al. 1963). This instrument is an evaluation of the functional independence or dependence of people in bathing, dressing, going to the toilet, transferring from bed to chair, and feeding. The higher the score, the greater the person's dependency. A functionally independent person, for example, would receive a score of 6, and a totally dependent person would receive a score of 18. On the whole, those who became acutely ill were very dependent; 81 percent received a score of 15 to 18 (severe functional impairment).

Respiratory and urinary tract infections are among the most commonly occurring acute illnesses in nursing homes. However, because no prospective study on the treatment of acute illness in nursing homes had been conducted, we chose to include the full range of possible acute illnesses, including diseases of the circulatory, digestive, genitourinary, and respiratory systems. (See Kayser-Jones, Wiener, and Barbaccia 1989 for a full description of categorization of acute-illness episodes by disease classification and primary symptom.)

DATA ANALYSIS

Data collected for each acute-illness episode were analyzed by the principal investigator (the author), the project director (a medical sociologist), and a physician/geriatrician with long-standing experience in caring for nursing home residents.

Data collection and analysis took place simultaneously. Throughout the data collection period, the principal investigator and the project director wrote *theoretical memos* (notes containing the results of inductive thinking). These memos helped to identify emerging themes and their relationship to one another. Furthermore, they served as an ongoing record of analytical insights and helped to focus future observations.

During data collection, the principal investigator, the project director, and the physician read the cases individually and met periodically to discuss findings. When collecting data and analyzing cases, we discovered patterns and developed categories. In some cases, for example, we observed that "appropriate treatment" was given and in other cases, only "partial treatment." When data collection was completed, the principal investigator, the project director, and the research team physician again read each case individually. We discussed each case in detail and developed a set of outcome categories. After thoroughly discussing and refining these categories, we determined eight final outcome categories:

1. Appropriate treatment
2. Partial or inadequate diagnosis or treatment
3. Appropriate management of the problem
4. Delay in approaching the problem or in beginning treatment
5. Drug of choice not given
6. Problems in monitoring care
7. Other
8. No treatment

Finally, we again read each acute-illness episode. Based on our total immersion in the field and our familiarity with the data, we agreed on the case's category.

THE FINDINGS

Of the 215 residents followed, 150 (60 percent) fell into a category we called *appropriate treatment* (treatment that would be considered the standard of care for a specific diagnosis). Many residents in this category were treated promptly and efficiently. Sometimes, though, the treatment of the acute illness was assessed as being appropriate, but problems occurred before the resident was treated. Some residents were treated appropriately but only because other factors, such as the presence of a family member, influenced the decision-making process.

For example, an eighty-eight-year-old woman with severe mental impairment developed pneumonia. Although cognitively impaired, she was socially active, and the nursing staff and her family felt that she had a good quality of life. Her physician did not want to treat her, saying that she was too demented. She was treated, but only because her granddaughter, who happened to be the bookkeeper in the nursing home, insisted on her transfer to an acute hospital for treatment.

In other cases, residents were treated because the physician had a close relationship with the resident and insisted on treatment despite the family's wishes. Mr. Zimmerman, for example, was a seventy-five-year-old, mentally alert man with periods of slight confusion. He had Parkinson's disease. Due to dysphagia (difficulty swallowing), a gastrostomy tube was inserted into his stomach to provide him with fluid and nutrition.

Mr. Zimmerman developed pneumonia, and the gastrostomy tube accidentally came out of his stomach. His wife did not want the tube replaced, and she did not want him transferred to the acute hospital for treatment. "He's suffered enough," she said. An interview with the granddaughter, who had lived with her grandparents for six years, revealed that their marriage was rocky and they led separate lives.

Mr. Zimmerman wanted the tube replaced, but he poignantly remarked to the nurse, "I know that I'm a terrible burden to my wife." The physician knew Mr. Zimmerman (a talented pianist) well because for years he had played the organ in the hospital chapel as a volunteer. On Mr. Zimmerman's admission to the acute hospital, the physician requested a meeting with the ethics committee. A decision was made to start intravenous (IV) antibiotics to treat Mr. Zimmerman's pneumonia. The gastrostomy tube was not reinserted, and he died a few days later. "It was a difficult case," the physician sighed. "I think he just gave up."

Twenty-one residents (8 percent) were placed in a category called *partial or inadequate diagnosis or treatment of acute illness.* The most dramatic case in this category was an eighty-two-year-old woman who was mentally impaired but socially intact. She developed a fever and a sore throat and was diagnosed as having parotitis (an acute inflammation of the parotid gland). Her physician ordered a medication to reduce her fever and an oral antibiotic. Because of severe throat pain, the resident was unable to swallow the medications. She was also unable to take any food or liquid by mouth. Six days after the onset of the symptoms, the doctor ordered an antibiotic by injection. No IV fluids were ordered, however. The woman became increasingly dehydrated and congested. Seven days after the infection began, she died (Kayser-Jones and Kapp 1989).

Eighteen residents (7 percent) fell into the third category—*appropriate management of the problem*—for example, residents who developed a fever. The doctor ordered aspirin, the temperature was resolved, but diagnostic procedures were not ordered.

Sixteen residents (6 percent) were placed in the fourth category, *delay in approaching the problem or in beginning treatment.* These residents had symptoms for many days before the problem was investigated, or laboratory studies were ordered, but medication was not ordered until several days later.

A seventy-year-old woman who had a history of urinary tract infections developed a fever of 101 degrees Fahrenheit. She also complained of burning during urination. The doctor was notified. He immediately ordered that a specimen of her urine be sent to the laboratory for a culture and sensitivity. It was a holiday weekend, however, and the urine specimen was not sent until three days later. Seven days later, the woman was complaining of chills and pain in her lower abdomen. An on-call doctor was notified. He ordered irrigation of her urinary catheter and suggested that the nursing staff "force fluids." Medication for the infection was not started until *ten* days after the symptoms began.

Seven residents (3 percent) fell into the fifth category, *drug of choice not given*. This category most commonly included residents who were not given the antibiotic of choice when they developed an acute infection. An eighty-one-year-old Chinese woman had a fever of 102.4 degrees Fahrenheit. She had ulcers with necrotic areas on the heels of both feet. When the physician was notified, he ordered aspirin for the fever and penicillin, intramuscularly. Data analysis indicated that this woman had developed sepsis due to microbial entry at the site of the ulcers on her feet. Penicillin was not an appropriate drug, given the severity of the infection.

Thirteen residents (5 percent) were placed in the sixth category, *problems in monitoring care*. Residents were treated, but there were difficulties in monitoring their condition and in taking appropriate action before, during, or after the acute-illness episode. An eighty-one-year-old, mentally alert, ambulatory woman suddenly began falling. She fell four times in two weeks. The nursing staff called her physician eleven times during that two-week period to report that the woman had fallen, was depressed, and had a decreased appetite and low back pain. The doctor returned the calls on three occasions and promised to visit but did not do so until two weeks after the symptoms were first reported. He then had her transferred to an acute hospital, where she was found to be in acute renal failure.

Nine residents (4 percent) fell into a miscellaneous category we called *other*. Usually, the patient had more than one acute problem. One problem was treated and resolved, but an evaluation of the other problem was not done because of the presence of cognitive or behavioral problems. These residents were often labeled "uncooperative."

Eighteen residents (7 percent) were placed in the category of *no treatment*. This group included a ninety-three-year-old man who refused treatment for acute leukemia and eight residents who were in the terminal phase of an illness such as cancer or end-stage renal disease.

When analyzing the cases involving residents who were not treated, we took into account many factors, such as their physical and mental status, their prognosis, their personal wishes and those of their family, and (some feel) the cost of care. After considering all these factors, however, we concluded that nine residents who could have been treated were not. Mr. R was an alert ninety-four-year-old man with moderate-to-severe confusion. He could not walk but moved about independently in a wheelchair. When Mr. R developed a fever, the doctor was called. The doctor said that he had pneumonia and ordered medication for the fever, an oral antibiotic, and oxygen by nasal prongs. He did not order a chest X-ray. The following day, Mr. R was not responding, and he could not swallow. The doctor gave a telephone order to "stop all oral medications." Although the nurses knew that Mr. R could not swallow, they did not ask the doctor whether he wanted the medications and fluid given intravenously, and he left no other orders.

Mr. R was a widower and had no children. He did, however, have a niece, who visited frequently. Five days after the onset of the fever, she became concerned because her uncle was not receiving any treatment. She called the doctor and angrily insisted that her uncle be given IV fluids. Shortly after the IV fluids were started, Mr. R died. The niece was angry with the physician and felt that her uncle had been treated poorly. She acknowledged that he was cognitively impaired but stated, "He's still a person, and he should have been given some kind of care." Significantly, Mr. R was in the nursing home for one year. The niece made lengthy visits to her uncle almost daily, but she had never met the physician (Kayser-Jones 1995).

Many residents in this study (60 percent) were treated appropriately and promptly when an acute illness occurred, but as already mentioned, some residents were treated only because an attentive family member insisted on treatment. In about one-third (30 percent) of the cases, either the acutely ill residents were not treated, or there were problems in the treatment and management of their acute illness. The partial or inadequate diagnosis and treatment, the delay in beginning treatment, the lack of monitoring treatment, and the use of inappropriate medications to treat acute infections are especially significant. As mentioned above, 53 percent of the residents were eighty years of age and older. Many were frail and therefore extremely vulnerable when they became acutely ill. Some suffered unnecessarily.

THE THEORETICAL FRAMEWORK—
ENVIRONMENTAL THEORY

When conducting research in nursing homes, we must examine the research problem within the environmental context of the nursing home setting. Building on the work of theorists in the field of environment and aging (Kahana 1982; Lawton and Nahemow 1973; Lawton 1975; Moos 1980; Moos and Lemke 1985), I have developed a conceptual model to illustrate how environmental factors affect the care of nursing home residents (Kayser-Jones 1992, 1993). Using a slight modification of this model, I shall describe and analyze how multiple internal (micro) and external (macro) factors, which I call the *environmental context of decision making*, influenced the decision-making process when residents became acutely ill (fig. 2.1).

Most studies have focused on four major features of the environment:

1. The physical environment
2. The organizational environment
3. The personal and suprapersonal environments
4. The cultural-social-psychological environment

The *physical* characteristics include architectural design, color, lighting, decor, and space.

Organizational aspects include policy, resident/staff ratio, financing, nursing and medical leadership and supervision, and philosophy.

Lawton (1975) defines the *personal* environment as the significant others who constitute the major one-to-one relationships of an individual (family, friends, and staff).

In the nursing home setting, residents' families and friends make up part of their personal world, but the nursing home staff constitutes the major part. The *suprapersonal* environment is defined as the modal characteristics of all the people in physical proximity to an individual (ethnicity, mean age, and mental status of other residents in the nursing home).

The *cultural-social-psychological* milieu refers to the norms, values, social activities, attitudes, and beliefs of the caregivers, and interactions of all who are a part of the institution (residents, staff, family, and visitors) (Kayser-Jones 1992). Residents and the characteristics they bring with them—their physical, functional, and cognitive status, diminished sensory-perceptual capacity, multiple pathologies, and social network—are placed within this complex situation.

First, using a case study, I shall illustrate how factors in various domains (in this case, cultural-social-psychological, organizational, per-

34

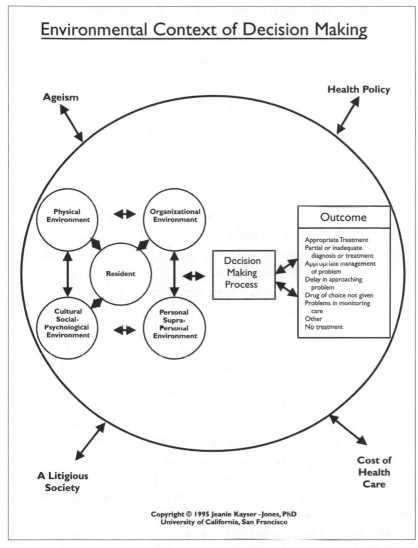

FIGURE 2.1

A conceptual model illustrating how multiple environmental factors influence the decision-making process when nursing home residents acquire an acute illness.

sonal, and suprapersonal) influenced decision making when an elderly nursing home resident became acutely ill. By presenting one acute-illness episode in detail, I hope to open the "black box" of decision making and examine the dynamics of the decision-making process. Next, I will discuss each of these domains in a more general fashion, describing the conditions under which we found decisions being made when acute-illness episodes occurred.

FACTORS THAT INFLUENCE THE DECISION-MAKING PROCESS—A CASE STUDY

Mrs. N was an eighty-nine-year-old woman who, after the death of her only daughter, had been transferred by her granddaughter from an out-of-state nursing home to Facility B. Her granddaughter (who worked in the business office) and her roommate (a social worker) were devoted to Mrs. N. One evening, while feeding Mrs. N, the granddaughter observed that she was cyanotic, pale, chilling, and shaking. She reported these symptoms to the charge nurse, who took Mrs. N's temperature and found it to be 102 degrees Fahrenheit. The nurse called the doctor (who was also the medical director); he asked to speak to a family member. He immediately asked the granddaughter whether she wanted her grandmother transferred to an acute hospital to be treated aggressively and whether she wanted him to "use cardiopulmonary resuscitation."

The granddaughter could not imagine why the doctor was asking her these questions when he had not seen her grandmother and did not know what was causing the symptoms. She felt "paralyzed" by his questions and confused by his asking her to make decisions she felt were inappropriate at this time. She told the doctor that she wanted to have her grandmother treated if her grandmother could be brought back to the quality of life she previously had at the nursing home. With this request, the doctor strongly stated, "But you know what your grandmother's condition is now. She has organic brain syndrome, and her quality of life is very bad! She is very old!"

The doctor's description of her grandmother offended the granddaughter. At times, her grandmother was not oriented, but she was normally very alert and gave much joy to the people around her, especially to the granddaughter and her roommate, who visited daily and often assisted her with care. The granddaughter said that her grandmother was still a contributing member of society because "there were people who still loved her and she was able to give those people pleasure." She believed that because the doctor did not know her grandmother as a person and had not even seen her since she had become acutely ill, he was not in a position to make a decision about how aggressively she should be treated.

After talking with the granddaughter, the doctor ordered oral antibiotics and "comfort measures." The following day, the resident's fever was still 102 degrees; the granddaughter asked for a conference with the doctor. The doctor advised against transferring Mrs. N to an acute hospital and against doing any diagnostic procedures. He told the granddaughter that he had done a urinalysis and that it was negative. The granddaughter challenged him on this point, saying that a urinalysis had not been ordered. The physician became angry, insisting that the report was negative. He reached for the chart to prove his point only to discover that, indeed, he had not ordered a urinalysis. He apologized to the granddaughter and agreed that IV antibiotics should be given. When the granddaughter suggested that Mrs. N be transferred to an acute hospital, the doctor warned her that her grandmother would be "most miserable" if she were transferred to an acute hospital. Many painful invasive tests would be done, he said.

The following day, Mrs. N complained of severe abdominal pain. Concerned, the granddaughter, without asking the physician, called an ambulance and had her grandmother transferred to an acute hospital, where she received excellent care. She was diagnosed and treated for urinary sepsis. Upon recovering, she returned to the nursing home. Painful invasive procedures were not required at the hospital. Blood was drawn for analysis, and an IV was started to administer antibiotics.

Because Mrs. N was transferred to the hospital without the physician's order, a meeting was called at the nursing home, attended by several members of the administrative staff, the physician, and the social worker. The physician was angry that the granddaughter had transferred Mrs. N to the acute hospital without his permission. This woman, he said, was "totally demented." He was concerned, he said, about what his physician colleagues at the hospital would think of him for transferring a "totally demented patient" to the hospital for treatment. At this point, the social worker again reminded the doctor that Mrs. N was the grandmother of an employee at the nursing home. The doctor appeared to be embarrassed by this and said no more.

In an interview, the social worker remarked that because this doctor (the medical director) had a heavy patient load, he often handled the workload by having a brief telephone consultation with families when residents became acutely ill. When he believed that a resident was "excessively mentally impaired or too old," he advised families not to have the resident treated aggressively and to have "no transfer" and "no CPR" orders written on the chart.

The Cultural-Social-Psychological Environment—Case Study

The case of Mrs. N clearly illuminates the influence of several contextual factors on the decision-making process. First, the culture of the nursing home dictates that physicians visit only every thirty days. However, when Mrs. N became acutely ill, the granddaughter's expectation was that the physician would visit her grandmother before making a treatment decision. She was confused when he asked her to make what she felt were inappropriate decisions about CPR.

Second, whereas the granddaughter valued her grandmother despite her cognitive impairment, the physician's statement, "Her quality of life is very bad! She is very old," illustrates that he did not value Mrs. N.

Third, the data further confirm that the physician's beliefs and negative attitude (cultural-social-psychological environment) toward elderly, cognitively impaired residents were major factors in the decision-making process. When discussing treatment of Mrs. N's acute illness, the doctor stated that he was concerned about what his physician colleagues at the hospital would think of him for transferring a "totally demented patient" to the hospital for treatment.

The Organizational Environment—Case Study

As already mentioned, regulations require that physicians visit their nursing home residents only once monthly. When residents become acutely ill, physicians often make decisions regarding treatment over the telephone (organizational environment). In the case presented here, a life-and-death decision was being made by one individual (the physician) who had little knowledge of this woman, her family, and their wishes. Without examining Mrs. N and without ordering a urinalysis for culture and sensitivity, the physician ordered an oral antibiotic, minimal (ineffective) treatment.

This situation stands in sharp contrast to the decision-making process described by Anspach (1993) in her study of two neonatal intensive care nurseries. Anspach describes how life-and-death decisions were discussed informally in conferences, presented on daily rounds, debated in formal conferences, and presented to parents. When an infant died, the case was reviewed in a morbidity and mortality conference (Anspach 1993:19).

In the hospital, a physician is more likely to discuss difficult decisions with colleagues. In nursing homes, decisions regarding residents are often made by telephone, and the doctor is typically the sole decision maker. Moreover, in the hospital, questionable decisions are likely to be debated by a committee of one's peers and superiors. In the nursing home, no such committees exist. The decision-making process in the nursing home is far less structured and organized than in an acute hospital.

The Personal and Suprapersonal Environments—Case Study

Next, we see how the physician's attitudes and beliefs (cultural-social-psychological environment) influenced his interaction with the granddaughter (personal and suprapersonal environments). Firm in his belief that elderly demented residents should not be treated aggressively, he used his influence and power as a physician, as well as deception (telling the granddaughter that her grandmother would be subjected to many painful invasive tests), to persuade the granddaughter to agree to minimal treatment. The physician knew, of course, that an eighty-nine-year-old woman with chills and a fever of 102 degrees was very ill and could die without the appropriate IV antibiotics.

Often, the physician's decision is not challenged, but in this case, the resident had an attentive, caring, knowledgeable granddaughter (personal and suprapersonal environments). Moreover, the granddaughter was an employee of the nursing home. She knew how to circumvent the physician's decision and have her grandmother transferred to an acute hospital, where she was treated appropriately. Thus, the physician's treatment decision was thwarted. Furthermore, the granddaughter's roommate (a social worker) had been employed in the facility for more than a year. She had observed that this physician sometimes persuaded families to his way of thinking by holding a brief telephone conversation with them when a resident became acutely ill.

Last, the granddaughter was not afraid to take the matter into her own hands when she observed that her grandmother's condition was not improving. Because of her intervention, Mrs. N received appropriate treatment and recovered.

FACTORS THAT INFLUENCE THE DECISION-MAKING PROCESS IN THE NURSING HOME

Having presented how multiple factors influenced the decision-making process in a specific case, I shall now describe, in general, how numerous environmental factors affected the decision-making process when an acute illness occurred.

The Physical Environment

Some nursing homes are physically very attractive and provide beautiful resident accommodations, but many are unattractive, physically and aesthetically. Residents are often accommodated in small, multi-bed rooms. Many remain in their rooms day after day, staring at a blank wall. Nursing homes are out of the mainstream of health care, and they lack necessary support services, such as a pharmacy and an X-ray department. The physical environment is unpleasant for the residents, their families, and the staff.

Lack of Support Services

With the passage of Medicare and Medicaid legislation in 1965 came a sudden increase in the number of nursing home beds (Harrington 1984). Before 1965, nursing homes provided primarily residential care to people who had chronic illnesses and needed assistance with activities of daily living (Streim and Katz 1994). Since the mid-1980s, however, the nursing home population has changed dramatically. Today, nursing homes are admitting people "sicker and quicker" after a short stay in an acute care hospital. These elderly people are typically very ill, fragile, and vulnerable. They have multiple pathological conditions and may suddenly develop an intercurrent acute illness that may be life-threatening.

When an acute illness occurs, physicians often need the diagnostic services of a laboratory, an X-ray department, and a pharmacy that can provide new or emergency drugs. Most nursing homes do not provide these services. In Mrs. N's case, because of delays in obtaining a urinary analysis, it was ten days before she received medication for a urinary tract infection, a painful condition that can be fatal in an elderly person.

In another case, due to the lack of on-site support services, it took five hours to diagnose and treat a woman in insulin shock. The unavailability of these services makes it difficult for physicians to treat acute illnesses in nursing homes. I asked a young geriatrician, "What are the problems you face in treating an acute illness in nursing homes?" Her reply succinctly summarized what physicians need when an acute illness occurs: "I would love for the nursing home to provide me with the right facilities to do acute treatment without having to transfer the patient. I would like, for example, to give intravenous [IV] feedings, to give IV antibiotics, if necessary, to have lab tests done quickly, and be able to take X-rays more expediently."

Unpleasant Surroundings

The nursing home milieu is often unpleasant. Offensive sights, sounds, and smells are ubiquitous. Residents, poorly groomed and dressed in bathrobes and slippers, sit slumped over in wheelchairs in the lounge or corridors, their clothing stained with food. One physician, when interviewed, said that he disliked making nursing home visits because "I go down the hallway and see all those little eyes, like Pets Unlimited."

During data collection, we repeatedly heard residents cry out for help. The overburdened staff walked by, ignoring their cries. A woman called out, "Help! I'm going to die before I get help." A resident in a piercing, desperate voice cried out, "Oh God, oh God, oh God Almighty!" A loud, mournful cry is heard from another resident. The nursing assistant shouted, "Stop moaning, Betty!" I walked to the room and found a blind woman sitting in a chair. She was tired and wanted assistance in getting back to bed (Kayser-Jones 1991). The son of a resident reported that he found a male resident, unable to walk, crawling out of his room on his hands and knees, crying for help. The visitor helped the man into a chair and called the nurse, who scolded the resident for being out of his room.

Because staff members fail to assist residents with their elimination needs, the offensive smell of urine and feces is everywhere. Our field notes document repeatedly the overpowering odor of urine and feces in the facilities. On one occasion, the odor of feces was so strong in the dining room that I could hardly bear to be in the nurses' station across the hall. Residents who were dependent upon the staff to assist with their elimination needs were made to wait for the bedpan. A ninety-year-old woman lamented, "I'm so sick. I'm dirty, and I am so unhappy here." When she asked for the bedpan, the nursing assistant placed it on her bedside table but would not assist her in getting on the bedpan. "Do it yourself," she commanded. Unable to use the bedpan unassisted, the woman was incontinent of feces and had to lie in a soiled bed for some time.

These unpleasant sights, sounds, and smells offend residents, visitors, and staff, and they are a deterrent to providing a high standard of care. When asked about the quality of life of nursing home residents, a sensitive, thoughtful physician replied, "Quality of life is pretty bad for all nursing home patients. Fortunately, with serious disease and disability, their perception is decreased, so they are not as aware of what is going on around them." When asked why he thought that their quality of life was so poor, he said, "First of all, they [nursing homes] all smell. That really bothers me. I don't know if it bothers other people, but it really bothers me." Many physicians said that they found nursing homes physically abhorrent. When asked how they would feel if they had to go into a nursing home, their typical answers were "I would regard it as a catastrophe," "I would take cyanide," and "I would commit suicide" (Wiener and Kayser-Jones 1990). The physical environment clearly affects physicians' attitudes toward nursing homes.

Unfortunately, a dislike for the physical environment of the nursing home has serious consequences for nursing home residents. First, because the physical environment is so unpleasant, physicians frequently do not make the required monthly visit. Second, because they dislike the nursing home, they also dislike the people who reside there. Mitchell and Hewes (1986) found that about 20 percent of the physicians in their study (N = 978) said that a dislike of nursing home residents was a reason for not making nursing home visits. Interestingly, when analyzing physicians' comments, they concluded that the physicians may be averse to the nursing home environment rather than to the residents.

The physicians in this study stated that nursing homes are inadequately staffed and consist of human rejects awaiting death. They spoke of the inhumane, depressing environment. "There is a degree of depression about old age, and it affects all those who take care of them," a medical director remarked. "Some doctors have a bad view of nursing homes, and they just won't go to the nursing home to see their patients" (Kayser-Jones 1986).

The Organizational Environment

The organizational environmental is a critical element in providing care. Policy issues, patient-staff ratios, nursing and physician leadership, and the philosophy of the facility influence every aspect of care. The consequences of the implementation of federal and state regulations and of understaffing are discussed here within the context of the organizational environment.

Legislation and Regulations

In the 1970s, there were numerous accounts of the poor quality of care in nursing homes (Mendelson 1974; Moss and Halamandaris 1977). During the 1980s, many efforts were directed toward improving the quality of care through legislation, consumer activism, and the initiation of the ombudsman program. Nursing home regulations have reduced some of the most egregious problems, such as fires, physical abuse, and extremely neglectful care (Kane 1988). Other problems—such as overuse or improper use of medications, inadequate rehabilitation programs, social isolation, lack of privacy, poor food, and lack of individualized care—continue to exist (Kane 1988; Harrington 1990).

Federal legislation to increase nursing home regulations to improve the quality of care has been the subject of much debate. In 1982, the Reagan administration announced that it would fulfill its campaign promise to deregulate America's private business sector, including a plan to reduce the regulatory process in nursing homes. Professionals, consumer groups, and their congressional allies responded vociferously to this announcement. After much debate, the issue was referred to the Institute of Medicine (IOM), which concluded that more, not less, regulation was needed (Institute of Medicine 1986).

To receive reimbursement from Medicare or Medicaid programs, nursing homes are required to meet state and federal licensing standards (Harrington 1984). To determine whether nursing homes comply with these standards, state survey agencies are authorized to conduct on-site surveys, usually on an annual basis (Harrington 1995). Even though regulations are essential, nursing home administrators and staff, who spend an enormous amount of time on the paperwork entailed in complying with the regulations, complain about what they call an "adversarial" relationship between the state surveyors and themselves. "We have to cover ourselves. We always worry about the state surveyors coming," said one director of nursing services. "They're not looking for good. They're looking for bad" (Wiener and Kayser-Jones 1989).

Regulation Implementation—Reporting Any Change
in a Resident's Condition

Because nursing staffs fear receiving a citation if they are not in compliance with state and federal regulations, they fastidiously comply with the regulations, especially on paper. For example, the regulations require that any change in the resident's condition, no matter how small (a slightly elevated temperature, an abrasion on the skin, a slightly abnormal laboratory report), must be reported to the family and the physician. Therefore, physicians receive a tremendous number of calls that they deem "foolish and unnecessary." "I have a patient who fell, and they called me, not because they cared about the patient but because of fear of liability. I asked if they wanted me to come and see the patient, and they said no. They just called to let me know. It's the regulations that are driving the system, not concern for the patient."

The nursing staff expressed the frustration they experienced because physicians did not return their calls and sometimes refused to visit residents who became acutely ill. To cover themselves and to avoid citations, they must persist in telephoning the physician and record in the nursing notes that the doctor has been notified. Additionally, they must cope with and attempt to allay the concerns of family members who continually ask the nursing staff when the physician will come to visit their sick relative.

The wife of a resident was upset because her husband had been feverish for a week. His doctor (the medical director) refused to visit him. After numerous calls requesting that the doctor visit the resident, the nurses reminded the doctor that the resident had a dental appointment at the Veterans Administration (VA) Hospital. The doctor then suggested that the resident also see a doctor while at the hospital. The nursing staff attempted to set up an appointment with a physician at the VA hospital. They were unable to accomplish this. The man was finally seen in the emergency department of the VA hospital. The wife, who had insisted that a doctor see her husband, said, "Acute illnesses don't get treated here."

Medicaid Reimbursement for Physicians' Visits

About two-thirds of nursing home residents are on Medicaid, a government program for low-income people (Jones 2002). Federal regulations require that physicians visit their patients only once a month. For some, this is adequate, but when residents become acutely ill, additional visits are sometimes necessary. If physicians make more than the required monthly visit, however, they have extreme difficulty getting reimbursement by Medicaid. Numerous physicians elaborated at length about the problems they have with Medicaid reimbursement. During an interview with one physician, he picked up a thick manila folder from his desk. "Maybe you would like to take a look at this," he suggested. He opened the folder and counted the letters he had received from Medicaid regarding reimbursement for a thoracotomy he had performed. The charge was $380. For months, he had been corresponding with Medicaid. He had received fourteen letters, and the issue was still unresolved. "Pretty soon," the doctor said, "they will have spent more on correspondence than I charged for the procedure."

A seventy-eight-year-old physician said that the bulk of his practice was geriatrics. "I have grown old along with my patients," he mused, and he was equally frustrated with Medicaid. His bookkeeper was angry about the additional workload placed on her by having to deal with difficult reimbursement issues. "Everything ends up going to claims review," she said, "and cases are held in suspension for a ridiculously long time." The paperwork had become so great that the physician had asked his daughter to help out in his office, solely to take care of reimbursement problems. Despite this difficulty, we observed that this elderly physician was extremely responsive to telephone calls, visiting his nursing home patients as often as necessary when they became acutely ill.

Telephone Medicine

The reimbursement for a visit to a nursing home resident is very small compared with what physicians receive when they see patients in their offices. Because of the low reimbursement rates and the difficulty of being reimbursed for additional visits, many physicians diagnose and treat by telephone when residents develop an acute illness. A decision regarding medical treatment is often made without the benefit of a clinical examination.

Providing medical treatment by telephone may be satisfactory in some cases, but sometimes it may have adverse consequences for residents and their families. When physicians do not actually see the resident's declining physical condition, they are removed from the personal, psycho-social-emotional component of illness and care. When elderly people become acutely ill, they look *very* sick. To see them in this condition and to become involved personally with their care may influence how the physician responds and treats the illness.

Also, when the nurse calls the doctor at his office, he is busy seeing other patients. The telephone conversation is hurried and brief. It does not allow for face-to-face discussion of the resident's care between the physician and the nurse and between the physician and the family. Families often do not have an opportunity to ask the necessary questions, and they cannot observe how the physician interacts with their sick relative. Similarly, physicians do not observe interactions between the resident and the family and therefore lack important data that should be a part of the decision-making process. This can be especially problematic when life-and-death decisions are being made, as was the case with Mr. R. If the physician had visited Mr. R and observed his close relationship with his niece, he might have decided to treat Mr. R when he developed pneumonia.

When the diagnosis and treatment of residents is conducted over the telephone, the physician must rely on the nurse's assessment. If the nurse is experienced and professionally competent, relying on her evaluation does not pose a problem. In the acute hospital, physicians are accustomed to working with professionally competent nurses. Most descriptions of nursing home staff, however, are unfavorable. Because of low salaries, difficult working conditions, and the lack of prestige associated with working in a nursing home, well-qualified nurses often choose to work elsewhere (Bowker 1982; Kayser-Jones 1990a). If the nurse does not accurately assess acutely ill residents, the physician lacks the data necessary to diagnose and treat them properly.

Further, the telephone, instead of facilitating care, has become an instrument of abuse and frustration for both the doctor and the nurse. As already mentioned, physicians believe that they receive many unnecessary calls from the nursing home staff; this takes up valuable time and annoys them. The nurses spoke of having to cope with the doctors' angry reactions and responses. Sometimes, physicians verbally abused the nurses on the telephone and terminated calls abruptly (Wiener and Kayser-Jones 1990). Unfortunately, when residents become acutely ill and it is imperative that the nurse give a detailed, accurate description of their condition, the doctor, frustrated by previous "unnecessary" interruptions, does not always take the call seriously and does not encourage the nurse to elaborate on the resident's condition.

The negative cultural climate within the nursing home (due, in part, to the regulation requiring the nursing staff to report any change in a resident's condition) and the physicians' difficulty receiving reimbursement for medical care are factors that create an adversarial situation not conducive to a professional relationship between physicians and nurses. Furthermore, it does not promote effective physician-nurse communication and good decision making when an acute illness occurs.

Physicians do not respect nurses who call repeatedly to report small changes in a resident's condition that require no intervention on their part. One physician, when asked about the quality of care in nursing homes, remarked, "There is a degree of ignorance in nursing homes about disease that is really appalling. It's just surprising how a nurse can call and say, 'The albumin is 3.9,' when the normal is 4.0, and then they'll say something like, 'Well, I just thought you might like to know.' Maybe they can keep people from getting bedsores, but when it comes to acute care, they are really very ignorant."

On the other hand, the nursing staff does not respect physicians who refuse to visit acutely ill residents. Moreover, they resent the fact that they must spend valuable time calling physicians repeatedly and writing to remind them that they are overdue for their visit. Interestingly, the burden is on the nursing home staff to ensure that physicians make the required monthly visit. If they fail to do so, the facility receives a citation from the state. "They never go after the doctor," one nurse lamented. "They always come after us."

Often, a conflict-ridden adversarial, instead of collaborative-productive, relationship develops between the doctors and the nursing staff. A research assistant in this study, who was also a doctoral student in nursing, said, "I have always worked in an acute care setting, and I am amazed at the lack of collaboration between nurses and doctors in the nursing home—it virtually doesn't exist!" The nurses in one facility were so intimidated by a physician who had repeatedly spoken to them angrily on the telephone that when he did come to the nursing home, they left the nurses' station for fear of having to interact with him. This eliminated any opportunity to discuss residents' care.

Unfortunately, the residents pay the price when communication is poor and the staff is focusing on complying with regulations. When analyzing the acute-illness episode data, we were struck by the fact that day after day the nurses recorded in the nurses' notes "Physician notified," indicating that they had notified the doctor of a problem needing medical attention. Still, the physician did not call back to leave orders, sometimes delaying treatment of an acute illness.

When asked about this practice, the nurses replied that the regulations require them to report any change in a patient's condition. Responsibility for the patient's care was seldom mentioned. It appears that the nurses feel that if they have reported a symptom or change of condition to the physician, they have fulfilled their responsibility. Making the call to the physician and recording it in the nurses' notes are what is important. Furthermore, after physicians return the phone call, they, too, feel that they have fulfilled their responsibility. The delay in beginning treatment or in monitoring the treatment of an acute illness, described above, illustrates how nursing home residents become the unfortunate victims of the nursing home culture. In an interview, one physician remarked on the lack of confidence he had in the staff's ability to monitor the residents: "The treatment would have to be very simple in the nursing home, for example, giving oral antibiotics or diuretics, but it's almost impossible to monitor. I have to call in and ask how things are going because they do not call me. They are not monitoring the patient."

Understaffing

An inadequate number of qualified nursing staff is a problem that has existed in nursing homes for decades. Because most nursing homes are proprietary, one of their goals is to make a profit. One way to control costs is to limit the number of staff hired. However, as noted above, today's nursing homes are admitting people in a sub-acute condition after a brief hospital stay—patients with nasogastric feeding tubes, gastrostomy tubes, tracheostomies, and other complex equipment and procedures.

In the study reported here, typically, one licensed staff—a registered nurse (RN) or a licensed vocational nurse (LVN)—oversaw the care of forty to forty-five residents. An interview with a geriatric nurse practitioner (GNP) recently hired at Facility B disclosed some of the problems facing nurses who choose to work in nursing homes. When asked how she was getting along in her new position, she replied that although she liked her work, she was overwhelmed by the amount of work. "They are going to have to make a decision about hiring more staff," she said. "Why do you say that?" I inquired. "Patients with tracheostomy tubes who should be suctioned every hour are maybe getting suctioned once a shift [once every eight hours]. If patients get pneumonia, they need to be suctioned often. Even if we give them IV antibiotics, they might not recover because they would not be getting the right nursing care. They are probably not going to get suctioned. They are not getting full treatment and care. If they wanted that kind of care, they should be in an acute care facility. If they [physicians] are interested in prolonging their life or in rehabilitating them, this is not the place to be."

"How would it be different if they were in an acute care hospital?" I inquired. Referring to a woman admitted with a tracheostomy, the GNP said, "If she were in acute care, she would be getting respiratory therapy. Ideally, she would be getting full range of motion every day. She would be suctioned more often. These would be the ideal circumstances, and they just don't exist here."

The Personal and Suprapersonal Environments

As mentioned above, the *personal* environment is composed of the significant others who constitute the major one-to-one relationships of an individual (family, friends, and work associates). The *suprapersonal* environment is defined as the modal characteristics of all those in physical proximity to an individual (the ethnicity, mean age, and mental status of others in the nursing home). In the nursing home, the nursing staff have the most interaction with residents. They provide the day-to-day care, observe any changes in residents' conditions, and often are the only people available to comfort and support residents when they become acutely ill.

The Nursing Staff—Foreign-Born Nurses

There are many concerns about the quality of nursing care in nursing homes and the multiple factors contributing to poor quality of care, such as understaffing, staff turnover, and low salaries (Harrington 1995; Kayser-Jones 1990b). Additionally, many nursing home employees are women who have limited knowledge of the English language and have been educated in cultures where women are inclined to be less assertive than American-born nurses. Certified nursing assistants (CNAs) with limited education provide most of the hands-on care, and they are overworked and underpaid.

In some parts of the country, nursing homes are staffed largely by immigrant nurses. On the West Coast, Filipino nurses (RNs, LVNs, and CNAs) provide much of the care. Many are excellent nurses, but some tend to be shy and easily intimidated by physicians. An elderly resident who was mentally ill had been abusive to the staff and other residents. The nurses wanted the physician to transfer her to a psychiatric facility. Instead, the physician said that he would double the amount of tranquilizer she was taking. Although the nurses were upset about having this woman on the unit, they were too timid to request a transfer. When speaking to the doctor, they were subdued and reluctant to insist that the woman be transferred. Knowing that they were not succeeding in their attempt to get the resident relocated, they turned to us (the investigators), asking, "How can we justify getting her out of here for a psych [psychiatric] consult?"

In addition to being shy, some Filipino nurses do not speak English well. When physicians cannot understand them, the physicians become angry and impatient, sometimes yelling at the nurses, which further intimidates and frightens them. A Caucasian nurse remarked that when she calls to report a change in a resident's condition, physicians sometimes yell at her. She responds by telling them in a straightforward manner that she will not listen to their shouting and yelling. If they want to offer suggestions, leave orders, or discuss a patient's care, she will listen, but she will not listen to them when they are yelling.

Most of the nursing staff in this study were minority women who had difficulty communicating with physicians. "It really makes a difference, who calls and how a case is presented to the doctor, in terms of what his decision will be," the assistant director of nursing at one facility remarked. "Some of the staff are very shy, and they don't have a lot of confidence in themselves, and their English is limited. There is one physician who never wants to transfer patients out of the nursing home, and he tries to kind of dump on the nurses by saying, 'What do you want to happen? Do you want them to go to the acute hospital, where they will be put on a respirator, hooked up to a lot of machinery, and bring in a lot of technology?'" She said, "He does that in order to convince the staff that acutely ill residents should not be transferred to the acute hospital for treatment."

When physicians use their power to control the situation, as we have seen, it may have grave consequences for nursing home residents, especially if they do not have family to advocate for them (which Mrs. N did have). Many of the nursing staff do not question the physician's decision. When asked to express their opinion about treatment of an acute illness, they often responded, "The doctor knows best." When nurses are intimidated by aggressive physicians and do not participate in the decision-making process and residents are without family, the physician has complete control. In the nursing home, physicians are not as accountable to other professionals as in an acute hospital, where many more professionals (nurses, physicians, pharmacists, and so on) are present.

In the case of the woman who died from an acute infection (parotitis), the nurses knew that she could not swallow oral antibiotics, food, and liquids. Yet, when her physician ordered oral medication, they did not suggest that antibiotics be given intramuscularly or intravenously, and the woman died.

Because nursing homes are isolated from the mainstream of medicine, physicians can, with impunity, make decisions that are not in the best interests of the residents. "There's no one to look over your shoulder in the nursing home," a physician said. "After the patient is dead, all that is left is a piece of paper," he remarked, referring to the death certificate.

The Role of the CNA in the Decision-Making Process

Although CNAs have the closest contact with the residents and often know them well, they are seldom asked to share information about residents who become acutely ill. Interviews with CNAs disclosed that they have unrecognized talents and possess valuable knowledge about the residents that is seldom utilized in the decision-making process.

Some of the CNAs, for example, have developed useful strategies for communicating with residents who can no longer speak. A twenty-eight-year-old, African-American CNA said, "Even if they cannot communicate, they understand what you are saying." When asked how she knew that they could understand her, she gave an example of a resident who she thought was not feeling well. She reported this to the charge nurse, who asked her to try to find out what was wrong. When she asked the resident whether something was wrong, the resident took the CNA's hand and moved it in a circular motion around her [the resident's] face. The CNA then asked, "Are you dizzy?" The resident nodded yes. Then the resident took the CNA's hand and placed it on her forehead. The CNA asked, "Do you have a headache?" The resident nodded yes.

Unaccustomed to being asked for their opinion, some CNAs were reluctant to be interviewed. Therefore, I conducted a group interview at Facility A with five CNAs who worked on a heavy-care ward, tending to residents who were severely impaired physically and cognitively. On this particular ward, twenty-five of the thirty residents were being fed via nasogastric tubes. Only two of the thirty residents could speak, and their speaking ability was severely limited. Staff turnover is sometimes high in nursing homes, but at Facility A, turnover was low. The CNAs knew the residents well and were often aware of subtle changes that might indicate the presence of an acute illness. When asked "How do you know if one of your residents is not feeling well?" they replied, "Sometimes the skin feels very hot, sometimes they refuse to eat, sometimes they have more mucous than usual, and sometimes they are crying as if they are in pain." "They may refuse to take a bath," one CNA remarked. "I know if I weren't feeling well, I wouldn't want to take a bath."

The CNAs were incredibly perceptive, yet they were seldom asked for an opinion. When asked, "Have you ever discussed your patients with their physician?" they replied, "No, they never talk to us. Maybe once in a while in an emergency, but they never really talk to us." On one occasion, a CNA told the charge nurse that her patient had pneumonia. The charge nurse did not examine the resident. When the doctor arrived on the unit, the CNA went to him directly and told him that she thought her patient had pneumonia. The physician examined the resident and found that she did have pneumonia.

Unfortunately, probably the most significant people in the world of the nursing home residents, the CNAs, are not given an opportunity to share information with physicians, an important early step in the decision-making process.

The Cultural-Social-Psychological Environment

Although many factors influenced the decision-making process, the caregivers' attitudes and beliefs were perhaps the most influential, especially the physicians' attitudes toward nursing homes and cognitively impaired residents.

There are three components to attitudes: cognitive, feeling, and action. The *cognitive* component of an attitude consists of a person's beliefs about an object or another person. The *feeling* component refers to the emotions connected with the object or person (that is, the object is felt to be pleasing or displeasing, or it is liked or disliked). The *action* component includes the behavioral readiness associated with the attitude. If, for example, an individual holds a positive attitude toward a given person, he or she will be inclined to help, reward, or support that person. On the other hand, if a person holds a negative attitude, he or she will be disposed to harm, punish, or act unfavorably toward that person (Krech, Crutchfield, and Ballachey 1962).

Physicians' Attitudes towards Nursing Homes

Earlier, I discussed how physicians, perhaps understandably, objected to the physical environment of nursing homes—the unpleasant sights, sounds, and smells. We cannot say precisely how these attitudes influenced the decision-making process, but it is useful to examine some physicians' statements expressing their perceptions of nursing homes.

In general, physicians stated that nursing homes provided a lower level and lower quality of care than one would find in an acute care hospital. They lamented the lack of support services, the inconvenience of making monthly visits, and the low reimbursement rates.

When physicians were asked whether they discussed an acute illness situation with the nursing staff, interestingly, 84 percent said yes, and 16 percent said no. Their answer often contained a reference to "competent" and "incompetent" nurses. This was a typical response: "It depends upon the nurse in charge. Some of the nurses are very competent. Then I always discuss it with them. It is very important to talk to the nurses. I like to get that kind of feedback. It's a pleasure to talk to someone on the phone who can give you some kind of judgment about the patient's condition. The nurses really have to triage for you, but some of them are just not capable of this at all." By and large, however, physicians stated that nursing home staff is incompetent. "In the nursing home, you find third- and fourth-level nurses who may or may not understand what you are talking about."

Many physicians also believe that the nursing staff is poorly equipped to provide acute care. "The nurses in acute care are better trained. They're more used to acute care medicine. The acute care hospitals are better staffed. Therefore, patients get much closer attention. The nurses are more up-to-date. They know more. When I give them an order, I know they will follow through. In the nursing home, there are a lot of foreign graduates, and they're shorter staffed," one physician explained.

One physician vehemently expressed his opinion about nursing homes: "I try to avoid having a patient in a nursing home any way that I can. I try to keep them at home. The staff is incompetent. They can't speak or write English." "They work hard," I interjected. "They don't work hard—they show up," he replied. "I don't like the place in any way. I don't like anything I have ever seen in a nursing home. I try to get family to care for them at home. If there is no family, there is usually a friend or the manager of the apartment house who can care for them. I do this for their sake. Once they're in a nursing home, they go batty."

Another doctor, in response to this question, said, "The care in nursing homes tends to be less personal. It is institutional care, and I have an institutional approach. If I'm still involved with the family or know the person, that helps, but I withdraw emotionally. I am less apt to be keenly interested. Their [the residents'] life in the nursing home is so limited. They are depressed. Even if they are senile, they know they are not at home. They want to die."

Other physicians, complaining about the lack of support services (laboratory, pharmacy, and X-ray departments), said, "It's like treating someone at home. You're out in the bush." Some physicians were very negative and fatalistic: "By the time the patient is in the nursing home, what that patient wants is creature comforts." One physician, in the process of "giving up" the nine patients he had in nursing homes, said, "It's too much of a hassle. The reimbursement is so poor—they're more trouble than they're worth." Another, who was also abandoning his nursing home residents, put it bluntly: "It is the human thing to want to be paid for what you do. It's just too depressing. That's why I'm quitting. You know how poorly doctors are reimbursed."

When physicians refuse to care for their nursing home patients, the patients are usually cared for by the medical director or by physicians who have developed a large nursing home practice, sometimes for the monetary rewards and because of the difficulties encountered in establishing a medical practice. The medical director at one facility candidly remarked that he became the medical director shortly after beginning to practice medicine. He needed to supplement his income, and another doctor suggested that he "do nursing home work." He went to nursing homes, handed out his professional card, and in a short time became the medical director for three nursing homes. "It's very hard work," he said. "It's very demanding. I usually receive ten to fifteen calls a day from the nursing homes. That's the reason good doctors don't do this for a very long time. As soon as they can, they get out. They refuse to go to nursing homes, and you get second-echelon doctors who don't care about the quality of care."

Another physician, who had picked up patients from doctors who no longer wanted to care for their nursing home residents, expressed an attitude of utter hopelessness about the future of nursing home care. This physician, nationally known for his work in geriatrics, had more than 300 nursing home residents in his practice. "I have very little hope that nursing homes will ever get better," he said. "I'm very pessimistic about this." Surprised by his statement, I inquired, "Why do you feel that way?" "Nursing homes—it's never going to work. It's useless. What we need to aim for is for people to die quickly. It's better to die on your feet. Putting them in nursing homes is abandonment," he continued. "People are useless when they are put into nursing homes. They are not an integral part of society. They are not productive. This country is never going to be willing to put the money into nursing home care that is needed." When I explained that in some European countries, such as Scandinavia and the United Kingdom, the quality of care in nursing homes is very good, he replied, "Well, maybe in some societies that are more socially minded, it would work, but it's not possible here." In describing the difference between hospital and nursing home care, he said, "First of all, there is a difference in the competence of care that the patient receives. Second, there is a difference in the philosophy of care. In the hospital, the aim is to cure, to improve the patient. In the nursing home, it's more of a 'hold steady.' There is more of a fatalistic attitude in the nursing home," he concluded.

These statements illustrate how physicians' negative attitudes toward nursing homes and the people who reside there may influence their treatment of acute illness. For example, there may be delay in beginning treatment, prescribing an antibiotic that was not appropriate given the severity of the infection, and providing no treatment at all to some residents even when families wanted their relative treated.

Physicians' Attitudes toward Providing Care
to Cognitively Impaired Residents

When and how aggressively to treat people who are cognitively impaired is a controversial issue. A large body of literature is devoted to age-based rationing of health care, whether and how aggressively to treat people who are functionally and cognitively impaired, and the escalating cost of health care, especially to elders in the last months or years of their lives (Begley 1993; Besdine 1983; Callahan 1987, 1993; McCullough 1984; O'Malley 1991; Pellegrino 1993). To discuss these issues at length is beyond the scope of this paper. Here, I shall present typical physicians' responses to the question "Does the mental status of your nursing home residents influence your decision regarding treatment of acute illness?" and then examine these responses within the context of the nursing home culture.

When asked this question, 78 percent of the physicians interviewed said that mental status influenced their treatment decisions; only 12 percent said that it did not. One physician, explaining why he treats mentally impaired people, said, "Demented people can suffer. If the patient is suffering with a fracture, take care of it. You don't want them to suffer." The response of another physician illustrates the importance of the presence of family: "No, I always treat an acute illness. Just recently I lost a patient who had been demented for ten years. His wife came every day to feed him. Several times it looked as if he was going to die, but on her request, I did everything for him." The response of a physician who adamantly believed that mentally impaired people should *not* be treated also illustrates the importance of the presence of a caring family member: "Mental status definitely affects the decision," he said. "It is very important. It is all-important in my mind! Somebody who is totally aware is probably more worthy of having resources expended on him than somebody whose brain is so affected that he is no longer participating in the human community. On the other hand," he reflected, "if there is a family who cares, this makes a big difference. An Alzheimer's patient with a caring family, yes, he should be treated."

Many physicians interviewed who said that mental status was a very important factor in the decision-making process were emphatic in their responses: "Absolutely! If the older person is in a vegetative state, senile, doesn't know what's going on, I would be slow to treat

57

vigorously." One physician said, "It's the most significant factor. Far and away, the most significant factor is the mental status of the patient. On a scale from one to ten, ten being the most significant, mental status would be a ten."

Some physicians treat mentally impaired residents who become acutely ill—not because they believe that it is what they should do but because they have to "cover themselves." "Yes, it's pretty important. Anyone mentally alert and oriented deserves much more treatment. Someone who is alert, ambulatory, and self-sufficient deserves every benefit. For the others, I may do everything that's expected, but I don't believe in it."

Other physicians treat an acute illness but do so less aggressively than they would if the patient were not mentally impaired. "The chronic mental status will affect how I treat. If they don't know or care where they are, they are likely to get less aggressive care," a physician remarked. Another physician thoughtfully replied, "I'm sure it does. I would be more vigorous with a person who was mentally alert than with somebody who was not." "Could you tell me what you mean by *vigorous?*" I inquired. "I would treat in a larger dose and perhaps prescribe medication more frequently," he explained. Another physician candidly said, "If the mental status is very poor, I'm less aggressive. If, for example, the mental status is very good, I'm more aggressive. In fact, it is the principal variable that determines my decision about treatment or nontreatment." This statement illustrates why physicians sometimes provide only partial or inadequate treatment when an acute illness occurs.

Some physicians, when responding, tried to place themselves in the position of a mentally impaired person: "If I, personally, were in that state, I would prefer not to be treated." Others had a tremendous fear of losing their cognitive ability. "Mental status, that is more important than anything else," a physician exclaimed. "All other organ parts can be transplanted, but the brain is unique. That's what makes us different from one another. Anyone who uses his head—a doctor, an engineer—worries." "What do they worry about?" I asked. "Going crazy!" he replied. "I worry about Alzheimer's or a stroke, being in such a position that I can no longer kill myself."

Many physicians stated that cognitively impaired people have a very poor quality of life. "Mental status strongly affects your quality of life." "Mental status is related to quality of life. It's the number one priority." "If the patient is totally confused, there is no life, no quality of life, and if there's no quality of life, I won't push as hard." These were typical responses.

One physician diligently tried to distinguish between mentally impaired residents who have some quality of life and those who do not. "If they are awake and alert, if they interact with staff, if they recognize family members, if they seem to enjoy staff, if they seem to take some pleasure in their food, eat their food with relish, they still have some quality of life. On the other hand, if they have no appreciation of their environment, no meaningful interaction with staff or family, it is not fair to put them through a lot of traumatic tests. It is kinder to let them die."

A few physicians, when discussing mentally impaired residents, used derogatory terms such as *goofy, batty, mentally damaged, nonsalvageable,* and *vegetable.* "Patients I would not treat would be those who are mentally damaged and nonsalvageable," the medical director of one facility asserted. "I have one patient who is blind, one who's goofy and whose legs clog up," another doctor remarked.

The use of the word *vegetable,* when describing people who are mentally impaired, probably derives from the medical term *permanent vegetative state* (an unfortunate choice of words), a condition in which the brain stem is intact but the cerebral hemispheres, which contain the function of consciousness or awareness, have been destroyed. The brain stem controls vegetative functions, such as respiration, and primitive stereotyped reflexes, such as coughing, gagging, swallowing, and pupillary response to light (Cranford 1988).

Unfortunately, there is much confusion among health care professionals concerning terms such as *persistent vegetative state, brain death, permanent unconsciousness, coma, irreversible coma,* and *dementia* (Cranford 1988). Because of this confusion, nursing home residents who are cognitively impaired are insensitively and erroneously labeled "vegetables." As health care professionals, we must ask how we would feel if our loved ones or we were referred to in this derogatory way. Using terminology such as *goofy* and *batty* when referring to nursing home residents is disrespectful and may have adverse consequences when treatment decisions are being made.

The director of nursing services (DNS) at Facility A (a city and county facility that provides care to the indigent elderly) remarked in an interview that all decisions must be made on an individual basis. "One physician," she said, "was going down the charts and writing *no code, no code, no code* on every chart, including that of a thirty-year-old woman who had tentatively been diagnosed as having multiple sclerosis." She noted that when this physician first began visiting residents at Facility A, he used very derogatory terms when speaking about them. She interrupted and corrected him when he spoke in such a manner. "He doesn't use this language anymore," she said, "but in his heart I think he still feels the same way. He feels they are a burden on the backs of taxpayers and doesn't feel they should be treated." This is one example of how attitudes, reflected in the language used, affect treatment decisions.

The Conceptual Model—The Environmental Context of Decision Making

I have described and analyzed how various factors of the nursing home culture influence decision making when an acute illness occurs. Elderly people with varying levels of cognitive and functional disabilities and multiple pathologies are placed within this complex, dynamic environment for long-term care. Some have devoted, knowledgeable families who can supervise their care and act as advocates when an acute illness occurs. Many are without attentive family and friends. When an acute illness occurs, the dynamics of the multiple factors within the nursing home environment, including the interactions of all those involved in the decision-making process, determine the following outcomes (refer to figure 2.1):

- Residents are treated appropriately.
- Residents receive partial or inadequate diagnosis and treatment.
- The problem is managed appropriately.
- There is a delay in beginning treatment.
- The drug of choice is not given.
- There are problems in monitoring care.
- Residents are not treated at all.

The two-way arrows between each component of the model in figure 2.1 (for example, physical environment and organizational environment) illustrate that, singularly or cumulatively, multiple factors in the nursing home environment influence treatment decisions. For example, an unpleasant physical environment (bad odors, the sound of residents crying out for help) may be due to lack of leadership and responsibility on the part of the administrative staff and their unwillingness to pay competitive salaries to an adequate number of well-trained staff (organizational environment). This leads physicians to believe that the quality of life is poor for nursing home residents. In turn, their belief influences their attitudes toward the treatment of acute illness (cultural-social-psychological environment).

The regulation to report any change in a resident's condition (organizational environment) could be implemented without annoying physicians if the nursing staff had confidence in their professional ability to distinguish between changes that need to be reported immediately and those that do not require immediate medical attention. However, because nursing homes are staffed by nurses who tend to abide by this regulation without exercising their professional judgment and because they have difficulty communicating with physicians (personal and suprapersonal environments), an adversarial relationship that is detrimental to decision making develops between doctors and nurses. Furthermore, because CNAs are not valued caregivers (cultural-social-psychological domain), their knowledge and expertise are not included in the decision-making process.

One of the most critical variables in the decision-making process is the physician's attitude toward providing care to mentally impaired residents (cultural-social-psychological domain). It is my hypothesis that these negative attitudes—along with factors such as frustration with state and federal regulations (organizational environment), interaction with nursing staff whom they view as incompetent (personal and suprapersonal environments), difficulties encountered in treating an acute illness due to a lack of support services and to unpleasant surroundings (physical environment)—cumulatively influence how physicians respond when an acute illness occurs. Taken together, these factors often create a cultural context that is not conducive to making decisions in the best interests of nursing home residents suffering from acute illness. Elderly nursing home residents are sometimes treated appropriately and expeditiously but at times are treated inappropriately or not at all. Without family members serving as their advocates, their situation would be even graver.

External Social-Cultural-Political Factors

The internal (micro) environment of the nursing home, described above, is, of course, greatly influenced by the external (macro) environment. Among the many external factors affecting treatment decisions are social, cultural, and political factors such as ageism, the rapidly increasing cost of health care, a litigious society with an increasing number of malpractice suits, changes in health policy (such as the introduction of Medicare's prospective payment system [PPS]), and, most recently, managed care.

Ageism

The United States has long been known as a society that worships youth and fears old age (Butler 1975). We value independence and productivity and look unfavorably on those who are dependent and unproductive. To be young is beautiful; to be old is ugly. This attitude is deeply ingrained in our culture. Material objects quickly become obsolete; we throw away old things in preference of the new (Erikson, Erikson, and Kivnick 1986:3301–02).

Furthermore, we live in an age-segregated society. The ultimate in segregation occurs when one is admitted to a nursing home, isolated from children, adolescents, young adults, and the larger community. A nursing home resident's status declines further when he or she becomes a Medicaid patient, having expended his or her financial resources on nursing home care. Disability in old age, accompanied by admission to a nursing home and the resultant poverty, is a fate feared by many. Because Americans tend to devalue even the elderly who are well, it is not surprising that we do not value those who are old, poor, physically and cognitively impaired, and institutionalized. These cultural values undoubtedly affect physicians. Perhaps this explains, in part, the attitude and behavior of some physicians when nursing home residents become acutely ill.

The physician who said, "What we need to aim for is for people to die quickly. People are useless when they are put into nursing homes...they are not productive," gives voice to the cultural beliefs shaping his perception of the elderly.

Cost of Care

Articles on the rapidly increasing cost of health care in the United States abound. Currently, the United States spends more on health care than any other nation (Charrow 1991:75). Health care costs in 1990 are estimated to have been $666.2 billion, about 12.1 percent of the nation's gross domestic product (GDP). It has been estimated that if existing programs such as Medicare and Medicaid do not change, national health care expenditures will rise to $16.0 trillion in the year 2030 (Burner, Waldo, and McKusick 1992).

Factors such as the development of expensive, new diagnostic and therapeutic modalities, increasing hospitalization and health care provider costs, and the emergence of new diseases and disorders are responsible for the escalating costs of health care. However, some believe that the increasing number and proportion of elderly people, especially the "oldest old," has had and will continue to have a significant effect on health care costs (Schneider and Guralnik 1990). More than one-third of the physicians interviewed in this study echoed these same concerns. Sixty percent of the physicians interviewed said that the cost of care did not influence their decision regarding treatment of an acute illness, 35 percent said that it did influence their decisions, and 5 percent were undecided.

One of those physicians who said that cost of care was *not* a factor in the decision-making process said, "Not at all! I don't think it should ever affect treatment. The cost of medicine should be left up to the accountants, lawyers, and politicians." Although many said that cost of care was not a factor, some physicians qualified their answers, saying that they try to be cost-conscious and are careful about ordering expensive diagnostic procedures, such as computed axial tomography (CAT) scans and magnetic resonance imaging (MRI). In an attempt to control cost, sometimes they do not transfer residents to the acute hospital when they become acutely ill.

A thoughtful forty-eight-year-old physician forcefully stated that the concept of cost had never entered his mind. "I want to practice medicine the way that I feel it should be practiced," he said. "I feel very strongly about that." Later in the interview, however, when asked whether he would treat pneumonia in a patient with advanced Alzheimer's disease, he responded that he would prescribe simple treatments but not complex therapies such as a respirator, endotracheal tubes, or blood cultures. After reflecting on his answer, he said, "I guess cost of care does enter the picture for me at times."

Physicians who said that cost is a factor in their decision-making process talked about the "astronomical costs of health care," their concern about spending money on people who have a poor quality of life, and the expectation of physicians to hold down the cost of care (although they are not taught in medical school about containing cost). "Until recently, the physician has been the advocate for the patient. Now we are supposed to be the social arbiter, and we don't know how to do that. We are cost-mindless," one physician remarked.

The response of one physician illustrates how cost of care in combination with the factor of mental impairment influences treatment decisions. "There are certain people where there is no quality to the life. If you have a nursing home patient who is demented, they're not doing anything, they don't know what's going on…if they develop pneumonia, this is the best way for them to go. It's a huge financial drain on the family and on society. Patients who are demented and don't know what's happening—I don't feel it's justified to spend thousand of dollars for their care."

The response of a reflective forty-year-old internist illustrates how cost of care influences decision making. When asked whether the cost of treatment of an acute illness influenced his decisions, he responded that he would like to say no but admitted, "Somehow I think it has sort of crept into my practice without my realizing it. It has a way of affecting your decisions, although you'd like to say it doesn't. In recent years, society is saying that we can't spend all this money on health care. There are some diagnostic tests, for example, that are not done because of costs. You try to hone down a bit." He then confided that with elderly patients, you do not have to worry so much about malpractice suits: "If you have talked it over with the family and they agree, they are just not going to sue you if the person is ninety years of age and you don't get a CAT scan."

Fear of a Malpractice Suit

Until recently, malpractice suits involving elderly nursing home residents were quite uncommon. Nevertheless, more than half (52 percent) of the physicians interviewed said that fear of a malpractice lawsuit was a factor in deciding whether to treat an acute illness; 48 percent said it was not. One physician said that fear of a malpractice suit was not much of a factor. "In the nursing home, the heat is off," he said, intimating that in an acute care hospital, there is greater cause for concern.

Numerous physicians remarked that involving families and listening to their concerns and opinions was a critically important factor. "It [malpractice] rarely influences my decision," a thirty-five-year-old geriatrician remarked with confidence. "I feel that documentation is key here, and if you've made a good decision involving consensus and supporting everybody involved…as long as the family supports the decision, there shouldn't be any problem…. It [fear of a malpractice lawsuit] affects my practice in that I pay more attention to family opinions. Their opinion really carries the weight because they are the ones that stay behind. They're the ones who are going to have to live with their decision." This geriatrician, along with many other physicians, said that she would never go against the wishes of the family.

Many physicians were fearful of being sued. "It's always hanging over one's head," a physician lamented. Another physician confided, "Everybody has to practice in a certain way because of a fear of a malpractice lawsuit. I'm being sued right now." A physician who believed strongly that patients with advanced Alzheimer's disease should not be tube-fed explained that, despite his beliefs, when residents stopped eating, he inserted nasogastric feeding tubes. "I'm not going to have my reputation ruined," he said. "I don't want to see my name on the front page of the newspaper!"

CONCLUSION

I have described and analyzed the internal and external factors that influenced decision making when nursing home residents became acutely ill. Ideally, residents, their families, their physician, and the nursing staff would collaboratively discuss and determine treatment decisions and develop a long-term plan of care. Seldom does this occur. This paper illustrates how multiple factors—such as an inadequate number of well-trained nursing staff, lack of support services, a tendency to focus rigidly on implementation of regulations, and the absence of physicians, who have the most power in the decision-making process but often the least contact with the elderly residents—create a cultural context for decision making that does not always serve the best interests of the residents. Understaffing, for example, leads to a poor quality of care, which, in turn, leads physicians to believe that residents have a poor quality of life and therefore should not be treated vigorously when an acute illness occurs.

This paper does not always present physicians in a positive light, but I do not mean to malign them. During the course of this study, I met many thoughtful, caring physicians who were troubled about having to make difficult decisions. Interestingly, many were eager to be interviewed because it gave them an opportunity to discuss these issues with us, to express their feelings, and to search for answers to difficult questions for which medical school had not prepared them.

Physicians have been at the center of the discussion because they are in a pivotal role in the decision-making process. Typically, everyone (nursing staff, families, and friends) turns to them when difficult decisions have to be made. It must be remembered that physicians are compelled to practice medicine and make decisions in an environment that is not conducive to the decision-making process.

In the introduction to this book, Phil Stafford discusses the concept of double burial and insightfully asks, "Is admission to a nursing home the *first burial?*" In the eyes of some, admission to a nursing home is a form of social death, a first burial. Many residents are cut off from family and society, and they are in an environment that does not facilitate decision making when an acute illness occurs. They are between life and death, and some physicians fear—in fact, abhor—a similar fate. They find it painful to see patients who were young, active, and mentally alert become old, disabled, and cognitively impaired. Sometimes, when an acute illness occurs, they have reservations about treating it because they believe that the quality of life in nursing homes is so poor. On the other hand, for ethical, personal, humanitarian, or legal reasons, they do not want to let residents die.

The environmental context for decision making as it exists now is woefully inadequate. Yet, we must not complacently conclude that death is preferable to life in a nursing home. Despite their isolation from society and the unpleasant circumstances of life in a nursing home, many elders cling to life and assert that they want to be treated, should they become acutely ill. In response to the question "If you should develop an acute illness such as pneumonia or a heart problem, would you want to be treated?" ninety percent of the 100 residents interviewed responded affirmatively. "Of course, I want to be treated," a ninety-nine-year-old woman replied. "It's better to be alive than dead!"

Social scientists and health care professionals must provide leadership and work collaboratively with elders, their families, the nursing home industry, and community advocates to change attitudes and, subsequently, conditions within nursing homes in a way that facilitates a culture of decision making conducive to treating elders with the care, respect, and consideration they so richly deserve.

3

A Use of Irony in Contemporary Ethnographic Narrative

Maria D. Vesperi

Dramatic irony arises from a relationship between the audience and the play. The audience knows that certain tragic events are destined to take place. It also hears some figure on the stage boasting of the good times to come. And in the audience, as *spectator,* arises dramatic irony. The audience is powerless to affect the course of events; at the same time, its sympathy for the characters makes it long to alter the course of events— and this divided attitude, a sense of being with the people as regards one's sympathies but *aloof* as regards one's ability to forestall the movements of destiny, this awareness of a breach between one's desires and one's understanding, this is ironic.

—*Kenneth Burke*

Kenneth Burke's description of dramatic irony frames a familiar challenge for anthropologists who study nursing homes, as well as for those who pursue field research in many other settings. Despite the conceit that lists *participant* first in the hybrid concept of participant-observation, our goal is to achieve understanding from several points of view. We strive to become good spectators, audience members who are credulous of plot and motive, culturally naive. Yet, our theories and methods train us to be masters of irony, privileged to observe the unfolding of cultural drama from many angles. According to Burke, irony develops from revealing the dialectic tension among or between perspectives, as when we say that there would be no cure without disease (Burke 1969) or no atheism without concepts of deity.

Such tensions abound in the contemporary nursing home. The institution itself would not exist without the frailties associated with advanced old age. Moreover, such facilities would not have adopted a medical model without the cultural construction of aging as a disease. Yet, given the contemporary medical focus on intervention, the fact that aging cannot be "cured" engenders predictable tensions with the goals of the model. Such tensions are further complicated by pervasive but vaguely specified cultural values that dictate humane treatment of the frail elderly.

It is here that the most poignant ironies reside. Burke's "figure on the stage boasting of the good times to come" is often an activities director striving mightily to rouse interest in Halloween, Mother's Day, or Valentine's Day, celebrations that often ring hollow in the absence of residents' children, spouses, and friends (Henderson 1995). Even those researchers who have participated as staff in the care of nursing home residents, such as J. Neil Henderson (1981, 1995), Timothy Diamond (1992), and me (1987, 1995), cannot avoid the overriding sense of being powerless to "forestall the movements of destiny" for our informants.

Burke's description of irony has another component that is relevant to social scientists who observe institutional life:

> True irony, humble irony, is based upon a sense of fundamental kinship with the enemy, as one *needs* him, is *indebted* to him, is not merely outside him as an observer but contains him within, being consubstantial with him. This is the irony of Flaubert, when he realizes that Madame Bovary is himself. (1969:514, italics in original)

Irony in this sense, as a dialectical relationship with the other or "kinship with the enemy," would most appropriately be explored as an aspect of nursing home research through candid interviews with residents themselves. Individuals who truly comprehend the ironies of their own lives are, by definition, tragic figures. They are people who do not exclusively blame others, understanding, instead, that their circumstances are the product of multiple agencies, including their own. As both actors and spectators, they know how the play will end, yet they continue to act and to hope. I have caught glimpses of such insight in many residents of long-term care facilities, settings that can be highly conducive to self-reflection.

In most cases, however, it has been difficult for informants to articulate their thoughts fully on this subject. Several factors are often at work: Their cognitive and verbal capacities may be impaired, they may be deeply depressed, they may not feel a level of trust and intimacy appropriate to such personal revelations, and they may fear recrimination, justifiably or otherwise. Most significant from the anthropologist's viewpoint, they may hesitate to give voice to the roles of significant others in the process that led to their institutionalization. Verbalizing the painful reality that one no longer has a place in the larger community signals a breakdown in social relations, which people are understandably reluctant to acknowledge, even to themselves.

The phenomenon of life review is a complex one that has been treated extensively in many genres. One early example, which relates specifically to the nursing home experience, is Samuel Beckett's 1956 novel, *Malone Dies* (1970). Beckett presents the stream of consciousness of a very frail man at the end of life; Malone is confined to bed and has apparently slipped beyond verbal communication with others. Sensing the immediacy of his death, he divides his time between the manipulation of a small inventory of objects—which fall out of reach, one by one—and a kind of life review organized around a series of fantasies. Malone's capacity for ironic reflection is established at the outset of the novel: "I must have thought about my time-table during the night. I think I shall be able to tell myself four stories, each one on a different theme....Perhaps I shall not have time to finish. On the other hand perhaps I shall finish too soon" (1970:3).

Kathleen Woodward has provided an insightful discussion of Malone's "transitional objects" in relation to the object-identification stage observed in very young children (1991:131–145). She remarks, also, on his "deflating self-irony" (1991:134) and what could be viewed as a dialectical tension between his fear of life and his fear of death: "He alternately and paranoically fears that his life will be prolonged by every available means possible by his caretakers *or* that he will be starved to death" (1991:142, emphasis in original).

Malone experiences neglect and speculates on the motives of those nameless others charged with his care: "Perhaps they think I am dead.

Or perhaps they are dead themselves" (Beckett 1970:81). Missing from Beckett's presentation, however, is the dimension of direct interaction between Malone and the caregiving other as a human agent. Instead, this other is progressively objectified to the point of abstraction: "In the beginning, but was it the beginning, I used to see an old woman, then for a time an old yellow arm, then for a time an old yellow hand" (1970:81).

Burke (1969:512–513) identifies a major fallacy in such presentations, namely that the dialectic can be reduced to meaningless relativism when the perspectives of individual characters are used to represent the whole and when these characters are presented as fixed entities who do not evolve as a result of the dialectical process itself. Malone does change during the process of his life review; he releases his hold on the objects and memories that bridge his presence in the world. This end-of-life novel is not primarily "about" institutionalization, however. The reader does not learn how long Malone has been in this setting, or precisely what kind of facility it is, or whether his vagueness on these points is a result of sudden trauma, dementia, or the numbing, long-term effect of indifferent custodial care.

Such questions are obviously of primary concern in texts that purport to offer a holistic description of the nursing home experience. Finding answers to them is another matter. The researcher is challenged both by the "spectator" problem and by a rigidly synchronic perspective on informants. In most cases, access to earlier periods in informants' lives is limited to their own recollections, augmented by the ethnographer's best effort to match their current behavior and speech patterns with this presentation of self.

Joel Savishinsky skillfully employs these methods to provide compelling portraits of the residents of Elmwood Grove in his nursing home ethnography, *The Ends of Time*. Bonnie Dumond, for instance, is a long-retired teacher in the early stages of dementia. She is acutely aware of her failing memory, and Savishinsky uses what she says about her past to help make sense of her fearful, frustrated responses to this awareness. "In the light of what Bonnie's own memory had become, it was ironic that words, and the very structure of language, had been two of the most passionate parts of her education," writes Savishinsky (1991:98). Bonnie had told him, "I loved to remember the hard words and pronounce them correctly, to diagram sentences, to learn the parts of speech: alliteration, metaphor, euphemism—those names were like magic or music to me. It was grand, in the elementary school I worked in, to teach all those lovely things to my pupils" (1991:99).

Here, subject and researcher work together to generate a synthesis from two poles of identity separated by time, space, and physical transformation. Bonnie is no longer the intellectually competent young teacher, but neither is she a vacant medical statistic. Irony helps us to appreciate her ontological status; she is not wrongfully confined to an institution, or is she? It is easy to see how either perspective, taken alone, would generate the distorting relativism against which Burke cautions.

Savishinsky is also aware of Bonnie's transitional objects, her old lesson plans from her days as a teacher. These were quite distinct from the snapshots and other items on her bulletin board, items "chosen for Bonnie by others" to represent her life. In contrast, Bonnie herself kept the lesson plans in a drawer: "She was not secretive about these, but was selective about who she chose to share them with. It was a sign of intimacy to have Bonnie take the papers out and to be invited into that part of her life" (1991:114).

Jay Gubrium uses a similar strategy in his delineation of "horizons of meaning" for nursing home residents (Gubrium 1993, 1995; Holstein and Gubrium 1995). His methodology includes extensive life history material, which enables the individual to emerge as a fully active participant in his or her construction of the nursing home experience. Thus, the subjective assessment of quality of life is revealed as a pattern of associations between pre-institutional life and current conditions.

Growing numbers of anthropologists are privileged to enjoy long-term relationships with the residents of host communities. As communities and individuals are revisited over time, the ethnographer gains a perspective that is increasingly independent of an informant's immediate presentation of self and concomitantly more reliant on his or her own experience of the informant. This is well illustrated by Margaret Blackman in her discussion of the death and funeral of Florence, a Haida informant with whom she had worked for twenty-four years. "Our relationship spanned my appearance in Masset...the attainment of a Ph.D., two marriages, the birth of a child, and an academic career as an anthropologist. It was publication of Florence's life history that assured my promotion to full professor and elevated her to the status of 'World's Nani' (grandmother), as she liked to describe herself" (Blackman, unpublished). For evident reasons, anthropologists who study nursing homes cannot usually anticipate interactions with residents whom they have known for many years and whom they have viewed from the perspectives of both youth and middle age.

"THE SMOKE IS HIDING EVERYTHING"

More than twenty years after I began investigating and writing about nursing homes, I found such an informant, almost literally, in my own back yard. He is a distant cousin, almost eighty-nine years old at this writing, a man I have known for my whole life and at least half of his. I was prompted to visit this cousin in 1990 during a trip to my hometown, because someone mentioned that a recent stroke had left him confined to his house. I brought along old family photographs of people and buildings I had been unable to identify, and we spent several enjoyable hours perusing them and talking about my mother, who had died two years before.

My cousin had lost the use of his right arm and leg and was receiving twenty-four-hour home nursing care. Until that point, he had lived alone with his wife, Frances, who was very frail.[1] He was the patriarch of a large Irish Catholic family, with five children and about twenty adult or adolescent grandchildren. Many of them lived in the area and visited the couple frequently.

Long considered one of the community's most successful business leaders, my cousin had established an independent pharmacy, retiring before such stores were overtaken by franchises and managed health care plans. He had speculated widely in real estate, acquiring a variety of commercial and residential properties. He was also a cornerstone of the community's most influential political power base. His guiding hand was felt in local elections and appointments for decades, and he had financed the early career of his younger brother, James, who became a high-profile state politician.

Clear memories of my cousin date from about 1955, when I was four years old and he was forty-nine. His drugstore, complete with variety goods, shiny chrome-trimmed stools, and a full grill and soda fountain, was an unofficial headquarters for Democratic politics. During the week, he was busy filling prescriptions and dispensing medical advice, while Frances ran the cash register and their teenage children or hired help kept the hamburgers sizzling and the cold milk shakes whizzing in their tall metal canisters.

The store was just two blocks from our house, and I was dispatched there frequently by my mother. It was a family duty to give my cousin "the business" to the fullest extent of his inventory, which at that time included milk, bread, pastries, candy, greeting cards, gifts, small toys, and a full line of toiletries for men and women. Often as not, no matter how small the purchase, my cousin would invite me with a flourish to sit down at the counter for a free half-pint of chocolate milk and a Devil Dog wrapped in waxed paper.

After church on Sunday morning, the drugstore was a mandatory stop for anyone involved in local politics. Then it was standing room only—a sea of legs to us kids, who were largely ignored while the adults argued and consumed endless cups of coffee. Later I came to understand that some of those cups were filled with "Irish" coffee, a beverage not widely available elsewhere on Sunday. That explained another inventory item, the shiny rows of whiskey bottles on display above the grill.

My relationship to this cousin was genealogically distant but socially close; my mother and her brother were members of his political circle. As a teenager, I became aware that those outside the circle were sometimes intimidated by this man; I heard the words *strong* and *difficult* applied to his personality. As an adult, I was impressed by his generosity in educating his children and supporting their careers. At the same time, I realized that the terms *strong* and *difficult* could also apply to his dealings with friends and relatives.

Thus, when he was placed in a private nursing home the year after his stroke, I was not surprised to hear that the family considered him too "difficult" to manage at home. Our small-town grapevine yielded the opinion that he had treated his home health aides rudely and that he demanded too much of Frances, who was physically unable to perform many caregiving tasks. In fact, I had caught a glimpse of these very problems during the several home visits I made. Given the size and apparent closeness of his family, however, I was surprised to learn that he had been institutionalized. I assumed—although no one mentioned it—that a significant physical or mental decline had precipitated the move. Surprise turned to concern when I visited him and found him fiercely alert, physically stable, and crying with humiliation at the turn his life had taken.

Since that time, I have visited my cousin on most trips to my hometown, at intervals of roughly four months. About two years ago, he was moved to a second facility, this one run by the community on town-owned land where the local "poorhouse" once stood. Frances has since died. My cousin's hope of eventually leaving the facility has yet to be realized, although his physical condition has remained essentially unchanged. He moves from his bed to a chair or commode with assistance, hears well, sees well at a distance with glasses but has difficulty reading, and speaks with the same wry expressiveness that has always been his trademark. His skin has assumed a flat pallor, however, and his facial expressions have become concentrated in his eyes, which register anger, humor, satisfaction, and concern with startling clarity. His approach to institutional life has shifted from self-pitying helplessness to a mix of openly calculated accommodation and active resistance.

In March 1995, I approached my cousin on the subject of an interview. The request did not seem to surprise him. He remembered that I wrote about aging as an anthropologist, that I had also worked as a journalist for many years, and that I had interviewed numerous people in the area—including him—for an unrelated project.

"No, but let me tell you about this article that I'd like to write, okay?" I began, regretfully interrupting his lively anecdote about betting on amateur sports. "Over the years, I've done some studies in nursing homes." Here he nodded in assent. "What I'm concerned about is that people understand what it's like to *be* in a nursing home. And like I said, a lot of the people, either they can't talk, or they're afraid."

"Yuh," he confirmed quickly. "Fear is a terrible thing. You're afraid of physical abuse. Most of the aides are 'efficient,' and some are really in a hurry. So if they're in a hurry, you gotta tolerate the—what is dealt out to you."

"Do you mind if I write some of this down?"

"No, go ahead," he said evenly.

"Here, too?" I asked, waving my Sony close to him. "On the tape recorder?"

"Okay."

Thus was consent for this project sought and obtained. During the last week of March 1995, I interviewed my cousin four times, averaging three hours per visit. I also conducted a follow-up interview on my next trip, four months later. All quotations that appear here are taken from the thirty-six pages of single-spaced transcription generated by these interviews. I sought consent from my cousin alone because I regard him as a mentally competent adult who happens to be living in an institution. His surroundings will be described only peripherally. I can say at the outset that this nursing home is better than average in several regards: It looks and smells clean, it is open to the community, and most residents enjoy exceptional opportunities for maintaining social contacts. The facility is quite small; there are approximately seventy patients.

After I obtained my cousin's permission to write about him, I discussed the project over dinner with his daughter, Annie, her husband, and two of his adult grandchildren. All were enthusiastic about the idea, despite their awareness that "Grandpa" was bitter about the nursing home placement and that his views on family behavior might be unflattering, especially in print. We had discussed his feelings repeatedly in the past, and I was satisfied that they appreciated the scope of what he might say.

If anything, these relatives were disappointed that I did not plan to use their father's name. I explained that confidentiality was a must and that even the name of the community would be altered. They persisted, pointing out that it was in the old man's character to be candid and that they would like to see his words preserved as a legacy. Then I told them that "Grandpa" had not only accepted this restriction but also had already chosen his own pseudonym.

The choice of a pseudonym was broached during our second interview, after my cousin had demanded to be moved from his chair to his bed because he was experiencing significant discomfort.

"A lot of pain, Maria," he said, as he shifted restlessly to find a comfortable position. "You know, they give you the bullshit, all our lives, 'the next world.' I don't care to explore it," he observed dryly.

I asked him about a painful-looking growth on his scalp, which led to a discussion of injuries he had sustained over the years. "It's a very vulnerable area, your brain. Mine's a good one and I'd like to preserve it. I enjoy talking," he said.

"Well, you have a lot to say. See—*I* don't know what to say," I added, with a nod to his surroundings. "I really appreciate your situation here. I really do."

"They ought to put this down and let me walk," he said, slapping the side rails on his bed with the palm of his hand. "If they'd do that, I'd have a chance, Maria. Otherwise, it's not gonna happen. Yesterday when I was up—I don't know when I was up—they let me use the telephone where the nurses are. I called Margaret [another of his daughters]. I remembered her number," he added, reciting it for me. "She's been good to me, and I pity her in a way 'cause her husband had a heart condition. You see, if Annie would, she'd take me. She won't do it. Her husband wouldn't stand—"

"I don't think that most people understand what it's really like to live in a nursing home," I interrupted. "I think if they did, maybe things would be a little different. Because nobody talks about it, see? Everybody says, 'Oh, hi, how are you?'"

"Yeah," he agreed, interrupting me.

"'You look great,'" I continued, mimicking the thin cheer I have heard so often in the voices of nervous visitors. "And then they go away."

"That's right," he said.

"I've spent a lot of time in nursing homes. I've talked to a lot of people because I feel that if more people could know what it's like, it would make a difference."

"I hope so," he said. "I'll tell you anything you want to know. I don't give a —. I'm not afraid of these people."

"Well, I'm not going to use your real name." Here I launched into a conscientious discussion of confidentiality in social science research, but my cousin seemed to lose interest as soon as I had conveyed the basics. He eventually broke in, his eyes alight with anticipation.

"You know," he began speculatively, "*T. D.* used to be the name of a clay pipe. The old Irish women used to use 'em."

Had I just met this man, I might well have interpreted his remark as a signal of dementia. Weren't we talking about the weighty matter of the protection of human subjects? Instead, I recognized his statement for what it was, an acceptance of my terms, an editorial dismissal of "the bullshit" that followed, and a constructive suggestion for moving the project forward.

"So you like that? *T. D.?* You want to be *T. D.?*"

His voice filled with pleasure and bemusement. *"Yeah.* That's okay. The smoke is hiding everything, the facts. There's a shroud of smoke from the pipe. And that concerns, really, what's in there."

"WHEN THE HAMMER STRIKES THE ANVIL"

"T. D.?"

"Yuh?"

"How long have you been in a nursing home?"

"I have no idea."

"You don't remember?"

"I think it was a matter of finance," he began, attempting to shift the conversation from *when* to *why,* his greater concern. "I had a few dollars."

"You were living over on Emory Street, right?" I countered, shifting it back.

"That's where—that should be my home."

"I remember visiting you there."

"Yuh, right."

"And you had people come to the house to take care of you."

"Yuh. Every one's a different personality."

"Were they good or not so good? At home?"

"They were more or less indifferent. I think all they cared about was the check at the end of the week. I don't think they had too much compassion. I believe, at that time, if they had walked me, I would have been able to progress on my own."

"And, of course, Frances was still there," I added gently.

"Frances died. I don't know what happened. Maybe a heart condition. And I always blamed myself."

"Why?" I asked, surprised.

"I thought I should have got her to Boston, where I had a heart bypass at the Mass. General, which has great, ah, great capabilities."

"But I'm sure she got good medical care, though."

"Who?"

"Frances."

"Frances's *dead*," he declared firmly. "She died. And I always blame myself that she didn't get better care," he repeated doggedly. "She was too good to me."

"Before you came here—"

"I was home most of the time. Well, I went to Newbridge," he amended quickly, with reference to his first nursing home placement. "I think I might have been there one year. They're quite proficient there. And a Mrs. Vanetti runs a good ship."

"So you liked it there better?"

"Not really. It was a dead end. I was going no place. They walk you once in a while, and it didn't seem to do the job. I needed more effort, walking. I don't think that the aides care to walk you...I think that putting in the time is very hard for an aide. They're waiting for the clock to go around." He paused, glancing briefly at his wall clock and the window beyond, where the thin light of a March afternoon was quickly fading away. "And the clock is slow, as you know."

"Yeah. When you were at home on Emory Street, how did it get decided that you were gonna go to the Newbridge nursing home?"

"I think, by word of mouth. Other people were there, and I was told that the trustees had an interest in me being there because I had a fairly well-known name, that would make it easy for other people."

"But did you want to go there?"

"Not really."

"Why did you say that you would go?"

"Because I had given power of attorney to my son, Will, and I think he had an idea, I think it was, I think the cost was too much. And he tried to preserve my assets, which I give him a lot of credit for. Which was probably a good motive."

"Yes, because you know a lot of people feel very badly that they can't leave anything to their family."

"I handled that matter pretty well, I think, up to a point. I remembered all of them."

"But you have given them a lot, all the time, over the years."

"I was proud of them because they all got through college and they all have families, very good children. *Numerous*." Here he smiled wryly.

"I'm mortified that a [person bearing his surname] is receiving some public funds," T. D. continued, moving from the pros to the cons of his family's efforts to preserve assets. "I'm too proud. Proud of my name. Proud of my brothers, James and Paul. Paul is in Canton, Ohio. And I'm proud of their war record. They both served, James and Paul, and *Martin*. He was probably my favorite. Then maybe James took over, because at heart I'm a politician."

T. D. understands that every action has its consequence. Neither cause nor effect, taken alone, could be considered ironic. Together, they are simultaneously unpredictable and inevitable, and herein lies the irony. First, T. D. transferred money and property to his children. Following the fiscally conservative principles he had taught them, they chose not to "spend down" on health care. As a result, T. D. now lives on Medicaid. While he did not anticipate the physical abandonment of institutionalization, he finds it difficult to condemn his son's actions without also praising his good business sense. During one of our conversations, he summed it up this way: "My father—that's when he was a blacksmith—he had a great saying that I like. He used to say, when something happened, 'When the hammer strikes the anvil.' "

"Yeah?" I asked, puzzled.

"What he meant by that was, when something occurs, there's a reason for it."

Here he lapsed into a long silence, which seemed to fill with unspoken regrets. "Well, I guess that's true, huh?" I said awkwardly. "Sometimes," I amended hastily, eager to avoid the implication that his problems were of his own making. "Sometimes, maybe not."

"Maybe not. You're right, Maria. So you tell me about O. J.," he invited, shifting without pause to a less personal example of ironic complexity, but one he followed keenly. "What's your version?"

Most of all, T. D. understands the heady, addictive qualities of power. Born in 1906, he grew up with three brothers and a sister in a small factory town beset with three-way ethnic tensions among the descendants of Revolutionary-era settlers and subsequent waves of Irish and Italian immigrants. His father died when he was a young adult. T. D.'s extended family included the wealthy and the very poor, and it contained several members—male and female—who were intent on

MARIA D. VESPERI

gaining access to local economic and political power structures. As Irish Americans in a community where virtually all the public sector jobs were controlled by "old Yankees," T. D. and his youthful peers sought to excel in academics, sports, street fighting, and gambling, in an order dictated by their respective talents.

T. D. gained a reputation as an outstanding high school athlete. All five children in his family went to college; T. D. and one brother, Paul, became pharmacists. As a young man, T. D. worked in a relative's store, where he learned how to dispense not only medications but also political patronage.

"In my hometown, to be Catholic was a disadvantage. The power lay in the other religious advocates, with the bankers and elected officials. If you wanted a school job, that was impossible," he said.

"But see, that's changed now," I said optimistically.

"I *hope* so," he replied pointedly. "We had patronage at Austin's store, from the Burns. And we felt obligated, in return for that patronage, to support Mike [a member of the Burns family who became a state politician]. He won the first time out."

During our conversations, T. D. made clear associations among his efforts to excel at sports, his labors on behalf of political candidates, and his ability to wield influence for the benefit of family and friends. Given that economic disparities and cultural bias made the playing field uneven, the end was often understood to justify the means.

"I wanted our town always to win," T. D. explained. "I never wanted to wear our uniform and get beat. I wanted us on the *top*. The *town*. I want *anybody* here to do well.

"And if I could help them at the Town Hall, I would. [Mr. Austin] wanted people taken care of, and I would go to the right agency. The assessors—you can lose your home with the assessors. And they could reduce the tax. Otherwise, they were afraid of the bankers, the Yankee element, which is very critical. The Yankees didn't want to spend a dime on education. Why? Because you were educating the Italians, and Portuguese."

"Yeah, that's true," I agreed, having heard many people discuss this subject over the years.

"They couldn't see that as making a good community," he concluded, clearly proud to have proven them wrong.

During my interviews with T. D., I was careful to make distinctions between what he had shared on earlier visits and what he was now telling me "for the record." Over the years, he had related some very colorful stories about politics and business, stories I accepted as truth because I had already heard them from others or because they were fully consistent with events I remembered in the community. T. D.'s repertoire was not limited to tales from the past. Even from his nursing home bed, he could pinpoint the details behind recent land deals or speculate reasonably about the apportionment of patronage jobs.

Shared knowledge was a key element of our interviews, of course, and of the portrait of T. D. that emerges here. However, I was concerned that T. D. might feel pressured to maintain the candor that had marked our prior conversations. For this reason, I avoided asking him to repeat stories he had told before, with one exception:

"You told me when I was here at Christmas time that you had gotten into a fight, you know, a physical fight with one of the aides. You hit somebody?"

T. D. nodded. "If they hit me, I punch back," he said simply. "I can't help—"

"What happens then?"

"Then they go to the top people, and they come in and give you hell. And I tell *them* to go to hell."

"Is that what happened when you did that before?"

"Yuh. I punched one of 'em, or kicked her."

"Then the boss comes in?"

"Yuh, they run to the boss," he explained, "and the boss has to placate them. Otherwise, they say they'll quit, and then the place is empty."

Here and elsewhere, T. D. is fully aware of the mutual dependency implicit in Burke's "kinship with the enemy." While he savors the fantasy of a staff walkout prompted by his resistance to authority, he also acknowledges the reality of the nursing home as a workplace created by his own need.

Another day, T. D. elaborated on his role in this ironically scripted drama with a story that helped to explain why resistance remains crucial to his sense of self. "My trouble is, I'm a physical type of person, always competitive and very resentful of opposition. I've had some real serious fights. There was a guy...tried to advance himself with a friend of mine. Reilly. Catherine Reilly. I was told about it, and I waylaid him, and I give him a goddamn good beating. And he came to the store the next day, and he wanted revenge. I said, 'Okay, I'll see you in back of the movie house, Friday, at twelve o'clock.' Then I got myself equipped with a Holy Cross and Boston College ring, one on each hand, Vaseline up here," he added, dabbing the fingertips of his left hand across his forehead, "and a tight jersey. I showed up there, and I hammered the shit out of him, cut him up pretty good."

At this point, we both burst out laughing; the disparity between the story and the circumstances of its telling could not have been greater. "I was proud of that," he continued smugly, smoothing the sheet over his chest. "I really liked those kids. Seven sisters, and two boys in the family."

"So how old were you when that happened?" I asked.

"How old was I? I was probably at least twenty-five. Crazy," he declared with a laugh, more rueful than the one before.

"So that was a while ago, huh?" I continued. "Has your attitude changed any?"

"Not really," he said casually, correctly interpreting my question to mean, might he still savor "hammering the shit out of" someone to avenge a friend, especially a female friend? Then he paused, and I could tell by the glint in his eye that my question was about to rebound with a wry twist. "I could understand," he amended, with mock solicitude for his former opponent. "That girl was really attractive!"

"EVERYBODY PLAYS THE GAME"

"In baseball, I used to steal a lot of the bases," T. D. told me. "We used to play in [a nearby town]. And Bobby [his close friend] got spiked over there. And I said to the guy that spiked him, I said, 'I'll be down to see you.' He was playing third base. So to get at him, I bunted the ball, which is not easy to do. They had a very good pitcher. So you bunt the ball....it's hard to field it. So I tagged first base. Then I headed for second. When I got near second, I got about seven or eight guys off me and headed for third. When I got close to third, I did the 'airplane slide' and put my feet up in the guy's chest. That started a fight. And I got put in the can over that."

"How come?"

"A big shot came out of the stand and told the cop at the game that I should be arrested for 'that type of baseball.' So he took me to the fire station. Downstairs was a cell. Nice odor of urine in the mattress. Beautiful."

When T. D. says "beautiful," he does not mean aesthetically pleasing, nor is he engaging in straightforward sarcasm. Instead, he alludes to a perfection, a balance, the inevitable completion of a circle, "when the hammer strikes the anvil." During our interviews, he used the term *beautiful* to describe the actions of the nursing assistants, whom he seemed to regard as dancers in a ballet dreamed up by a highly cynical choreographer.

"So today, the lady, Marta, she's the boss, second boss, she came around with six pills, and I refused them," he reported during one of my visits. "Because it makes no sense. You see, they want to give you six immediately, so they don't have to come back. They give you six all at once, and of course, that's a contradiction, a chemical contradiction. You take six pills and swallow them, they're not going to do the individual job that they're designed for. Ha, ha! That's a laugh." I laughed, too.

"See, now, if the one that has *that* job, they have a book and they notate the frequency of the kind of pills that you get," he continued, warming to the subject. "They claim that the doctor—believe me, the doctors don't know what—this is a free ride for the doctors. They're not competent. Nobody checks the MDs, so everybody plays the game."

Another time, we returned to the subject of physical resistance. "Well, if they switch and turn me in cleaning, it hurts, and I'll strike back," T. D. said without hesitation. "And you can't do that. They have like a union. They threaten management that they're gonna quit, walk out. The guy's stuck. How's he gonna operate without help? And the state, I think—my own opinion—the state is indifferent. They don't supervise as they should."

"You mean they don't supervise conditions?"

"Each specialist plays their own game."

"Well, how is it structured, then?" I asked.

"What, dear?"

"How is it structured in terms of authority here?"

"There's a manager, Joey something. He has a funny last name. Then there's 'experienced supervisors,' which I think is weak," he commented in an editorial tone. "The ordinary worker here needs to be checked and impressed with authority. I think they resent supervision. It interferes with their routine. In the morning, they can come in, have a cup of coffee or whatever, or a muffin. Which, the kitchen does a pretty good job here," he added in the interest of fairness. "This morning, the dull affair was cereal and toast, with coffee."

"And that was okay?"

"They also start out with orange juice. A vitamin is added to it, and I try to consume it, with the hope of benefits from the supplement. It's probably a powdered vitamin. I don't know what it is. They insist—I think the state approves their test for longevity.... *Geriatric,* right? Which is a laugh. *Ha ha.* I don't think they expect you to last too long. *Expectations of the future are very cloudy,*" he pronounced in a tone of theatrical solemnity, but with a twinkle in his eye.

"And it's my own humble opinion that families are indifferent and should be made to accommodate their relatives, and if not, they should be taxed for it," T. D. continued. "If that happened, they would soon take the family members home and maybe rotate them." Here he paused, thinking through the implications. "Which, in a sense, would be an intrusion on several members of a family, who have their own small, new family, which gets all their attention. And it's costly," he concluded in a dispirited tone, "in today's world."

T. D.'s view of the medical profession is based on his career as a pharmacist and his role as a local mover and shaker. Politics, in his experience, is a game to be played with one's spikes on. He continues to follow local and national politics, and this blunt advice for Bill Clinton earmarks his approach: "What the President should do is get the records of these Republicans—how much they've spent on airfares—and hammer the shit out of them."

One March morning, T. D. voted in a local election by absentee ballot. The experience prompted the following recollection when I arrived for our interview later that day:

"When it came to absentee votes, we voted a shithouse full of 'em. [Once] about seventy-seven absentee votes went in for the Democrats on Election Day. I would go to [the town clerk], get the application. Then I would go to Dr. G, or one of the doctors, get his signature. See, the person voting at home, the requirements were that they were unable to walk to the polls. That's why the absentee ballot was supplied the voter. And you had to produce the evidence, by the doctor's signature, that the person was homebound and couldn't go to the polls to vote and had the right as a citizen to vote under supervision. So I got the doctors lined up, and then we would take the application to the town clerk...and a ballot would be issued. Then we would ask the clerk who received the ballots, and we would go to the home with a notary public—we had about six guys doing it—and we would get the vote for the Democrats."

"APRIL FOOL"

T. D. shares a semi-private room with Rob Winston, another stroke patient. Mr. Winston is rail thin, mobile, and visibly frustrated by his severe aphasia. His verbal communication is restricted to the perseveration of "Yuh, yuh, yuh." Our conversations invariably go something like this:

"Hello, Mr. Winston."

"Yuh, yuh, yuh."

"I hope you're feeling well today."

"Yuh, yuh, yuh."

"I'm here to see T. D. again."

"Yuh, yuh, yuh."

Mr. Winston can perform routine self-care activities. He subscribes to the local newspaper, enjoys visits from family and friends, and wanders the halls in a hesitant shuffle. He and T. D. have a cordial and vaguely symbiotic relationship. Mr. Winston, for instance, is clearly amused by T. D.'s stories. A particularly outrageous tale can cause him to beam like a little brother who, to his own surprise, has been trusted to tag along for a day of mischief.

At the same time, as I did not realize until I transcribed our conversations, T. D. has largely substituted "yuh" for "yes" in his own vocabulary. T. D.'s conversational style is otherwise quite formal, despite the obligatory cursing that marks accepted masculine speech in his cultural environment.

"Hi, Rob. *Mr. Winston*," T. D. said heartily one day as his roommate picked his way cautiously from corridor to bed. Then to me, but loud enough for Mr. Winston to hear, "He's a Manchester gentleman. The Winstons came from Manchester in the Revolutionary period.

"He tries to walk every day. A lot of courage. I admire him. Sometimes when I drop something—he's very, very good to me." T. D. paused. "I think he thinks I'm a pretty good guy," he concluded softly.

"Well, you are," I agreed.

"That remains to be seen," T. D. countered sharply, his eyes flashing dark humor.

"How old are you going to be on your next birthday, T. D.?" I asked him.

"I will be close to ninety, I think. That's terrible. I'm afraid of it. I don't want to grow old. My advice is, don't do it."

"Why not?"

"There's no purpose served, as long as you are incapacitated by whatever happens to you, sickness or anything else, a shock. [T. D. and other local people of his generation use the term *shock* interchangeably with *stroke*.] There's people here with shock. That's too bad, and they could do better if they could get walking. They could help themselves and be happy. Most of them are very unhappy. They want out."

"What do you mean, they want out?"

"They want to be back to their homes. The home influence is very positive, and it means a great deal. This place has the semblance of a jail, and the aides are looked upon by most patients as jailers. They have reason to be here, financial reason."

"Why do you think a person would pick *this* work, instead of —?"

"Why? Because the demands of the economy are such that a few dollars a week on the side is extremely important to a family. And they soon have accommodated themselves with friendships and interests with the other aides. They probably socialize some."

"Why do you say that?"

"Because I hear them talk: 'They're going to go out tonight and have a toddy.' And, of course, the subject of conversation is always their personal experience. They talk back and forth. They exchange, for companionship, conversation. It's all self-interest."

"How about with you?"

"What do you mean?"

"Do you feel that they talk with you directly?"

"Occasionally. Some of them are very kind to say 'hi' or 'hello.' Some of them are good. They're good nurses. They're good people."

A bank of windows next to T. D.'s bed faces obliquely on the yellow brick wall of an adjoining wing of the nursing home. These windows are large and the building is low, so he also commands a patch of grass and a smudge of sky. In this part of the country, the intensity of light against buildings and trees reveals a lot about the weather and the changing seasons.

"Do you know how long you have been here, in this place?" I asked him, curious about the sense of time afforded by his fixed view of winter, spring, summer, and fall.

"I have no idea," T. D. said, pinning me with a keen look. "I'm afraid to ask. I don't know if they would tell me. I haven't asked in quite a while, probably two or three months. If they don't watch me, I'm gonna die here. And I don't wanna die. I'm afraid of death. And I can do a lot of things. My brain isn't that bad."

"Not at all," I agreed readily. "That's why if you can talk about the experience of being in a nursing home, other people can learn something about it."

"You ask me any question you want. I'll give you an answer," he said magnanimously. I said nothing for a moment, so he gamely volunteered: "The food here is not bad. Margaret's been very good. She brings fruit, like pears or peaches, and I enjoy the consumption. And that also activates the bowels, which can be a bother, because then you're gonna soil the bed and soil yourself, which can be somewhat painful. You have to get used to pain. It takes a lot of courage, which I don't have."

"Yes you do," I countered.

"And I feel bad for some of the ladies here," he continued, noting my comment with a slow blink. "They're helpless. They should be walked every day. And a guy like me, to get me going, *I* should be walked twice a day, morning and afternoon."

"*Do* you walk around?"

"I would. If I got up, I would help a lot of people because I know a lot of people."

"Can you use your leg at all?"

"I can move it, with a great effort."

"But it won't bear weight, huh?"

"It will not respond to what I want to do....If I had a cane, I can do fair with it. My cane is not here."

"What about one of those walkers, like that lady has?" I asked, gesturing toward a woman who was making slow progress along the corridor.

"It would be worth a try," said T. D., craning his neck to watch as she disappeared beyond his doorway.

As our attention shifted back to the room, a calendar caught my attention. "T. D., do you keep track of the date?" I asked.

"It's very hard. My mind doesn't seem to want to do it. The date? I think now we're into March."

"Yes, that's right."

"I remember St. Patrick's Day."

"Yeah, that was last week, right?"

"If I could get out of here, I'd *go* to Ireland," he declared. "I wanna go to Dublin," he continued, his eyes sparkling as he warmed to the subject, " 'cause, you know, there's a pub there that I could use as a headquarters." He mentioned a postcard someone had sent him from Ireland that showed a drugstore connected to a pub. "Which is quite *necessary*," he said wryly.

"Yeah, I know what you mean," I said, remembering the rows of whiskey bottles over the grill. "*Your* store used to be a headquarters, didn't it?"

"Yes, it did," he agreed with satisfaction. "Not only that, but we played cards at night. Also played checkers for money on the side. Played a game of checkers for five dollars. That was very interesting."

"The reason I'm asking you about the date is because I'm wondering if people in the nursing home keep track of time."

"I don't think they do. They don't have a calendar. And how are they going to mark a calendar, or change it, if they're bedridden?" he asked.

"What about the year?" I persisted. "Do you keep track of the year?"

"I try, but it's not easy. It's *hard* to remember. I think now it's about ninety-th—ree, ninety-four, or ninety-five."

"Ninety-five," I said encouragingly. "That's right, ninety-five."

"It *is* ninety-five," he said confidently. Then he shifted once again to a topic that he found handy when he wanted to change the subject, collecting opinions about the O. J. Simpson trial. Debating current events was a skill he had thoroughly mastered during his working years, and he was still hungry for viewpoints that could be gathered and shared.

"What do *you* think about him?" I asked.

"I think the detectives are involved in narcotics," he offered.

"It doesn't add up, does it?"

"No, if you take it for a subject of conversation. I sent him a check, small check. Also, a check for that environmental thing, the loss of animals. I sent a small—*had Will* send a small check," he corrected promptly, as if honoring a vow to keep in scrupulous touch with reality. "And I sent to Africa, to the blacks there who had a hard time."

"In Somalia or in Rwanda?" I asked.

"In South Africa, Johannesburg, is that it? Yuh. That's too bad because someday this whole world of ours is going to be Spanish and partially black."

"People have a lot of prejudice, don't they?"

"Yuh, prejudice is going to defeat the nation....Where are you gonna get citizens? Where are you gonna get people to join the service?" he mused aloud.

At the end of our week, I returned to the subject of calendars. Looking back on this conversation, I can see that my ethnocentric fixation on knowing the date was of little consequence to T. D. I was frustrated that a man who could discuss diplomacy in Northern Ireland, welfare reform in the US Congress, and the potential for nuclear aggression by North Korea was being deprived of such a key measure of reality orientation. Now I realize that I had not really listened when I asked him whether people in nursing homes kept track of time. For T. D., marking the calendar was "do gooder" behavior, the domain of activities directors. It was a nod to superficial niceties, at best, and from another perspective, a cruel irony. At the time, however, I persisted:

"Can you *see* that calendar over there, T. D.? Can you read it?" I prompted.

"No, I can't see it," he replied indifferently.

"Not doing you much good over there."

"No, you're right," he agreed amiably, but without much conviction. "It would be better if it's put under the clock."

"Yeah. Cause you *can* read the clock, right?"

"Yuh. That's about it."

"Anyway, today's April Fool's Day, you know."

"The first of April?"

"Yeah."

"That April Fool applies well to me," he responded, his interest sparked by the prospect of word play. "I've been well fooled. I think I've been bullshitted."

"THE CHAIR IS KILLING ME"

"I know what it is to suffer from injuries as an athlete," T. D. said one afternoon, when his discomfort threatened to disrupt our interview. He was sitting restlessly in the big padded chair next to his bed.

"How would you compare that to the pain you have now?" I asked.

"I've had pain before, legs injured, and the head through the windshield. Then I went through a window in the armory, playing my man. See, I had to stop him and he had to stop me," he declared with relish, remembering an old basketball game.

"Do a lot of people have visitors on the weekend?" I asked, distracted from the topic of pain by loud greetings as a woman made her way down the corridor. In this small community, visiting family members might encounter their former teachers, neighbors, or co-workers before reaching their own relative's bed.

"Yes, there seem to be quite a few," T. D. said. "Not enough," he added pointedly.

"Umhum. Do you think people have it better if their families come?"

"Oh, yes," he said definitively. "It's important, to break up the monotony and keep their spirits up. They owe that to their relatives, particularly if they're blood relatives, which is really the trying point. Friends *will* come once in a while, but relatives are—" he hesitated, then abandoned the search for an adequate term, "are terrible. They ought to be ashamed of themselves."

Then a nursing assistant arrived, placing a tray on T. D.'s adjustable table. "Hello there," T. D. offered. As she acknowledged his greeting, T. D. turned to me and asked cordially, "Do you want something to drink?" For a moment I felt as if I had just joined him at a restaurant and the nursing assistant was a waitress, eager to take my order.

I declined and the illusion was broken. "Linda?" He addressed her almost plaintively.

"Yes, sir."

"I'm in a lot of pain."

"I know, but *you don't take your pain medicine.*" This last was enunciated in a slow singsong, as if to a child.

"Well, that's not your business," he retorted, anticipating that nothing would be done and retaliating by alluding to her status as a nursing assistant, not a nurse.

"Well, no, but I'm trying to explain. That's why you have pain," she said, momentarily flustered.

"That's not your affair," he reiterated loftily.

"Well, why do you tell me about your pain? We try to help you and you won't listen."

"That's not the way to help. *I need to get out of the chair. The chair is killing me,*" he said emphatically.

"Oh, okay," she replied dismissively. Then, half to me and half to T. D., she asked, "Are you writing a letter, or something?" It was a reasonable question; I was holding a steno book and a pen.

"Yes, I'm gonna write to the President," T. D. shot back sarcastically.

"Ooo-*kay,*" she responded, matching his tone. "Tell him what to do, will ya? Give him some good advice." Here they both laughed, but not together and for quite different reasons. "He could use it."

"I have great affection for him because he comes from Little Rock," T. D. countered grandly. I knew that T. D. had been a college sports star in Little Rock as a young man, that he had experienced religious prejudice in Arkansas, and that he had witnessed brutal acts of racism. The experience of living in the South was rare among his age-peers and had helped define his liberal views on social issues.

To the nursing assistant, who knew none of this, T. D.'s remark must have been the ultimate non sequitur. She laughed, and her voice took on a humoring tone: "Oh, GOOD. That's—all right. Finish your letter." She took a good look at him then, slumped in his chair and obviously in pain. "I, ah, what time is it?" she mumbled to herself, checking her watch. Next, she startled me by shifting abruptly to a very loud voice, as if the preceding conversation had not been conducted easily at a bantering level: "WOULD YOU LIKE TO GO TO BED AND FINISH YOUR LETTER IN BED?"

"Yes, ma'am," said T. D. quietly.

"Okay," she confirmed, beginning to move pillows from the chair to the bed.

"This is a high-priced secretary I have here," T. D. joked, indicating me.

The nursing assistant laughed. T. D. had broken the tension.

"SEE HOW THEY SELL YOU?"

"Hi!" a nursing assistant said brightly as she made a quick visual inventory of T. D.'s supper tray. "How are you doin'? You didn't eat much today."

"Not very good," T. D. answered. It was unclear to me whether this remark referred to the food, his state of health, or both.

"Wasn't very good?" she echoed.

"No." Then impatiently, "Take that away, will ya?"

"Wouldn't you like to keep your coffee?"

"I'll try it. Take that dish out of the way, please."

"All right. I'll leave you some water, too." She hesitated, then commented in a neutral tone, "That's your, ah, *supplement,* you know. That pudding is your vitamins."

T. D. eyed the bland-looking contents of a small bowl with sharp suspicion. "Really? I don't know."

"Well, are you sure you don't want that?"

"I'll try it," he said, tempted by the promise of sweetness. "It tastes good."

"'Cause it has all your, ah, the goodies in it, you know?" she continued, obviously working to keep her tone noncommittal. "You really ought to put that in your tummy."

"I don't believe it. What is a 'supplement'? What *is* it?"

"It's called, ah, *biopudding*. It has all kinds of vitamins and stuff in it." At this point, she turned and left, obviously relieved to have avoided an outburst.

"I wonder," T. D. mused. "See how they sell you? They've got a story for everything."

"Do they know that you're a pharmacist, though?" I was appalled by the condescending way T. D.'s questions had been sidestepped.

"They throw that at me once in a while. They say, 'You should know better.'"

"But they're not *telling* you anything!"

"You're right," he agreed, working his spoon into the bowl. "That tastes good," he conceded. "I don't know what the hell it is." Then, with an invitation that was really a command, "Taste it."

T. D. stared expectantly as I raised a healthy spoonful of the stuff to my mouth. It was vanilla pudding, but with a distinctive chalky aftertaste. "What is it?" he asked eagerly.

"Not bad. It has a vanilla taste. Vanilla pudding."

Soon, however, I began to feel an odd pressure inside my head. T. D. launched into a complicated story, but one or both of us lost its thread. It was late anyhow, so I went home, where I played that portion of the tape in an effort to recapture what the story was about. T. D.'s words were notably slurred. "He sounds drugged," remarked my daughter's husband, who has never met T. D.

Later I was able to make sense of the **nursing** assistant's elaborate casualness and T. D.'s insistence that I taste the pudding. His family told me that tranquilizers and antidepressants had been prescribed, that T. D. had refused them, and that they had hesitated to push the issue one way or another. The "pudding" was apparently a compromise; it avoided the battle over pills. T. D. knew that something was "wrong" with it; he also knew that he was fighting a losing battle on this front.

"Are you taking any medications, T. D.?" I asked on another occasion.

"It's been prescribed, but I know, in most cases, they want to give you six pills at once. That's a conflict; one pill makes negative the other. And that's time-consuming, to come back and serve you six medicals."

"So what do you do?"

"I don't like to take them. I know from my experience as a drug-gist, that's absurd, and it serves no useful purpose. Like today, the girl said, 'It's for your heart.' I know better."

"What do you think it was?"

"I think it was potassium. I think it was potassium chloride, which I don't think is necessary, is good—"

"But low potassium is a problem, right?" I interrupted reasonably.

"Yes it is, up to a point," he agreed. "A food like a banana is sup-posed to be laden with a good amount of potassium, and it's said to be helpful for your heart."

"So, do you eat bananas?"

"Yuh. If they give you a banana, I ask them to put it in the cereal, or eat it as is. It's not that bad. It's easy on your system.…It's hard for a patient to peel it. You cannot peel a banana in a prone position."

"What about for pain? What do you take for pain?"

"Yes, they do relieve your pain on request."

"What do you get?" I pressed, curious to test his knowledge on this point.

"I imagine it goes back to the narcotic, such as maybe it's a by-product of, uh, codeine. Which is not good for the system because you ultimately become dependent. It's an easy out for this place. Then you go back the next day, and everything is the same as the day before," he concluded bitterly, ready to drop the subject.

"What do *you* think would be the best pain medicine for you to take?" I persisted.

"It's *got* to be something with codeine," he conceded grudgingly, mentioning a drug by a series of numbers and then translating. "It has an eighth of a grain of codeine." This seemed to contradict his initial objection, until he continued with his reason for dreading codeine.

"If the bowel acts up, now you're gonna soil the bed, and your skin is gonna break down. I'm afraid of that. I don't wanna die from bedsores. Also, a lot of pain is involved, before you collapse. Then you're gonna starve to death. Starvation is a real possibility…" he trailed off grimly. I was reminded of Kathleen Woodward's comment about Beckett's Malone, who was fearful of neglect and starvation while equally apprehensive that his misery would be extended through heroic means.

"Now you know, there's people who have tubes," I said.

"I don't want that. A tube into me?" he retorted sharply. "They *do* have that. I think that's terrible. They suffer. I saw a fella by the name of Camelli. That's the way he was here, and I really felt bad for him because I knew him. He was an early baseball star."

"Have you told people that you wouldn't want something like that?"

"You're never asked," he proclaimed haughtily.

"Well, you can be, you know. You can sign a form that says you don't want that."

"*Really?* I'll sign it. I don't want that kind of—I don't want to live forever. What good is it?"

I told him about living wills, surprised that he was unfamiliar with them. He knew, for instance, the name and mandate of an ombudsman who visited the nursing home, and he was generally apprised of his legal rights.

"I'll mention it to Annie," I offered.

"I wish you would."

"You have to sign it in front of a witness."

At this, he began to look dubious. "You know what I believe, Maria? I believe that the doctor's philosophy affects Annie's thinking. [Annie's husband is a retired physician.] I think her husband, these medical people, come to a certain conclusion. You know?"

"I know what you mean. I don't know about [living wills], but I've seen that before with doctors."

"I laughed to myself," T. D. continued. "I said, pretty good. You've got two doctors in the family and two druggists."

With that comment, the six decades of T. D.'s support for his family fanned out before me. I remembered the drugstore, open roughly fourteen hours a day, seven days a week. I briefly considered the school tuition bills, the houses, the acreage, and the countless forms of material and social capital that had passed from T. D. to his siblings, children, grandchildren, and beyond.

"So, you think that's ironic, then?" I asked.

"That's right. It's a self-made joke."

"THE CLOCK IS NOT OUR FRIEND"

"I was going to ask you what it's like here at night."

"At night? It's very routine. They come in and check you, to see if you need to be cleaned, and they work in pairs. And one of them will roll you, and the other will use the cleaning tissues or cloths. They call them 'wipes.' Usually, you're either sweating or you have a bowel movement, which is not good, 'cause that will break down the skin if it's not—if you're not cleaned, and the feces will eventually kill you. Bedsores," he predicted grimly.

After a brief discussion of preventative care for bedsores, I asked, "Do you sleep through the night?"

"Not the best. I try to watch television, to kill the night. Then they'll come in, they'll—one of them will grab the glasses, take them off. They say, ah, 'No television after 10.' Gotta shut the damn thing down....They give you that bullshit—the glasses, if I go to sleep, I don't need the glasses."

"Hmmm."

"See, the big thing now with everybody that's here is the time, passage of time, which is very slow. The clock is not our friend." There was a long pause; I could not think of anything to say. Finally, T. D. glanced out the window at the fading day and picked up the thread of conversation: "Isn't there an hour change coming up now?"

"Yes. It's tonight," I said.

I left the room for a few minutes while two nursing assistant helped T. D. into bed. "Now you see, Maria, with her nerve, she just put that damned urine bottle there," he complained when I returned. "Very uncomfortable," he added, gesturing between his legs to the visible outline of a urinal under the sheets. "I suppose that's 'preparation.' They work as teammates."

"Umhmm."

"So that means that if I don't—if the bed isn't wet—the next one won't have to change it. So they work as pals. Then, when they give you a bath, I can see what it does. If you take that whirlpool bath, see, you'll be dressed in the bath when you get out of the tub. It's not a *tub*," he corrected, "It's some kind of metal container for the water.

"And the one that operates that, oh boy, is she cruel. She even shaved me the other day. They can't stand to look at me. I'm ridiculed as 'Santa Claus' or 'Adams.' They made a picture of some guy by the name of Adams. He was supposed to be a, a man of the country, a hill man. 'Fuzzy.' They call me 'Fuzzy.'" T. D. was clearly unfamiliar with the television program *Grizzly Adams*. I was unsure whether knowledge of its content would have assuaged or increased his outrage at the comparison.

"That's not good, to ridicule anybody," T. D. continued. "That breaks your spirit. You're mortified—like today, this big one that helped put me out of the chair into here. A big woman. She's very strong.... Ha! I told you when they shaved me, one held my arm so I couldn't push them away or hit them—"

"Yeah, you did tell me that."

"And the other one held my head up so the one with the razor could bear down, and she did. Now today, this one shaved me under pressure. That really hurts."

"What did she say?"

"She kep' at it. She was determined that I would be clean-shaven, and the hair on my neck was pretty long. That was not shaved—with that electric—it was like burning off your beard. They put the pressure on very hard. That takes away the whiskers. And that really is a painful procedure."

"Well, what do *you* want to do? Do you want to shave yourself, or do you want to grow a beard?"

"I'd just as soon have the beard and shave myself if I can. Without a mirror, you don't know what the hell you're doing."

"They have mirrors they could hook on your bed over there," I said, indicating the rail. "On an arm, you know?"

"Yuh. That would be a big help." But he sounded discouraged.

"Do you ever shave yourself?"

"I try, dear. It's not easy. Will shaved me yesterday, a couple of days ago. I wish he'd come and do it today, instead of her. See, they domineer. I think this place gets to them. Too much pain for their patients, and *difficult* patients. We all have our problems. I'm very sensitive. My daughter Margaret says, 'You have sensitive skin, Dad.' Because everything hurts."

T. D. tilted his head to draw my attention to a nursing assistant who was walking down the hall. "That one goes up and down the corridor there, singing. She thinks she's a singer. She's not. Ha! She hustles by.

They keep going. They will not come in to check you, to help you. And that singing performance is for the management, to hear how interested she is in her work. So she's singing away, happily."

Once again, T. D. mined his insider's vantage point for full ironic effect. As a businessman, he could imagine how the nursing assistant's performance might be music to the ears of her supervisor. An alert resident such as he, who observed her work habits directly, might interpret her singing quite differently. Last but not least, an old man with good hearing was certainly entitled to his opinion. "'I Don't Know Why I Love You,' that's her theme song," T. D. informed me. "Ha, ha! She can't sing a note."

"LIFE IS TOO ATTRACTIVE"

The presence of irony in ethnographic texts has been widely critiqued (Clifford 1986; Fischer 1986; Krupat 1992; Marcus 1986). Fischer offers a promising discussion of its use as an intentional device: "Irony and humor are tactics that ethnographers have only slowly come to appreciate, albeit recently with increasing interest" (1986:229). He points out that the resultant introduction of subtlety "seems often (but not necessarily) to run counter to the canons of explicitness and univocal meaning expected in scientific writing" (1986:230). More recently, Fernandez and Huber (2001) bring together a range of important insights on irony in relation to anthropological inquiry in the introduction to their welcome collection, *Irony in Action*. A discussion of Kenneth Burke by James Boon is included in this volume. Among the many useful bridges to the wellspring of Burke's thought is an exploration of "kinship with the enemy" in relation to Boon's (2001: 118–132) own fieldwork in Bali. Reading this essay, I was struck anew by the anthropological relevance of Burke's work on irony and how powerfully it has informed both research and interpretation among ethnographers who, like me, were exposed to his ideas as students.

In contemporary practice, the univocal approach—Burke's extreme relativism—is regarded as less than adequate for the representation of ethnographic contexts and the situation of selves within them. The author who does not speak is really the only speaker, no matter how often he or she might reproduce the words of the other. Thus, I have tried to present my conversations with T. D. in the context of our shared knowledge, both personal and cultural. Sometimes this knowledge took the form of a concordance, used by each to elicit meaning from the other's statements. At other times, it became a mirror in which we checked to ensure that our own words had been accurately received.

T. D. and I had our last interview in July 1995, a week after we attended an eightieth birthday celebration for his brother James. This party, with almost 600 in attendance, was the acknowledged capstone of a long political career that T. D. had helped to create. He told me in March that he had every intention of being there; he knew the details of who was running the event and how the speeches would be organized. He was mentally rehearsing a speech of his own, and he tried out a couple of anecdotes on me.

T. D. arrived at the party with his son, who had hired a wheelchair van and a driver for the thirty-mile trip. Like the other men, he was impeccably groomed and dressed in a fine suit and tie. Although this was a daytime affair, some older women wore formal clothes. The dark hall was designed to create the illusion of an evening party; brocaded gowns captured pinpoints of light from the dramatic chandeliers.

During the two-hour presentation that preceded the meal, testimonial speakers were concealed behind a stage curtain. Each read his or her remarks and then stepped forward to congratulate James. The first voice was Will's, reading his father's little speech. When he pushed T. D. from behind the curtain, there were audible gasps. Clearly, no one expected T. D. to make the trip; out-of-towners had probably assumed that he was dead. The crowd rose and applauded wildly, and I saw that several people at nearby tables were crying.

No interpretation was needed to tease the irony from the contrast between that day and our last formal interview two weeks later. T. D. was back in his sparsely furnished room, staring blankly at a news broadcast on his small television. "If I stay here, I'll go insane," he announced immediately.

"What do you mean?" I asked. "Your mind is fine."

"Well, I'm afraid. I worry so much. I don't want to die here. To me, that's a disgrace, to take any charity, and my kids owe it to me. I've been good to them. If they have any family pride, they wouldn't let it be known that I'm here. I betcha they pass it off: 'How's your father? Oh, he's fine.'"

He told me once again that he feared dying in the nursing home and added that his daughter Annie had promised that "she wouldn't let that happen." He dispassionately reviewed the prospects among his children: available space, health, lifestyle, objections from spouses. There was a painful silence. *"That wouldn't be bad if I could live with one of my kids,"* he uttered longingly, as if thinking aloud.

T. D. said that his family had "aborted their responsibility" to care for him. "Put the member of their family in one of these places, and they can go on with their business and forget ya. They don't give a damn. It's too bad, but life is too attractive."

During his working years and during his second career as a nursing home resident, T. D. has been able to see himself both as an individual and as a component of a well-oiled machine. He is able simultaneously to *tell* me his feelings and to *reflect* on himself speaking as an old man in a bed, conscious that he is being interviewed for an article about nursing homes. "You keep hope alive, you know," he observed with a self-deprecating grin. "In the back of your mind, you want to go back to the old days. 'The old days are too old.' Quote."

T. D. appreciates that my view of him is, itself, polyvocal, a frequently discordant chorus of imagery from the present and the past. Such dissonance can embarrass nursing home residents, and visitors often cite it as a reason to stay away. As one friend said, when I suggested a visit to T. D., he preferred to "remember him as he was." Yet, T. D. himself still hungers to be known for who he *is*. A storyteller with sharp political insight, he is fully aware of the irony behind the sound bite, the distortion inherent in allowing a part to represent the whole. Metonymy and synecdoche are never enough. As he himself put it, the smoke from an old clay pipe can speak plainly of fire while shrouding the burning heart within.

Postscript: This article was completed in 1996. Nearly a year later, T. D. died in the nursing home, attended by family members.

Note

1.   The names of people and locations have been altered to protect confidentiality.

4

"Bread and Butter" Issues

Food, Conflict, and Control
in a Nursing Home

Joel S. Savishinsky

In the diet and weight-conscious culture of the United States, some people eat to live and others live to eat. American nursing homes are places where both these contrasting attitudes are played out, sometimes in dramatic fashion. Geriatric residents and staff clearly share a concern for the health and nutritional status of the elderly. Food, of course, is not the only issue that carries emotional and symbolic weight inside the institution: Loss, death, morality, nurturance, intimacy, autonomy, and privacy also loom large. However, these other concerns are often expressed in how residents deal with meals on a daily basis. This essay examines how such "bread and butter" issues connect to these other areas of meaning. It draws on research conducted at Elmwood Grove Nursing Home, an 84-bed skilled nursing facility in a rural area of upstate New York. The focus is on the significance of meals there as they relate to sociability, pleasure, anger, control, and responsibility.[1]

The data presented here derive from an ongoing study of Elmwood Grove that my students and I began in 1983. Initially, we were drawn to the institution as part of a project designed to assess the effectiveness of a pet therapy program that community volunteers were conducting at Elmwood and three other geriatric facilities in our area. The pet program's primary goal was to humanize these institutions by reintroducing an element of domesticity that most residents had been compelled to give up upon entering these facilities. After concluding a yearlong evaluation of this program, we decided to continue our work, focusing on one nursing home in order to study its institutional culture in a more comprehensive way.

We selected Elmwood Grove for several reasons. Its small size— seven dozen residents in a compact, two-story building—would allow us to examine all facets of its operation in a holistic way. Its local reputation as a good facility would permit us to study how a decent institution handles its responsibilities and human relationships. Although most of Elmwood's residents and staff were female and from predominantly white and rural communities, a number of patients and employees were of an African-American, urban, or European ethnic background. By the time the comprehensive phase of our project began, we had established good ties with staff, community volunteers, and many residents and their families. This enabled us to pursue our fundamental objective, to study how each of these different constituencies experience the same institutional world.

Several research methodologies were employed. While studying the pet therapy program, my students and I participated in and observed this community organization as volunteers. We visited the facility each week with our own or borrowed animals and also began to spend more time with individual residents and staff. When we started to study Elmwood in a more focused way, we supplemented our ongoing participant-observation at the home with structured and semi-structured interviews and the collection of life narratives. The latter approaches, first done with patients, were eventually extended to employees, volunteers, and relatives. As we became better acquainted with staff, volunteers, and the families of residents, we occasionally visited them in their own homes to talk in a more private setting. Most interviews were tape-recorded, and we made some use of video and still photography to document the details of the home's daily life. When possible, we also followed up on people who had left the world of Elmwood, residents who had been discharged, employees and volunteers who had quit, and families whose elderly relatives had died. The symbolic and substantive meanings of food were not major issues at the inception of our project, but they emerged as matters of considerable personal and social significance as we became better acquainted with the women and men of Elmwood.

FOOD AND SOCIABILITY

People entered Elmwood Grove, as they do all nursing homes, for a variety of reasons, a basic one being their inability to live independently and carry out the ADL (activities of daily living). One of the most fundamental of these activities is the capacity to take care of one's own nutritional needs, that is, to buy, prepare, and consume food. Although many residents regret and resent being in a nursing home, a number of Elmwood's patients were relieved that their move to the institution eliminated their daily anxieties about safety, security, and nutrition. Impaired health had made it difficult for them to obtain and prepare food. Those who had been living alone commonly found little joy in their solitary and often meager meals. For them, life in the nursing home was a major improvement in both nutrition and its social context. Not only was more and better food available, but also they were more likely to eat and enjoy it because of the structured and sociable environment in which it was served.

A charge nurse at Elmwood noted that a significant portion of each resident's day revolved around meals. Especially for the more mobile patients, nearly six hours per day could be devoted to getting ready for meals, going to the dining room, eating the food, and returning to the unit. As well as structuring time, meals shaped people's perception of time. Many residents talked about the other activities in their lives (family visits, physical therapy, baths, and recreational events) as occurring before or after particular meals. Visitors or staff who were walking down a hallway or working in a patient's room were often asked *not* "What time is it?" but "How long is it until we get served dinner?"

The latter question reflected a preoccupation with food and also an interest in the sociability that meals signified. People who did not see one another during other periods of the day could count on meals to bring them together. In some cases, a few critical junctures like this were the seeds from which friendships grew. Bonnie Dumond, an eighty-five-year-old woman with severe arthritis and mild confusion, who had been living at Elmwood for three years, recalled her very first day at the home: "They wheeled me into the dining room for lunch, and this woman, Barbara, she motioned me over to sit in the empty spot at the table next to her. Well, now we're good friends, and we've been eating together ever since." Eating companions who were not "good friends" also valued mealtime as one of the more social events of the day. Even the less talkative exchanged comments about their health, the weather, family occurrences, institutional gossip, or, at the very least, the food itself.

Through their own efforts, residents created food-centered events. These actions showed that the symbolic and sensory meanings of food lay not just in what people could eat but also in what they could give. The relatives of certain residents, for example, periodically brought in food to share with them, an act recreating the kind of family caregiving that relatives—as outsiders—were otherwise unable to provide. One astute relative regularly turned her act of nurturance into one of self-nurturing for the resident. In the summer, Stavros Costa's daughter Katina brought him vegetables and herbs grown in a garden he had started more than twenty-five years ago. She made a point of presenting the peppers and basil to him with the words, "Here, Dad, these are some of *your* vegetables." In some cases, kin brought boxes of candy or baskets of fruit and vegetables, not only for their relative to eat but also to share with other residents and staff. The food offerings became a social currency through which these patients could reinforce their ties to fellow residents and reward those staff whose attention they especially valued. These exchanges were sometimes done privately, and at other times they were the occasion for publicity. Stavros would quietly give some beans or peppers to his nursing assistant when she left her shift at the end of the afternoon. Another resident, Frank Healey, loved to announce to the floor staff that he had put out a basket of fruit at the nurse's station for them to share.

Another example of food sharing as a form of connectedness emerged from the weekly pet therapy program. When community volunteers brought in their cats and dogs each Friday afternoon, certain residents who regularly participated in this program gave some of their own snacks to both the human and the animal volunteers. At first, volunteers tried to dissuade patients from doing this, fearing that they were depriving themselves. Eventually, the volunteers came to recognize how important it was for the elderly to be able to offer something in return for this companionship they so appreciated. Bonnie Dumond—whose girth easily filled her wheelchair—would brush aside volunteers' objections by saying, "Your dogs need it more than me." Feeding their own pets had been a part of their domestic life. Now, offering tidbits to these animals provided a new kind of nurturant opportunity. That many residents came to look upon the pet volunteers (and their animals) as a "real" or "new" kind of family added even more domestic meaning to this form of sharing. Whether they shared food with pets or with people, in public or in private, these acts, collectively, lent support to the relevance of the exchange theory for an understanding of the details of meaning in nursing home life (Dowd 1975; Kayser-Jones 1981).

One other example of an invented food event came from a number of Elmwood's male patients, men who were, at best, reluctant participants in the home's organized activities. Several individuals had established a pattern of gravitating to a corner of the dining room between meals in order to sit over coffee and tea. None of the three to five men in the group were roommates. Two of them, Stavros and Frank, had roommates they could not stand or to whom they could not relate. A third man, Dave, shared a room with his disabled wife and joked about having "a roommate I see and hear too much of." With the help of a sociable, neutral space and the ritual of the cups, these men had created, outside the bounds of rooms and marriage, a *kaffeeklatsch* camaraderie that offset the strained silence or abrasiveness of other relations. In talk or in silence, over full meals or steaming cups, times such as these were an expression of the literal meaning of *companionship*, a word that denotes the joint consumption of *panis* (Latin for "bread"), an act of being together that is nourished and defined by the food that is shared.

PLEASURE AND ANGER

The *content* of food, not just its context, can also be loaded with meaning. Stavros, for example, was a self-effacing man of Greek ancestry who found the bland American fare of Elmwood a burden to his Hellenic sensibilities. Nonassertive by nature, Stavros was visited almost daily by an outgoing, dutiful daughter, Katina, who often interceded with staff on her father's behalf. She had arranged, for example, to have the charge nurse change the location of his call bell, she asked the maintenance staff to alter the layout of his room so that he could move around it more easily, and she had Stavros transferred to the care of a different nursing assistant when an earlier caregiver had proved too rough and crude for his taste. After hearing her father complain several times about the taste of the food ("too much tomato sauce and over-cooked chicken"), Katina again took the initiative and began to bring in lemons and basil each week so that her father could flavor his food to his own liking. This not only pleased his palette but also turned food into yet another medium for the expression of family ties and personal concern. It nurtured both Katina and her father.

Some staff were particularly sensitive to the sensory pleasure food gave to people and sometimes performed small acts at variance with the strict rules for patients issued by doctors and the dietary department. A number of the home's residents, for example, were diabetic and kept on a closely limited sugar intake. They sometimes pleaded for the treat of a cookie or a piece of cake and learned which staff members would accommodate them. One nursing assistant, who confessed to minor indiscretions of this sort, explained: "You're told to watch your diet so that you can live to old age. Well, somehow, they've made it, but what's there to live for? If they can't even have a cookie, what was the point?"

Things did not always work out this well or this innocently, however. Frank Healey, one of Stavros's coffee companions, was a far more outspoken and demanding individual, a person whose artistic ambitions and romantic passions found little room for expression in the nursing home world. Even though his son, Patrick, and daughter-in-law, Effie, tried hard to help Frank make the most of his situation and the staff supported their efforts, these caregivers all encountered frequent frustration. The main impediment was Frank himself. This came out dramatically in what people at Elmwood came to call "the bread and butter incident." This event left a mark not only on the floor but also on everyone concerned. Of the many foods that appeared on his meal tray each week, bread and butter was the one Frank found most objectionable. It seemed a minor and curious choice for complaint, but he was insistent and serious about his displeasure. Finally, Patrick and Effie brought it up with Nina Breckner, the social worker. She put them in touch with the dietician, who agreed to switch whole-wheat slices for white and a whipped spread for a hard pat.

Even the best-laid trays can go astray. When Florence, a dietary aide, proudly put the new fare in front of Frank one lunchtime, he sat and stared at it, said nothing for a moment, and then exploded, saying that he had asked for rye bread. Then he picked up the tray and hurled it at her, splattering Florence's dress and the floor with meatloaf, gravy, peas, whole-wheat crumbs, and butter.

Patrick was left to "pick up the pieces," socially if not literally. He was called in that afternoon to calm his father. He sought out Florence to apologize and then arranged with Nina to discuss the whole incident. Later that day, when Nina and Patrick met in her office, they traded weak, rueful smiles. They thought that they were going to make some small progress this time but, instead, found themselves going over the wreckage. Nothing permanent had been destroyed, only the week's expectations, but they were tired, worn down by their would-be beneficiary. Nina's view was that their attempts to help Frank "had only made him feel more helpless. It's unpredictable. In this case, it simply added fuel to his anger. It's a real double bind," she continued. "Each time we try to do something he wants, he is reminded that only *we* can do it for him."

Patrick found himself pleading, "But he is already dependent in so many ways. Can't anyone do *anything* for him without his getting resentful?"

"Maybe. Sometimes," Nina offered. "But that is what we're up against. He has so many reasons to feel this way. *That* is what he really threw at us today."

CONTROL AND RESPONSIBILITY

The emotional intensity surrounding food could also take on a moral dimension. Frank seized on food to displace his anger about his loss of autonomy. Other residents took this one step further, turning food into a literal life-and-death issue. These were the people who refused to eat, whose final effort at control was to take charge of their own death. Some staff were conscious and supportive of these decisions and permitted people to act out this last wish in comfort and without interference. This decision earned them the enmity of co-workers who felt that allowing residents to act in this way was tanta-mount to being an accomplice to suicide. Even though the same kinds of conflict surfaced over implementing DNR (Do Not Resuscitate) orders, nutrition was sometimes an even more contentious issue because, unlike the critical, momentary nature of a resuscitation deci-sion, food was a chronic, daily matter continually confronting people: Its withdrawal set in motion a process, not just a single event.

The same moral difficulty over food went beyond disagreements among staff to conflicts between residents and their relatives. This came out most dramatically at Elmwood, as it does in the courts, when fami-lies, patients, and the institution cannot agree on when to discontinue artificial means of nutrition (compare with Kayser-Jones 1990b; Olson 1993:558). In one case at Elmwood, a family insisted on a life-sustaining nasogastric (NG) tube, which the resident had once verbally indicated that she would not want. The nursing assistant who cared for this woman railed, "If I was Celia, you know what I'd say? 'If you put me through that [kind of torture], I'll haunt you for the rest of your life.'"

Responding to people's wishes and advanced directives was not the only food-related issue that haunted staff at Elmwood Grove. They were responsible for people's overall well-being and nutrition, and they were answerable to the state for any apparent failings in nursing, hygiene, or dietary services. In New York State, the publicity surround-ing patients' rights, the existence of a toll-free complaint hotline for people to call, the promptness of investigations when complaints were made, and the presence of an efficient state health department that made periodic, unscheduled inspections all served to put nursing home administrators on their guard against deficiencies and dissatis-faction.

That many of Elmwood's articulate residents found fault with the food was very much imprinted on administrative consciousness. Aware that complaints of this sort are ubiquitous in institutional settings, Elmwood's top staff members were nevertheless sensitive to having their facility put in a bad light for this reason (Savishinsky 1995). They were responsible for the food and wanted some control over how it was portrayed. Without intending to, my students and I stumbled into this sensitive area during the early phase of our study, and we unwittingly offended a number of people. During the first part of our research, we collected the life stories of certain Elmwood residents and recorded their accounts of how they had adapted to institutional existence. In one of the progress reports we circulated at this time, we quoted resident Peter Marsh's acerbic remarks about meals in a narrative detailing how he felt about a typical day at the home.

The criticism consisted of only a few lines in one of several extended narratives, but these caught the eye and the ire of Gordon Morrell, one of Elmwood's top administrators. He castigated us for citing such explicit language and for selecting Peter, "a well-known malcontent," as one of our subjects. Gordon explained that the facility had been working hard to improve dietary services and that such a quote would demoralize the staff in that department. His comments revealed that the issue was even broader than this. Gordon felt that nursing homes, in general, were struggling to combat a very negative public image. A quote of this sort—presented without explanation or contrasting opinions—undermined Elmwood's best efforts. His reaction also highlighted for us the "issue of representativeness" as an ethical concern in publications on aging populations (Rowles and Reinharz 1988:25–26).

Not all staff were as sensitive to pointed remarks as this administrator. Louise Santorini, one of Elmwood's more experienced nurses, felt that what seemed like small matters or petty complaints to some staff—the kind of bread served, how a plate was laid out, who got his tray first—were not instances of residents merely being "picky or fussy or troublemakers." In Louise's opinion, it was really a matter of people with very little power trying to assert some control in the few areas where they felt they might have some efficacy. The difference in how Louise and Gordon viewed such incidents was telling. It helped us to appreciate that not only did residents have control issues surrounding food and other amenities but also some staff were equally concerned with controlling the way the institution served others and how the institution itself was perceived.

COMPARISONS

As suggested by the stories of Stavros's lemons and basil, Frank's bread and butter, and Bonnie's dog treats, by the feelings of Celia and her nursing assistant, and by the responses to language shown by Peter,

Gordon, and Louise, food carried more than just nutritional weight at Elmwood. Nurturance, control, ethnic identity, sensory pleasure, anger, perception, and moral responsibility were also being served up. Some people felt that residents' health was "at risk," and others argued that it was really their autonomy at stake. What was ultimately at issue, then, was not just life and death but meaning, with food occupying the place of both means and end, substance and symbol.

Although Elmwood had its unique mix of characters and characteristics, its array of food-related issues was indicative of situations that have been observed in other ethnographic research on nursing homes. In a series of studies published since the early 1960s, various authors have described a range of social, symbolic, nutritional, and emotional aspects of institutional food. Each reveals the centrality of food as a contested domain in the geriatric world. Specific attention has centered on questions of nurturance, reciprocity, gender identity, autonomy, and dehumanization.

One of the earliest anthropological descriptions of extreme deprivation in a nursing home was Henry's (1963) account of Rosemont—a 100-bed, private facility he called "Hell's Vestibule" (1963:406). In a section titled "Hunger," Henry (1963:413–422) detailed the chronic inadequacy of the diet, the odor of excrement mixed with food smells, and the delusions, denials, and fantasies about meals through which Rosemont's residents tried to cope with being chronically hungry. The persistent lack of sufficient or appetizing nutrition reduced the elderly there to a canine-like existence. Henry called this process "pathogenic metamorphosis," one in which "pathogenic institutions metamorphose inmates into specific types [of animals or objects] and treat the perceptual apparatus of the inmates as if it belonged to the metamorphoses—dog, cockroach, child, et cetera" (1963:419). Patients exhibiting canine traits begged for food, licked their plates, and hid leftover bread just as dogs bury bones for future consumption (1963:417). The degrading aspects of Rosemont's meals and food became a primary means of dehumanization.

Less extreme cases have been instructive in other ways, providing insights into the obsessions of residents and the social categories created by staff. In her autobiographical account of a month-long stay in "Golden Mesa," a 100-bed Arizona nursing home, seventy-nine-year-old

anthropologist Carobeth Laird explained to readers her preoccupation with food, bowels, and bladder: "If I seem to dwell with obsessive
repetition upon the functions of the body in this work, you must
remember that the lives of those in Golden Mesa, and similar facilities,
essentially revolve around eating and excreting" (1979:2). Laird went
on to recount how food was central to the two ways that staff classified
residents: those who were mobile enough to be taken to the dining
room for meals and those whom employees had to hand-feed in their
rooms, the "feeders" (1979:63).

Kayser-Jones (1981) highlighted the institutional differences in the
content and control of food in her comparison of Scotsdale, a National
Health Service facility in Scotland, with Pacific Manor, a private institution in California. She found that the former had a significantly better variety, quality, and amount of food and a much higher level of
patient satisfaction with meals. Scotsdale's selective menu and the
access of its residents to personal money for purchasing food at the
hospital shop enhanced the nutritional aspects of people's lives. At
Pacific Manor, by contrast, the quality and quantity of food were
judged inadequate, meals were unattractively presented, and the odor
of urine detracted from the dining room environment. When patients
or their kin tried to supplement the diet with food from the outside,
people commonly found that these items were stolen from storage
places within the facility (1981:25–27).

At Murray Manor, a 360-bed, nonprofit facility in the American
Midwest, Gubrium (1975) found significant differences in the tenor of
meals among residents within the same facility. He described how the
healthier people on the lower floors were served food in a more
relaxed and comfortable setting than the disabled patients on the
upper nursing units. For residents, meals were times of maximum visi-
bility, so they wanted "to appear and be treated as 'normal, competent'
elders" (1975:131). Patients, by contrast, were given their meals in a
more impersonal, rushed manner and were waited on by aides who
treated them in a less subservient way. Complaints about food were a
ubiquitous topic of conversation throughout Murray Manor.
Nevertheless, Gubrium found that preparing for and talking about
meals were major ways in which people passed time at this institution.
Patients would "look forward to [these events], some with simple

pleasure and others with the firm knowledge that 'it's something to do here and you can depend on it'" (1975:160–161). Discussing and waiting for food, in fact, occupied more time than eating the food. Finally, some clients at Murray Manor simply sat in silence in the dining room between meals or walked "back and forth from their own rooms to the dining area most of the day" (1975:174). Others created more purpose and meaning around food events. Some of the home's residents took on the self-appointed role of helpers by collecting trays during mealtimes, and various people shared food with each other as one of the social obligations arising from friendships.

The difficulty the elderly face in finding emotional and social satisfaction from food was emphasized in Shield's (1988) study of Franklin Nursing Home, a Jewish facility located in the Northeast. Dietary mistakes did occur within this institution's bureaucracy, but far more serious was the loss that residents experienced because of their inability to control and offer food to others (compare with Gubrium 1993:136–139, 145). Shield observed that many residents felt "the loss of their refrigerators keenly" (1988:134). Food could be kept in a communal refrigerator at the home but was likely to be eaten by others. She noted that women, in particular, wanted to be able to offer guests something to eat and that certain individuals kept a jar of hard candies for this purpose. Such a practice could not truly fulfill some of the other symbolic meanings and associations food had for people, including its messages of nurturing and being taken care of and its central place in the role of women as mothers. To the extent that preparing and offering food defined "women as women" through their capacity to nourish and entertain, nursing home life could not offer female residents a form of fulfillment that had been theirs in the past (1988:134–135).

The symbolic meaning of food and its special significance for older women were also stressed in Vesperi's study of institutional life in a 50-bed, private facility in New England that she called "Martindale Nursing Home." Although meals were sanitary and nutritious there, they also had a monotonous, disheartening quality. Because Martindale lacked a communal dining room, "the self-contained meal, served at bedside" reflected and reinforced the isolation of residents (1983:234). That meals were no longer a shared experience among family, friends, and co-workers, as well as the loss of pride in cooking, was particularly painful for women. Vesperi noted that two ways in which residents protested the dehumanizing conditions of their existence were through incontinence and the refusal to eat. What went into and came out of the body became sources of conflict and control. A few patients had recourse to suicidal hunger strikes as a desperate last resort to define their lives. Others, in a less dramatic but still food-centered protest, rejected the impersonal and isolating meals as a way to contest both their own dependency and "the institution's ability to adequately perceive and fulfill" their needs (1983:234).

Two more recent ethnographies (Diamond 1992; Foner 1994) focus on the work experiences of nursing assistants, the primary caregivers in all geriatric institutions. In both projects, the nursing assistants these researchers studied and worked with were overwhelmingly women of color, and their responsibility for hand-feeding frail, often demented and impaired elders required considerable skill, patience, and understanding (Diamond 1988:45; Foner 1994:34–35). The experiences of nursing assistants revealed various other facets of how food was dealt with in the institutional setting. In Foner's study of "Crescent Nursing Home," a 200-bed, nonprofit, skilled nursing facility in New York City, she found that the nursing assistants' response to a demanding and highly bureaucratic work environment lay somewhere between "cruelty and compassion" (1994:38). Neither monsters nor saints, periodically subject to abuse by residents, the nursing assistants sought to preserve their autonomy and, in many cases, their emotional ties to their patients. Sometimes, however, the nursing assistants' "strategies of resistance" compromised the best interests of residents. For example, informal pressures among nursing assistants not to do extra work meant their cutting back on compassionate care. Nursing assistants would be reluctant to get an extra cup of coffee for a resident because co-workers feared that more patients would demand such a service (1994:132–134).

Diamond's work resulted in a "collective story" of three homes in the Chicago area (1992:5). He found that residents wanted to give, not just receive, in their relations with staff. Against the rules in these facilities, residents offered their caregivers tips and food (1992:91, 195). When it came to the residents' experience with food, several problems confronted them. The time between meals was long, and residents were frequently hungry. Food was a constant topic of conversation, but meals were consumed with "silent voraciousness" (1992:109). Because of the multiple layers of authority in the home, residents found it frustrating to correct mistaken or missing items in their diet, so they learned to stop asking and just eat what was given to them. To refuse to eat was to risk having one's behavior charted and, potentially, being force-fed (1992:95). Although bureaucratic record keeping pervaded these facilities, official documents did not catalog the reasons people rejected certain foods or refused to eat. Government inspectors passed the homes on the factor of nutrition because they looked mainly at the records and did not investigate people's sentiments about—or the quality of—what was put on their plates (1992:190–191).

CODA

In his classic study, *The Wisdom of the Body,* physician Walter Cannon described human reactions to hunger and distinguished between food intake motivated by nutritional need and intake prompted by a desire for certain sensations of delight. In the latter case, he said, the person "seeks satisfaction, not relief" (1939:75). Cannon considered this the difference between "two motivating agencies—the pang and the pleasure…" (1939:76).

In the decades since Cannon's pioneering work, a series of nursing home studies have helped us appreciate the many pleasures the senses stimulate in the elderly and how many meanings food may carry for them. At Elmwood Grove and the other institutions discussed here, food was associated with nurturance, domesticity, reciprocity, sociability, control, autonomy, power, protest, and family, ethnic, and gender identity.

Several ethnographies cited have noted that food can be a critical area in which residents can participate in exchange and reciprocity and exert a degree of control over their daily lives. The attention of patients to the timing of snacks and meals also reveals how food events become key anchors of temporality. The fulfillment of feeding visiting or resident pets has been noted by other observers (for example, Thomas 1994:122–123). More "thick description" (Geertz 1973) of this kind would undoubtedly reveal other important and previously unrecognized elements in food-related behavior in institutions. High and Rowles (1995:105–106, 114), for example, cite case materials from their study of four Kentucky facilities that highlight the importance to family visitors of bringing a favorite food to their relative or of making interventions to aid their nutritional intake (compare with Rowles and High, this volume, Chapter 7). Other authors in this volume (Perkinson, Shield, Stafford, and Vesperi) similarly note how families continue to function as food providers, feeders, or dietary advocates for their institutionalized relatives. All these behaviors undoubtedly enhance the nutritional well-being of patients (compare with Kayser-Jones 1993:2208).

People who live in nursing homes can also take a very active role in getting and using food and defining the meaning of meals. Henderson, for instance, has shown that residents engage in elaborate "food procurement strategies" in order to be able "to eat food that is in its proper condition" (1995:53). Studies of residential and day centers for elders, such as the one examined in England by Hazan (1980), reveal that in facilities for the relatively healthy or able-bodied aged, food and meals also emerge as areas of daily life where issues of authority, rebellion, independence, and client-staff conflict are acted out (for example, Hazan 1980:56–66; Hornum 1995:157–163). Specific situations described elsewhere by Hazan (1992:20, 39) in one Israeli facility include residents taking food from the dining room or kitchen against the rules, criticizing the quality of meals, objecting to others' table manners to distance themselves from the stigma of being institutionalized, and giving gifts to staff in exchange for being served special kinds of food. If, as several ethnographers and theorists argue, the ability to engage in exchange and the sense of control over one's life are major contributors to people's feelings of well-being, the social and emotional roles of food in these regards need to be given full recognition (compare with Dowd 1975; Groger 1995:64–69; Rodin 1986). Food's importance as a medium of exchange should be considered along with other goods and services that nursing home residents offer as social currency, including gifts, money, the provision of help, and expressions of interest and gratitude.

Residents at most institutions complain about food or the way some of their peers eat (for example, Gubrium 1993:137), yet meals continue to be "the highlight of their day" (O'Brien 1989:142). The foods consumed at such times "are especially weighted with emotional significance" (Vladeck 1980:26) because eating remains one of the few sensory and social experiences left to many people. The opportunities that meals provide for demonstrating love, nurturance, and security and for creating friendships and social ties have been noted in numerous geriatric settings, reflecting the fact that food events become stages for expressing a variety of meanings (for example, Hornum 1995:157–163; Kayser-Jones 1994:81–82). Although the widespread complaints of nursing home patients may reflect real deficiencies in what they are served, residents also communicate many of their other pleasures and displeasures with life by displacing them onto the quality or quantity of institutional food. Nursing home administrators can be particularly sensitive to such charges, but an awareness of the dynamic process of displacement at work here may help people understand what the elderly are really expressing.

Finally, weight loss, complaints about food, and the refusal to eat are connected to difficult ethical and treatment issues in nursing homes. These include staff-resident conflicts over people's food needs and preferences (Kayser-Jones 1994:81; Silverman and McAllister 1995:217), the difficulty in using advance directives when patients fluctuate between competency and incompetency (Shield 1995:114), staff threats to report, force-feed, or use NG tubes on uncooperative patients (Diamond 1992:95; Kayser-Jones 1990a:472), and controversy about the meaning and diagnosis of "failure to thrive" (FTT) among elders.

For clinicians, food often becomes merely a medicalized, measured commodity, assessed mainly in terms of what goes into and out of the body. Individual and ethnic food preferences may be overlooked except on special holidays. Medical assessments of nutritional status may miss key factors because doctors are frequently prone to seek pathological causes of weight loss rather than look for sources rooted in nursing home staffing patterns, meal scheduling, food aesthetics, the environmental context within which meals are consumed, and the psychosocial status of patients (Kayser-Jones 1993:2206–2208). Ethically, clinicians, caregivers, and kin may face dilemmas about withholding or withdrawing nutrition and hydration and their degree of obligation to respect patient wishes and advance directives, or the necessity for them to act in the absence of such guidelines (Kayser-Jones 1990a; Olson 1993). Clinically, the role of depression—as well as dental, oral, and organic causes of an elderly person's disinterest in or rejection of food—needs to be carefully assessed. Alternatively, refusal may constitute a resident's reappropriation of his or her body from those who clean, dress, fill, and empty it. The cultural and religious values of staff and patients can also play a critical role in shaping people's responses to such situations (Davidson et al. 1990; Hirschfeld and Ziv 1989). FTT, a syndrome first identified and developed in pediatrics, is now recognized as "a common occurrence in institutionalized and hospitalized patients" (Palmer 1990:47). Its symptoms include weight loss and reduced appetite, and its complex etiology is most often connected to factors such as dementia, depression, delirium, drug reactions, and chronic diseases (Palmer 1990:48–55).

These ethical and diagnostic issues, and the spectrum of meanings and feelings about food shown in nursing home ethnographies, reflect the complex of medical, social, emotional, and symbolic factors impinging on nutrition among institutionalized elders. As Gubrium observes, "One can be a 'good eater' but nonetheless be ready to die" (1993:19). Collectively, these issues and meanings may be taken as a caveat for critics tempted to jump to quick conclusions about the content and format of nursing home meals. The experiences of people at Elmwood Grove and other facilities studied indicate that, in some cases, inadequate nutritional intake may not be a cause of the failure to thrive but, instead, a symptom of it. People who are deeply displeased with life may lose their appetite for it and manifest this in literal, nutritional terms. Such elderly individuals are at risk not because of the food they are being served but because of how they feel about the way they have been served by the nursing home, society, and life itself.

Note

1. This paper is based on a research project that has been examining the nature of life, labor, and voluntarism in several nursing homes in rural areas of upstate New York since 1982. The study has been supported, in part, by grants from the Center for Faculty Research and Development and the Gerontology

Institute at Ithaca College and by a fellowship from the National Endowment for the Humanities. Results of the project have been reported in several earlier publications, and some major findings from the first phases of the work have been summarized in a book (Savishinsky 1991).

5

Homebodies

Voices of Place in a North American Community

Philip B. Stafford

Many observers have noted that the nursing home maintains an ambiguous status in the cultural order, owing to its being composed of elements drawn from oppositional spheres of meaning—home and hospital. Having elements of both home (in that people are residents) and hospital (in that people are patients), the institution is both yet neither. A structuralist interpretation would suggest, following Leach, for example, that when "a boundary separates two zones of social space-time which are *normal, time-bound, clear-cut, central, secular*...the spatial and temporal markers, which actually serve as boundaries, are themselves *abnormal, timeless, ambiguous, at the edge, sacred*" (Leach 1976:35). It is this liminal, betwixt-and-between status of the nursing home that engenders a collective discomfort on the part of our citizenry.

Mary Douglas might have predicted that the patient qua resident, as a member of this marginal space, provokes a kind of disgust reaction from some visitors to the scene: "I can't stand to go into the nursing home." "They are all so pitiful." "How can you work in that place?" A more benign response, also predicted by Mary Douglas's schema, is seen in those who look at nursing home residents as somewhat sacred beings, needing the special care and feeding one might give an infant or a sacrificial animal.[1]

Whatever space the nursing home occupies in our cultural cosmology, the institution in its current form is clearly a significant *presence* in our society. Nearly two million persons live within nursing homes; 1.2 million persons work within them as full-time employees (Foner 1994:9). One could estimate that at least twice as many are directly affected by them as family members of residents, as volunteers, and as friends. This major social institution has arisen (in its present form) in the short space of approximately forty years and consumes a huge portion of the health care budget in the United States. The existence of the institution itself, however, has never been seriously questioned. It has become a necessity taken for granted in a modern world where medicine keeps people alive (but not always healthy) and families (the former caregiving units) are pulled out of the home and into the wage-based economy to survive (compare with Johnson and Grant 1985).

In this paper, it is my intention to explore the home side of the home/hospital opposition. The question *Can a nursing home be home-like?* obviously can be grounded only in a thorough discussion of the notion of home, wherever it appears. Therefore, I touch not only on the manifestation of home within the nursing home but also on the manner in which home is defined (or experienced) in the wider context of the community. For that purpose, I draw upon the voices of older residents of nursing homes, as well as the voices of older and younger residents of our local community.[2]

Ethnographers of the nursing home scene have, of course, asked whether the nursing home can be home-like. Savishinsky reports that the staff of Elmwood Nursing Home consensually acknowledged that decorations and ornamentations, although worthwhile, could not make the place truly home-like. He quotes a nursing assistant:

> For some…[the loss of a home] is more devastating than losing a husband or wife. I don't say that to sound cruel or make people seem callous, but having to move can be worse than dealing with a death. When someone dies, you lose one part of your life. But when you have to leave the place where you lived, it's like you fell out of your life. Everything that was familiar, everything that made it feel like a home, all the

things you had memories about, you can't replace those.
(1991:114)

Stavros Costa, an Elmwood resident, concurs, saying, *"Home.* That is a very distinguished word, and no nursing institution can be that. Here, instead of paintings, age hangs on the walls" (Savishinsky 1991:74).

Lily Robinson, a nursing home resident interviewed by J. Gubrium, discusses the concepts of home and hospital:

> I think they all seem about just alike. I stayed in the hospital quite a long time when they amputated my legs, and the nurses are friendly, but it's not like home. No place, no hospital, no nursing home is like your own home, not to me.... Peace of mind, I think, at home makes you different. You run your home. These people here run the nursing home. At home, you're the overseer. You take care of everything, and I think that's more like a whole being. Here you're just a part. When you're home, you're whole. You're a whole person. You're taking care of everything, and everything comes to you by your means, and it makes you feel more at home. (1993:128–29)

Stavros, Lily, and the nursing assistant are making very important, fundamental observations about the notion of home. We can learn from these expressions of place. Do we usually listen? Not often enough. The notion of home, as *professionally* constructed, moves on a different plane. Many professionals state that a nursing "facility" can't be home, but an attempt is made, nevertheless, to create a simulacrum. Hence, the ritual trappings of domesticity are displayed: the monthly birthday parties (compare with Laird 1979), the cooking class in which beating batter in a bowl simulates the kitchen,[3] the wingback chairs and false hearths in the lobby, simulated *Main Street* signs at the nurses' station, reminiscing groups who make use of poetry about the smell of some generic mother's homemade cookies. The examples could be multiplied fourfold.

Moreover, the intended representation of home makes use of only the positive side of that experience and, hence, even as a signifier, doesn't fully represent the signified. (Martha Gilbert, in Gubrium's

PHILIP B. STAFFORD

Speaking of Life [1993], makes this point quite well.) This is to say that the professional strategy is a *semiotic* one. It tries to re-create home through its symbolic representation.[4] As such, it trivializes the notion of home and, indeed, often has the opposite effect on the resident. The very attempt to re-create home draws attention to its impossibility.[5] If we truly listen to the authentic voices of the residents, we *can* learn much about the notion of home. We can learn that home and self are intertwined, that home and spouse can be identities, that home has to do with human agency, *and* that nursing home residents are good at interpreting the hidden meanings of bureaucratic practices.

LOCAL VOICE, OUTSIDE THE WALLS

In Bloomington, Indiana, we have been engaged in a community dialog about the meaning of place.[6] To that end, we have involved both old and young people in activities designed to give expression to notions of place: creative writing groups, neighborhood focus groups, intergenerational interviewing, public lectures and discussions, ethnography, and household surveys. Of late, we have added the voices of local nursing home residents to the discussion. The practical goal of this community project is to enable us to become more aware of the relationship between health and environment. The words of Tony Hiss speak to the spirit of our endeavor:

> Our ordinary surroundings, built and natural alike, have an immediate and a continuing effect on the way we feel and act, and on our health and intelligence. These places have an impact on our sense of self, our sense of safety, the kind of work we get done, the ways we interact with other people, even our ability to function as citizens in a democracy. In short, the places where we spend our time affect the people we are and can become. (1990:xi)

Even though place and self (person) are intimately related, as Hiss suggests, we do not assume, as Hiss does, that place affects person in a simple cause-and-effect manner. Rather, place and person are in a *dialectical* relationship, each affecting the other. *Space* in the mundane sense may be said to affect people, but it is the creation of *place* that interests us. Yi-Fu Tuan has sensitized us to the distinctions between space and place. He notes how space becomes place through use. Intimate exchanges between people have "a locale which partakes in the quality of the human encounter" (Tuan 1977:141). The study of place, from this perspective, is a study of meaning, not forces or causes.

Our collection of stories about local place and the meaning of home was published in a local volume, *Experiencing Place,* in 1995. At the risk of diminishing the stories by interpreting them, it behooves us to try to learn from them. A number of themes have emerged.

Place is not adequately described by the visual. The spatial experience is multisensory, involving the whole body. Elder Sally Wegener's reminiscences are overwhelmingly olfactory, not surprising if you grow up around the Chicago stockyards:

> No scent of sun-warmed apples
> From bee-filled back-of-field orchards,
> Nor fragrance fresh of new-cut hay,
> Nor hillside stands of pungent pines
> Recall for me, my childhood.
> Acrid smells instead,
> Of tanning hides and bestial blood
> Of carnal butchering,
> The smells of slaughter conjure up
> For me, my early city life.

An anonymous young author (age about eleven) experiences place as auditory:

> Papers turning, teachers talking, kids walking, kids talking, kids running around getting ready for a rehearsal, doors closing, and Joe coughing. I hear Simon snapping his pencil on the floor, Mrs. Holt talking to Johnnie. I hear Emily writing and Tiff asking her same old questions. I hear Emily making funny noises. I hear all of this stuff because I listen.

Betty Ray's reminiscences of her father's factory long ago likewise draw upon the ear, not the eye:

> You could hear that noise two blocks away. There was a distinct, regular rhythm about it, and my father knew the moment it skipped a beat, and he would run to investigate.

> Every season, about a week or two before the factory started processing, my father would get a quicker step in his walk and make phone calls to verify employees were going to be there for the big moment of start-up. Everything around our house changed because the family life revolved around this important time in my father's canning factory. You didn't want to get in his way, because he was concentrating on getting the operation under way…. I've never forgotten the sound nor the rhythm of the pumps. Many years later, when I lived in Long Beach, I passed a petroleum processing plant and heard a familiar rhythmic *Whoosh, Clang* noise. The immediate flashback was to my father's factory.

Although these experiences of childhood occurred sixty-five years apart, each is rich, fresh, and organic. To be fully alive and aware of our environment is to call up the primal senses and suspend our usual, detached observation. This suggests a second theme characteristic of our local voices: Environments are experienced as peopled. I like the definition of a healthy neighborhood offered by eleven-year-old Andrew Remak: "One thing you need to make a neighborhood healthy is one spot where everyone meets. In our neighborhood, it's my house."

For Andrew, this central tendency results in a suburban roller blade hockey game.[7] In Parshall, North Dakota, about fifty years ago, surely that central meeting place was the "Big Store" owned by author LeRoy Sanden's father. For LeRoy, the place can be described only by the people who moved through it, mostly Native Americans from the Fort Berthold Reservation and immigrant Norwegian farmers. (What great good fortune Andrew and LeRoy share, to have been brought up in the neighborhood meeting place!)

Personal possessions are, of course, an important part of the material environment. Madison Avenue notwithstanding, it is clear that possessions, even for children victimized by television advertising, take on their value and significance through their representation of prized personal relationships. Young Ben Mason's cherished Thurman Thomas rookie basketball card is his favorite because his younger brother gave it to Ben and paid for it out of his own pocket. Eleven-year-old

Elizabeth Galoozis's favorite possession is her Heidi doll, given to her by her Greek grandmother, her "Yia Yia."

> I love Yia Yia very much, so this might be part of the reason I love Heidi.... Heidi has lost a porcelain foot, and I have had to sew her arms back to her shoulders an innumerable amount of times. But she somehow seems real to me. If I lost Heidi, I don't know what I'd do.

Likewise does Melissa McClung (age eleven) rely on her Grandma Blanket to feel connected: "I go to it when I'm feeling lonely or just had a fight with someone. I know that some people might think it's ugly, but to me it's beautiful."

That even a rock takes on special meaning when it enters into human relationships is well stated by young Robert Zendajas: "I am going to tell about my special rock. My friend and I found it, but this time he gets to have it for the day. But tomorrow, I get it for the day because we trade it."

As these little parables suggest, possessions take their value not only from their ability to represent valued relationships but also from the very tangible power they have to pull people together into relationships. The rock is not Robert's. It truly belongs to both boys.

Age, moreover, makes little distinction on this score. Invariably, when charged to write about place or thing, our older writers describe *persons*. The implicit association between person and place is nowhere better described than in Gleeda Hillenberg's loving recollection of "Daddy." Downtown Saturday night in Bloomington, Indiana, in the 1940s can only be understood in the context of Gleeda's attachment to her father. Saturday night was the only night a quarry worker had the time and money to shop and socialize with family and friends.

The inherent connection between persons and the *natural* environment is also revealed by the numerous references to animals and trees in the work of our young authors. The reader of these stories meets hamsters, birds, skunks, mean dogs and good dogs, cats, cats, and more cats. Trees, no less than animals, are part of the human community and take on qualities of friendliness, self-doubt, and charity. (No wonder Shel Silversteins's book *The Giving Tree* is so popular with children young and old.)

Gary Snyder, in *The Practice of the Wild*, notes how children experience the environment in a primary and tactile manner:

> The landscape of childhood is learned on foot, and a map is inscribed in the mind—trails and pathways and grooves—the mean dog, the cranky old man's house, the pasture with a bull in it—going out wider and farther. All of us carry a picture of the terrain that was learned roughly between the ages of six and nine. (It could as easily be an urban neighborhood as some rural scene.) Revisualising that place with its smells and textures, walking through it again in your imagination, has a grounding and settling effect. (1990:26)

As Snyder notes, "We might also wonder how it is for those whose childhood landscape was being ripped up by bulldozers or whose family moving about made it all a blur." Young Mark Wilson describes such an experience:

> My backyard was once a woods. My mom or sister used to take me mushroom hunting during the spring. I never went into the woods all by myself.
> One day, people chopped down the trees and made apartment buildings. Then they put a fence in for everyone that lived in Walnut Woods, so the people who did not live there could not come over, which I think is wrong because I lived there ever since I was two.

The jarring sensation of having one's childhood landscape sundered can affect one long after the place has been left behind, as elder Frances Sanden explains:

> A couple of years ago, after a long absence, we made a sentimental journey to the old neighborhood and realized the truth of the saying *You can never go back*. Gone was the casual and tolerant informality in lifestyles, along with the former graciousness displayed in area neighborhoods. Victorian houses had been razed and replaced by imposing new mansions, creating an atmosphere of wealth and even arrogance. New stores had ushered out the old familiar ones. New York merchants, with high-priced offerings, had moved

into a huge, elaborate shopping mall a few miles distant. The lovely little village we cherished had vanished—like Brigadoon—and been replaced by ostentatious wealth and class distinction attesting to moneyed success.

These stories, vernacular in the best sense of the word, demonstrate how people, both young and old, live within a nourishing web of human and natural connections. As such, they don't represent the dominant, rationalistic Western model of man as the "solitary knower" of his environment, "just a self and a world," in Snyder's terms:

> In this (Western, rational model) there is no recognition that grandparents, place, grammar, pets, friends, lovers, children, tools, the poems and songs we remember, are what we think with. Such a solitary mind—if it could exist—would be a boring prisoner of abstractions. With no surroundings there can be no path, and with no path one cannot become free. (1990:60)[8]

LOCAL VOICE, INSIDE THE WALLS— NARRATIVES OF THE NURSING HOME

If we learn anything from the preceding stories, it is that *home* is a much more comprehensive and wide-ranging term than suggested by its simplistic professional construction in the nursing home. The notion that home does not *represent* self but *is* self and that objects don't merely *stand for* home but *are* home suggests a method of research other than the semiotic one. If we are to understand the affecting presence of home and possessions, we must, as Husserl said, go "to the things themselves." A phenomenological anthropology seems called for. To understand the lived experience of the nursing home, we must enter into the experience bodily and not simply rationally. Along with interviewing, we must participate. Along with participating, we must take the role of the other. We must learn to listen to the sounds as they are listened to. We must watch and be watched. This method sees knowledge as a "coming to know," as Michael Jackson explains, citing Dewey's test for the adequacy of inquiry, a test based in a radical empiricism: "Does it render ordinary life experience more significant, or more opaque?" (1995:163). Echoing the title of J. Gubrium's (1991) valuable work on nursing care and home care, *The Mosaic of Care*, Jackson proposes a "mosaic philosophy—a philosophy of plural facts, which aims to give all modalities of experience their due" (1995:164).

Max

A genuine sadness overtook me as I said my goodbyes to Max on his last day at adult day care. For us, the staff, day care involved a desperate struggle to help families keep their loved ones with them at home. We had come to admire and love Max for his unending gentlemanliness and integrity. As a creative and productive electrical engineer, Max had patented many inventions for his company, helping his boss become one of the true early pioneers in the fledgling television industry of the 1950s. At adult day care, his identity as an engineer was sustained rigidly, in the face of increasing dementia, through a constant reference to himself, his peers, and his company—in the corpus of a pictorial history of the company, authored by a local industrial historian. This dog-eared book was Max's constant companion and provided ready access to Max's past and present. To say that the book merely represented Max's former self would trivialize it. Indeed, the book became Max, and Max the book. Whenever the book was out of sight, Max was "out of mind."

Alas, the tribulation of supporting Max at home, with his wandering becoming unmanageable, meant that he would leave adult day care to enter a nursing home. In his inimitable way, Max was taking care of us on his last day as we said goodbye, albeit, I grant, he did not know what was in store for him. His words had a prophetic, Zen-like quality. "We'll be around as long as we can be," he said to me.

Now, as Max wanders the halls of the nursing home, I think that perhaps there is a secondary reading of that phrase, which I take to be "We'll be, as long as we're around." *Being around, going around.* That is the primal character of Max's life now, and I see his behavior as a kind of Ur form for us all, with its metaphor of the journey as a going and a coming home. As Michael Jackson might describe the peripatetic home life of the aboriginal Warlpiri of central Australia, existence is defined by the path, the track of Dreaming:

> It got me thinking about the motif of the journey, which

crops up again and again in Warlpiri myth: the dialectic of coming out...and going back in...which at once suggests the passage from birth to death, from day to night, from waking to sleep. (1995:134)

Martha

With a dementia less profound than Max's but with no caregiver at home, Martha found herself being admitted to the nursing home near the adult day care program. Her boisterous personality offended some but endeared her to most as she danced her way through the day at adult day care, incessantly reminding us about her many years tending switchboard at the university, taking care of the president's calls from abroad, and tendering care to her beloved husband, never quite well after being gassed in the War. We genuinely felt the loss of her spirited presence after her departure. As she continued to have strong days in the nursing home, she had weak ones, too, and often the doldrums seemed to leave her sails flapping. Yet, through her dementia, her wisdom rose to the surface. When visited by the day care coordinator a few weeks after her institutionalization, Martha described her fate clearly: "They've taken the home out of me. This is a business here, and I'm not used to that."

Martha clearly understood and voiced the identification of home and self. In Jackson's words, "The human body and the body of the land share a common language. Person and place coalesce. Whatever happens to the one, happens to the other" (1995:125).[9]

Martin Heidegger has spoken extensively about the identification of self and place, of dwelling and thinking. The etymological history of the word *dwelling, bauen* in German, means "to build," but has as its cognate the word *bin,* as in *ich bin,* "I am," *du bist,* "you are," and the imperative form, *bis,* "to be":

What then does *ich bin* mean? The old word *bauen,* to which the *bin* belongs, [suggests the] answer: *ich bin, du bist* means I dwell, you dwell. The way in which you are and I am, the manner in which we humans are on the earth, is *Buan,* dwelling. To be human...means to dwell. (1971:147)

Heidegger proceeds to elaborate on the old definition of *home* to mean "to remain," "to stay in a place." He compares it to the Old Saxon word *woun*, which also means "to be at peace." Hence, the word *home* comes to mean "retreat," "a place of safety and security."

As Michael Jackson notes, Heidegger's identification of house and building with self belies a Eurocentric bias emergent with the rise of middle-class, propertied values in the seventeenth century. Before that, Jackson (1995:86) explains, citing John Berger, the notion of home connoted village, a group of kin, a state of being. Nevertheless, although Martha's home was her house, it constituted an essential part of her being.

Insofar as we can become attached to a dwelling, the feel of the house becomes as much a part of us as its surface appearances. Indeed, we can walk through a familiar place with our eyes closed, not because we hold consciously to a cognitive representation of it but because our *bodies* know the place. It becomes a part of our *habitus*. Bachelard, in *The Poetics of Space*, describes this process through which so-called mundane household routines enter into our being and take on a reality not appreciated by those who would separate work from play, work from life. Bachelard quotes author Henri Bosco, who describes the quiet and persistent work of an old servant, Sidoine, as she cleans a wooden bowl:

> The soft wax entered into the polished substance under the pressure of hands and the effective warmth of a woolen cloth. Slowly the tray took on a dull luster. It was as though the radiance induced by magnetic rubbing emanated from the hundred-year-old sapwood, from the very heart of the dead tree, and spread gradually, in the form of light, over the tray. The old fingers possessed of every virtue, the broad palm, drew from the solid block with its inanimate fibers, the latent powers of life itself. This was creation of an object, a real act of faith taking place before my enchanted eyes. (Bachelard 1994:68)

As Bachelard describes the intimate daily process of building a house "from the inside," so Wendell Berry, in his novel *The Memory of Old Jack*, beautifully describes the process by which the old Kentucky farmer Jack Beechum melds with the landscape around him:

He had known no other place. From babyhood he had moved in the openings and foldings of the old farm as familiarly as he moved inside his clothes. But after the full responsibility of it fell to him, he saw it with a new clarity. He had simply relied on it before. Now when he walked in his fields and pastures and woodlands he was tramping into his mind the shape of the land, his thought becoming indistinguishable from it, so that when he came to die, his intelligence would subside into it like his own spirit. (Berry 1999:30)

These are Jack's fields, yes, but they are not his *property* in the crude sense of today's so-called property rights advocates. The fields and the work pull Jack into a relationship with those who came before and those who will follow:

The work satisfied something deeper in him than his own desire. It was as if he went to his fields in the spring not just because he wanted to, but because his father and grandfather before him had gone because they wanted to—because since the first seeds were planted by hand in the ground, his kinsmen had gone each spring to the fields.... He remembers those days for their order, the comeliness of the shape his work made in each one of them as it passed. It was an order that came of the union in him of skill and passion, the energy that would not be greater in him than it was then. (1999:30)

Hack

On our first meeting, in the corner of Hack's room in the nursing home, I am reminded of Burt Lancaster in *Birdman of Alcatraz*. Tall, lanky, and graceful, although slightly bent, Hack is silhouetted against the window, his back toward the room as he tends to living things—the pigeons and sparrows that visit his second-floor birdfeeder, the two-foot-long seedlings sprouting from white styrofoam cups. One seedling is a hackberry, and I'm struck by the coincidence of naming, even more so as Hack explains to me his connection with the hackberry tree standing out back of the nursing home. The hackberry, he explains, is an ancient tree: "You don't see too many of them around here anymore.

They're called *hackberry* because the bark looks as if it's been all hacked up." The one out back, he notes, has some kind of injury to it. Almost overnight, a butterfly-like growth had appeared on a crotch of the tree. "A way it kind of repairs itself," he says. He fans out his fingers to show how it looks. He tells me which tree he's talking about among the several behind the facility.

A couple of days later, as I leave by the back door, I check out the tree. Sure enough, about twenty feet off the ground the immense tree displays the shelf-like growth Hack described. The nursing home employees casually enjoying their cigarettes under the shade of the huge tree have, as in Shel Silverstein's book, an entirely different connection with that tree. I doubt that they have noticed the growth, and I bet that they don't know its name.

In another visit, as I chat with Hack's roommate, we are politely interrupted by Hack, who wants to show me the praying mantis, now mummified, that flew through the window into his room a few days before.

> HACK (pinching it gently between his fingers): "They're like lady bugs."
>
> PHIL: They eat a lot of stuff.
>
> HACK: They catch 'em. Just like that [shows motion with his hands]. Faster than a man can draw, that's what they say. I sit and watch 'em, 'til I get real close, and they know exactly, like rabbits.
>
> PHIL: They stay real still?
>
> HACK: Just like you bat your eyes.

He explains how this one came to join him in his room.

> HACK: This one flew in the window. I told Myron, "Look at that!" and that thing flew in here. I said, "Where'd he go?" and I looked and looked and looked. I was afraid that thing would get in bed with me. And I finally found it. Fact is, there [pointing], I caught it settin' up there.
>
> PHIL: Yeah, now you got a trophy.
>
> HACK: I'm gonna try to mount it.

PHIL: Mount it with a pin?

HACK (moving to the wall to show the spot where the mantis will be displayed): Put him on there. I don't know. I've got so much to do. I've got a list over a mile long.

Our discussion turns to other items on his wall: one of those bird's-eye photos of a farmstead taken by itinerant pilots and sold to the relevant farm families and a photo of a small bungalow, framed in front by a stone arch at the beginning of the sidewalk leading to the house. The arch has no accompanying fence. As such, it seems out of place. Hack mentions how his son used to mow the grass across the road at Opha Small's house. (I am amazed at how the circle turns. Opha, now in her nineties, lives in the next room!)

HACK (pointing to the arch): He sees now what old Dad did. I did that.

PHIL: You did?

HACK: A windstorm [blew it down]. My son said [to the insurance man], "There's nobody gonna fix that unless they put it back exactly like Dad had it!" This guy [handyman] looked at it and said, "I'll put it back exactly like that," and he did.

HACK (pointing to the stone work): I cut every one of them with a pitchin' tool.

PHIL: You cut it with pitching tools. You mean you dug them out of the ground?

HACK: You face it.

PHIL: You call that pitching it?

HACK: Yeah. Pitching it is making rock face out of it...and squarin' it up. It's a breakin' tool [shows me the movement of the tool with his hands]—something like a big wide chisel, but it's cut on just like that. You get that just right, and it'll break the rock. But you line it with a square and then cut it. Put your rock face on it.

PHIL: Did you work in a rock quarry, too?

(I am beginning to wonder whether there is anything Hack has not done.)

> HACK: My uncle was a stone carver. He cut stone [for the] WPA. He cut on what they called a banker, made out of heavy four-by-fours, in fact, like a [unintelligible], so they won't bounce. It's gotta be solid or the rock won't break just right. These banker tables was made so they didn't give. That's where they broke the rock. They put it on there and hit it with a wooden maul—made outta hedge apple.[10]

> PHIL: Oh, really, yeah?

> HACK: 'Bout as hard as you can get. You get a root. Make it out of hedge apple. Most of 'em had a wooden pin.

> PHIL: What kind of head did the maul have?

> HACK: It was round.

(He discusses how a good maul won't split.)

> PHIL: Does your son still live there?

> HACK: My youngest boy's there. Stevie.

> PHIL: And the arch is still standing there?

> HACK: Yeah. A big storm came right up Vernal Pike.

> PHIL: Yeah, I remember that.

> HACK: And they didn't get no warnin'.

> PHIL: That was about five, six years ago.

> HACK: Back in, oh [pause] it broke trees all down in there. After the trees was all down and the people was gathered around there, the siren went off.

(I laugh.)

> HACK: My son says, "Why in the hell, that shows they're really on guard." You'd better believe it. And when it comes out in the paper, it was "high winds."

> PHIL: High winds

> HACK: When it twists the trees off [shows with his hands in a wringing motion], that's awfully high winds.

PHIL: I'd heard that a hedge apple tree was hardwood. You can't split it.

HACK: It's curly. You can see the grain go 'round there. I used that for a long time. My uncle used to work on the WPA. You know the stone wall around Rose Hill [the city cemetery]?

PHIL: Sure, '33? Something like that? '34?

Hack: Well, I was just a kid. I'm seventy-nine now. I imagine I was about fourteen. Hard times.

PHIL: Yeah [pause] well, were you born in this house?

Hack: My kids were. I bought that in 1939. My wife and I was married in '38.

PHIL: You set up housekeeping there?

HACK: Yeah, that's where all the kids were born. Five kids. I had six kids. Lost the second boy. Didn't know how to breathe.

PHIL: Happened to me, too.

HACK: All they needed to do was put him on a respirator, but back then they didn't know what to do.

PHIL: Yeah.

HACK: There's a double garage out there, with a breezeway [pointing]. Here's that old building. [unintelligible] Anderson bought the land all the way through to Packinghouse Road, and I tore that old building down.

PHIL: Why did you move from there [pointing to the first picture] to there [pointing to the picture of the farmstead]?

HACK: My second wife, we married in '69, and she owned that piece down there, and when we was goin' together, that's what we said: When we'd both retire, we'd go down there. That was an old school building [pointing to the house], called Red Cut, 'bout three quarters of a mile from Koleen, right down in an old lake bed. Thousands and thousands of years ago, all that stood in water, but an extra big

rain happened thousands of years ago and washed the lower
end out, and that lake drained. There's still a creek.

(The conversation moves on to his time in this house near Koleen.)

As Hack talks about his life, I generally stand in awe. He possesses
only a basic education but a wealth of knowledge. I am reminded how
much I love the work that brings me in touch with smart old guys like
him. When he talks about doing some "water witchin'" as a kid of nine-
teen and not finding a peach fork, he lets me know how he improvised
with a coke bottle and a "number nine" wire. When he tells about the
man from Texas who came up to drill wells, it's important to remark
that he used a number five casing, "not a number six, like they use
around here." When he got his water from a rock spring out at his
Greene County home, it was cold: "It was at least 51 degrees, and that
water in the wintertime would feel good on your hands."

As he talks, his body enters into the conversation. The objects we
use to construct our conversation, the pictures on the wall, help
cement the relationship between us and place us in the landscape we
are noting together. The stone arch is significant. Yes, it does have a
symbolic import—it's a symbol of his artisanship and a vehicle for a
son's pride in his father—but it's more than that. It's a presence, in and
of itself. As Hack stands there and "faces" those rocks, that arch is
rebuilt, re-created anew, just as Bosco describes Sidoine's housework as
acts of creation.

It also occurs to me that the picture of the arch is not taken looking outward from the house but, rather, looking in. The arch is not an
exit but an entrance, an entrance to a home and a family. The absence
of any attached fence makes sense now. This is a home that welcomes
and invites. It speaks to hospitality and neighborliness, not property
and enclosure.

As Hack talks of his life in these places, he is not merely reminiscing. He is reliving, re-experiencing them. The slight bend in his
upper body suggests not age but a physical yearning for a place.
Perhaps old age replaces the horizontal journey of youth with the ver-
tical journey towards the earth.[11] Western culture seems to denigrate
the low, the earthy, the fallen. (Perhaps these metaphorical associations are universal, as some [Lakoff and Johnson 1980] would argue.)

Indeed, the "fear of falling" has become, in American society, a heavily charged issue and a pivot point around which major "policy" decisions are made, within both the public and private spheres. The family asks, "But what if Mom should fall?" and places her in a nursing home to assure that she won't. Just how is her fall prevented in the nursing home? By tying her to a wheelchair and calling it "up, with restraints" (Diamond 1992:213, on the language of record-keeping). Another wise and creative old "informant" of ours, Nathan, is aware of this death-delaying tactic and prefers, as he says, "to just slide into the floor" when it's his time.

Hack is a man like Jack Beechum, a man with a sense of scale, a man who, like the child, sees the small wild things and, with the wisdom of years, sees the traces of events much larger than those in our small lives—the ancient trees, the washed out valleys. In the nursing home, he carries on this way of being in the world. Amid the rushing and clanging, the hard shiny surfaces of the nursing home, Hack moves in a different but parallel dimension. A natural man in an unnatural environment, Hack maintains his equanimity and only rarely criticizes what he sees around him. Once, he reports, they got mad at him for trying to catch a man who was falling. "They'd have to cut my arms off to keep me from doing that!" he says.

In our ethnographic freeze frames, we often portray informants as static beings whose lives have no valence or existence beyond our fieldwork. As I write, Hack has resumed his "horizontal journey" and has moved out of the nursing home to a small apartment in a nearby small town. "There's everything I need," he explains, "a park across the street and a tavern that's s'posed to sell tenderloins this big." He shows me with his hands. I'm anxious to visit him and carry on. "It's number eight," he says.

Jewel

Just down the hall from Hack's room, Jewel lives with and among her things. There, one finds a veritable storehouse of knickknacks, crafty things, teddy bears, clothing on hangers, bottles, and party leftovers. She knows that she's pushing the official limit on this issue. "Some think it's junk, and I know it's tacky, but it's my junk," she explains. As we do a tape-recorded inventory of each and every object (a task beyond the scope of my capability as a fieldworker with limited time), Jewel comments on the significance of each. The history of some objects is lost to memory but usually noted as something "someone gave to me." Being the recipient of many little gifts has significance for Jewel, but not in any boastful sense. The handmade afghan at the end of her bed epitomizes the relevance of gifts to her. It had belonged to the woman across the hall and, upon her death, was given by her son to Jewel. "You always smiled at my mother," he said, "and we wanted you to know we appreciated that."

In the corner are stacked two large cardboard boxes, buckling under the weight of additional items piled on top. "In there is my frying pan, and I'll never give that up," Jewel says. I am reminded of my fieldwork visits years ago to Lu McDonald in her tiny, frail house in Switz City and the relevance of her frying pan to her. "My house'd burn down, but I'd still have my fryin' pan" was the way she put it. That image of the frying pan, strong as the woman who handles it (or wields it, as in the cartoons), fits Jewel. To see it, one has to look past her southern, ladylike gentility from a Jackson, Mississippi, upbringing and past her own frail visage, diminished by Parkinson's disease.

Folklorist Henry Glassie came upon another fine southern lady a few years ago while engaged in a search for the meanings of home:

> I was once down in southern Kentucky, driving around and looking, as I did in those days, for old houses. I came to one, and I wanted to take its picture. The woman of the house understood that I wished to take a picture of her home, and so she assembled for me a little still life. Her name was Mae Young, and in her still life what she did was to gather everything about her home that mattered. Boards didn't matter. The walls didn't matter. The fact that it conformed to one of Fred Kniffen's architectural types surely didn't matter to Mae Young. What mattered to her was her grandfather's little stoneware bottle. What mattered to her were the clumsily carved things that her grandfather gave her when she was a little girl. What mattered to her was the ring her grandfather beat out of pennies when he was a prisoner, starving in a Yankee prison. What mattered to her was a picture of an

uncle whose name she didn't even remember. What mattered to her were the scissors she'd found when she was digging in the garden. What mattered to her was the family Bible. Wherever she is and those things are, that's home. Home doesn't need any walls at all. It can be a collection of possessions. (1995:16)

Most nursing home residents with whom I've talked have reached a certain level of acceptance regarding the loss of things, telling me that although being among "your things" is important, bringing everything along with you is unrealistic. How one separates from things makes a difference. Concern about the disposition of things is reflected, for example, in the violent phrase so commonly used, "breaking up the home."[12] This loss is mitigated significantly if the resident is able to exert some control over where things go. Anna Simpson described to me the systematic method by which she distributed family heirlooms upon her entry into the residential wing of the facility. She speaks highly of those younger heirs who can be trusted to "keep things in the family." The importance of this control was also reflected in Anna's willingness to continue paying rent on her apartment for three months after her move, enough time to carefully distribute the furnishings. For some residents, the luxury of time in these circumstances is limited. Long-distance family members may sweep into town for a few days to get it done all at once and return to their own lives. The process must feel more violent when it happens that way.

Knowing the persons who inherit one's things ameliorates the loss. *Not* knowing who is getting your things can exacerbate grief. Another scholar discussing the meaning of home, Korosec-Serfaty, speaks of the experience of being burglarized (a similar loss) and summarizes the implications:

The word *rape* (used by interviewees who had been burglarized) moreover emphasizes the articulations of the home experience and the body as self.... Says a forty-year old man, "They've violated our privacy, these people who broke in here. We tell ourselves, well, they *saw* things which belong to us, which are, well, they're our own little secrets, they're not anybody's business, we don't tell them to anyone. That's it,

> it's this aspect of the thing, rather than what they stole."
> [emphasis mine] This foreign gaze, imposed, loaded with
> deceit ("we've certainly been watched"), ransacks what is
> "nobody's business" and which is generally closed: the
> boxes, chests, drawers, closets, and the dressing table, "where
> you always keep a few things" [sixty-year-old woman]...."
> (1985:78)

Violations of secrecy and the converse—the keeping of hiding places—constitute basic negative and positive conditions of the home experience. Bachelard devotes a chapter of *The Poetics of Space* to the subject of drawers, chests, and wardrobes, noting the manner in which objects such as these create intimacy in our lives:

> An anthology devoted to small boxes, such as chests and cas-
> kets, would constitute an important chapter in psychology.
> These complex pieces that a craftsman creates are very evi-
> dent witnesses of the *need for secrecy*, of an intuitive sense of
> hiding places. (1994:82)

As Bachelard notes, "the homology between the geometry of the small box and the psychology of secrecy does not call for protracted comment" (1994:83). Yet, common sense notwithstanding, attention to this issue in nursing home settings has increased only within the past few years as patient rights concerns have grown. Despite well-meaning policies that require knocking on doors and increased attention to residents' modesty and privacy in bathing, toileting, and so on, many lapses in privacy still occur, as documented clearly by several ethnographers of the nursing home scene. In my own research, I have noticed that such lapses are more common with residents who have dementia or are otherwise powerless to voice protest. A resident deemed to be unaware is more likely to be treated with disrespect, to be left exposed, in the literal sense, to the gaze of others passing in the hallway.

To Bachelard's commentary on the significance of boxes and other containers, I would add mention of the practice of "placing things." I need only revisit my own childhood to recall the many hours spent arranging my toy soldiers in an endless variety of configurations on the living room floor. Now, as I watch my eleven-year-old daughter arrange her horses on her shelf, spirit away her valuables into a small pink box (with a key, of course!), and arrange a veritable menagerie of waterproof animals on the floor of the shower, I think of the quiet satisfaction that comes from such activity. A recent movie we attended together, *The Indian in the Cupboard,* suggests that the power to place things is not brutish but, rather, magical. In the movie, a small boy is given a tiny locking cupboard. He discovers that a favorite toy placed within it, a tiny Indian molded of lead, comes to life when the cupboard is closed and then opened.

As I think about the magical or sacred qualities we ascribe to boxes, I wonder about the effect of the innocent disregard for these spaces by nursing assistants who rifle through dresser and drawer in search of clothing and accessories as they strive to help their residents. Would the mark of good care not be, then, precisely this appreciation of the sacred quality of personal space?

Carl Selby

My friend Carl, who has cerebral palsy, has been a resident of institutions since age seven. Carl was first placed in a state institution after being diagnosed as retarded, which he certainly is *not.* Now, at age fifty-three, Carl looks back on eighteen years as a resident of a local nursing home (the length of time we have known each other). Although Carl keeps his valuables in an olive-colored lock box in the bottom drawer of his bedside table, he is still concerned about theft. In the box, he keeps his penny collection, pens, pencils, and other sundry items. One would think that the box is inviolate, yet, for Carl, it's a bit of a ruse. He keeps his most important possessions in a cardboard box on a shelf in a closet of a local human service agency. The secretary in that office has shown the sensitivity to keep Carl's items there for nearly ten years. What is in this secret cardboard box? Nothing less than Carl himself, represented in numerous birthday cards, notes, newspaper clippings about him, and letters from kindly others. Carl, with what I think is an eidetic memory, knows *exactly* what is in the box. About two years ago, we visited the box to make sure that everything was still there. My own file cabinet has since become an additional secret cupboard for Carl, which has bolstered the intimacy of our relationship. Carl now tells me that I'm like a brother to him.

PHILIP B. STAFFORD

ENDINGS AND BEGINNINGS

What can we learn from these simple, poetic expressions of place voiced by ordinary persons both inside and outside the nursing home? We can learn much if we suspend interpretation and listen to the words themselves in their emotive and practical context, a context that, we should remember, includes the fieldworker.

Michael Jackson, in his beautiful ethnography of the Warlpiri, shows clearly that the concept of home can easily transcend the mundane walls within which we reside. He relates the true story of the negligent destruction of a tree *(watiya)* that marked, and sprung from, a Warlpiri sacred site (a Dreaming) in the desert of Central Australia. Jackson remarked how struck he was by the depth of grief expressed the preceding year by the old woman Nola Nungarrayi when she found a limb broken on the tree during one of their many joint excursions. Nola's daughter Wanda explained to Michael that Nola's father had died against the trunk of the tree years before: "He bin pass away here, turn into this tree" (1995: 56).[13] With the tree damaged, there was a risk that the father's *pirlirrpa* (glossed here as *spirit*) would leave the spot.

A year after the visit to the sacred spot, a crew of "whitefellas," carelessly trying to extract a vehicle from a rut, uprooted the tree. This time, the grief over the loss of the tree was felt by all Warlpiri in the area. Anger rose as well, and the Warlpiri demanded compensation from the whites, realizing that the way to hurt them would be to extract money ("the whitefella Dreaming"). The Warlpiri make use of the tree as a metaphor for the family; trees, like people, have limbs and trunks. Their roots descend deep into the soil, holding the branches, the offspring, in place. (As Jackson notes, such "genealogical images have more force for Warlpiri, perhaps, than Westerners, as Francine and I had seen a year ago when Nola Nungarryi wept at the sight of her father's broken limb" [1995:139].) Indeed, Jackson inferred that the tree was not simply a metaphor, a representation of ancestors, akin to our memorials and monuments. "That wasn't a tree," Nola's sibling explained. "It was a person. A person's Dreaming. It was the life-essence *[pirlirrpa]* of a person. When those whitefellas knocked down that tree, they hurt the Dreamings and the ceremonies there" (1995:138).

The ceremonies, the continual visiting of such places on "walka-bout" (which describes the very nature of Jackson's participative field-work) is, moreover, the mode through which places take on meaning.

> My experience at the business camp (a kind of men's cere-monial center) reinforced my conviction that a sense of home is grounded less in a place per se than in the activity that goes on in a place. Whether the body is engaged in dancing or in mundane labor [one recalls Jack Beechum], concentrated activity is experienced as a quickened relation-ship between oneself and whatever one works upon. Inert matter, the ground under one's feet, the shield or spear one fashions—becomes infused with the energy and effort that goes into the work. The object comes to embody the life of the worker. This means that before Warlpiri recognize a metaphorical fusion between person and place, this fusion is felt in bodily praxis... (Jackson 1995:148)

When the labor is jointly conducted with others present, or as an extension of the labor of previous generations, as was Jack Beechum's, the place in which it is carried on partakes of its vital energy.

> It is the stepping up and concentration of activity during ceremony that lends a site the depth and density that makes it "sacred." As if the earth at that place were stamped and impregnated with the vital force of the activities carried out upon it. (Jackson 1995:148)

Marx clearly saw the process by which some products, in capitalist modes of production, lose the connection with their source, with the energy and human action that led to their origination. Jackson sees as the task of anthropology "to close this gap, exploring the practical and social underpinnings of abstract forms of understanding, disclosing the subject behind the act..." (1995:148). For Warlpiri, as for Jack Beechum, this connectedness with earth, with generation, is the meaning of home.

> The meaning of home cannot be sought in the substantive, though it may find expression in substantive things like land, house, and family. Experientially, home was a matter

of being-at-home-in-the-world. It connoted a sense of existential control and connectedness—the way we feel when
what we say or do seems to matter, and there is a balanced
reciprocity between the world beyond us and the world
within which we move. (Jackson 1995:154)

These experiential rhythms *can* be found within the nursing home.
Surely the hospital codes do exert a powerful force to define. They provide what might be called the *givenness* of the institution. The work of
anthropology, quoting Jackson once more, is to ask, "How do people
transform givenness into choice so that the world into which they are
thrown becomes a world they can call their own..." (1995:123).

The phenomenal world of the nursing home does exhibit continuity with the rhythms of the external world. There is *home* as defined
by the path:

Bloomington elder Lilian, residing on the "outside," speaks fondly
of the fact that her home is next door to that of her daughter: "There's
a path between our houses." This path was produced by the daily trek
of her grandchildren seeking after-school cookies.

Ruby Coplin, residing "inside," speaks to ethnographer Jay Gubrium
about her life of giving to others in return for what she has been
blessed with:

A very close friend. She's Madeline...she wasn't bad when I
first came in, and I am very close to her. I feel that God has
put her in my path, you know, to kind of look after her. And
then there was Mrs. Edison here...we'd wheel her to and
from the dining room. If she was cold, we'd go get her
sweaters. And then she died. When she left, she had a lot of
nice things. [After she died] I walked in [her room].... This
nice gentleman comes up and says to me, "I want to shake
your hand." He said, "Mrs. Coplin, you're the most wonder-
ful person I've ever known.... The way you were with my
mother." She was two doors down from me, and I felt like
she was my grandmother and...I kind of adopted her as my
family. (1993:52)

For Lilian and Ruby, the path expresses their participation in a valued chain of familial (if fictive) relationships. For others, the image of the path can be taken more literally. Several times a day, and often late at night, Etta (on the "inside") makes a cautious but determined trip to the canteen, taking the elevator one floor down from her room. There, over cigarettes and coffee, she meets her regular gang to chat, laugh, reminisce, and talk about what's going on, both inside and out. When asked what her definition of home would be, she replied, "I guess a place where I can go." Her room is sparsely detailed. It is the place where she goes to rest, between visits to the canteen.

Participants in adult day care (on the "outside") echo this theme of coming and going in a collective poem:

> I have several homes
> I know a home is a home when I can
> Go there
> Stay
> And go out again

Another individual writes:

> Home is where the dog goes
> When it gets too cold to roam
> When winter's coming on
> That's when I want to go Home

The constant coming and going of some nursing home residents, albeit in circumscribed space, may be as much a consequence of the staff's actions. The daily routine of the nursing assistant involves much time moving patients here and there—shrouded and coded in clinical language as "ambulation"—to the day room, to the dining room, to the activity room, back to the "bed" room. Visitors and family members as well participate in an extensive ritual movement of patients from one place to another. The reasons for this are often not verbalized; it seems to be something that "should be done." In this regard, front-line staff, particularly the nursing assistants, are the real caregivers, for they are the ones helping the residents to participate in the ancient rhythm of movement to and fro. As Foner (1994) points out, this labor, valuable as it is, is not recognized as part of the reward system dictated by the bureaucratic organization of the nursing home.

When reduced to its most primitive and skeletal form, the path, the rhythm of to and fro, presents as the wandering behavior of the patient with dementia. The meaning of the wandering, as *professionally* constructed, misses the point again. "She's searching for home" is the typical explanation for the behavior. (True, it is often expressed verbally as such by the patients themselves.) Home, again, is taken to be some cognitive representation, a mental entity. Yet, recognizing that the path itself *is* home, can we not reinterpret the behavior as a kind of homemaking, in and of itself? The behavior is persistently repeated, not because home is *not* found but because it *is* and is constantly being re-created in the journey from there to here. Taking the behavior back to its most primal roots, can we not see its ultimate (and original) extension in the rocking back and forth of the nonambulatory patient with dementia, the tap, tap, tap of the palm on the chair, the creation of noise, however guttural, as the movement away from silence? We come full circle to the "peek-a-boo" game of the infant, framed as a dialectic of self and other.[14]

I am taken back again to the Warlpiri and the meaning of home. Scott Sanders, who has also commented on the Dreaming, gets the point about the relation of home to the journey. In a commentary on the travel essay "The Songlines," by Bruce Chatwin, Sanders notes that the nomadic life does not correspond with the life of the vagabond praised by Chatwin. Indeed, the purposeful wandering of the Australian Aborigines "may suggest a way for us to harness our restlessness, a way to reconcile our need to rove with our need to settle down," according to Sanders.

> Unlike vagabonds, who use up place after place without returning on their tracks, the Aborigines wed themselves to one place, and range over it with gratitude and care. So that they might continue as residents, they become stewards. Like the rest of nature, they move in circles, walking again and again over sacred ground. (1993:110)

There is a final return, however, a point at which the journey (on this earth) ends. We are aware of those nursing home residents who are ready to stop traveling. They are the ones who are prepared for death; the ones who find no compelling reason to attend the birthday party; the ones who stop eating; the ones who enter the curiously named "vegetative" state. (I am not referring to the "resistant" ones here, who refuse to do these things for quite different reasons.)

> To endure the most critical moments in life—birth, illness, death—we must disengage from the world about us. We must be in touch with ourselves. (Jackson 1995:135)

This is the point at which we begin to see the home as a retreat, a refuge—not a place to come to but a place to stay. There is a kind of diffuse awareness that nursing home patients who reach this point have somehow entered into a new state of being, near death. They have turned away from us, from the world. Their journey is ended, but they have not yet reached home. As they cease to participate in the social world, their personhood dissipates. Some are treated with dignity, and a silent watch is kept for them. Others are treated shabbily, allowed to be exposed and either forcibly retained in this world or treated as already gone. In so-called primitive nomadic societies, they may be allowed to stop as the group moves on without them. In our society, these are the ultimate marginal ones, existing at the brink of death. As such, their danger and our ambivalence do not derive from the fear of death (which has its own clarity as the next home) but from the fear of dying, the fear of homelessness.

Notes

1. Shield (1988:183ff.), Gubrium (1993:183), Savishinsky (1991:248), Diamond (1992:212ff.), Hornum (1995), and, of course, Carobeth Laird (1979) all observe that the nursing home exhibits liminality in its paradoxical status as home and hospital. Shield has elaborated on the argument to a considerable degree, discussing the nursing home experience as an incomplete rite of passage—the liminal state is entered, but the rite of incorporation doesn't follow.

2. This chapter is drawn from research conducted as a part of a more encompassing research program conducted in Bloomington, Indiana, with funding from the Retirement Research Foundation, Inc. We are grateful for the foundation's support. I am grateful for the valuable insights of fellow ethnographers Julianne Short and Bridget Edwards, who participated in the collection of narratives, to folklorist Erika Peterson-Veatch, who facilitated the creative writing project, to folklorist Nicole Kousaleos, who has assisted in numerous ways, and to the Evergreen Research Team, for inspiration and shared enthusiasm for our goals.

Also, I am indebted to the participants and staff of Bloomington Hospital Adult Day Center for their insights into human behavior, as so well demonstrated in the chapter. The project goal is to promote the development of healthy urban environments for elders.

3. This example is derived from Shield (1988).

4. It might be more appropriate to refer to the strategy as semiological. I am speaking of those forms of analysis that focus on the referential function of symbols—the Saussurian tradition carried on by British Social Anthropology, for example.

5. Foner (1994:139) describes a similar dynamic in the nursing home she studied. At Christmas, the administrative staff would "turn the tables" and act as servers in the dining room. In the end, this only highlighted the split between the upper and the lower echelons.

6. I use actual names when the individuals have so agreed. I use first names in certain instances, not out of disrespect but out of familiarity. These are persons with whom I am on a first-name basis.

7. Wendell Berry phrases this aspect of "good places" beautifully: "A human community, then, if it is to last, must exert a sort of centripetal force, holding local soil and local memory in place" (1990:155).

8. Levi-Strauss's familiar dictum, *Myths are good to think,* takes on a newly relevant meaning when considered as part of this line of thought.

9. Martha also is perceptive when it comes to identifying the underlying capitalistic organization of the institution.

10. William Least-Heat Moon writes of the hedge apple in his book *PrairyErth,* an absolutely remarkable history of place (Chase County, Kansas). After speaking of the tree's unusual fruit, he notes,

> It is, of course, the wood of *Maclura (pomifera)* that men have for several thousand years admired: one of the heaviest on the continent, a cubic foot of it in a natural state weighs more than half that of an equal size chunk of limestone, and is nearly as hard, taking the edge off a lathe chisel or saw blade immediately; yet the wood is two and a half times stronger than white oak while still marvelously flexible: an Osage orange bow made from a good sapling properly seasoned and strung with bison sinew could drive a dogwood arrow up to the fletching into a buffalo, and to this day some archers believe the wood superior to yew, the stuff of the famed English longbow. (1991:283)

11. I certainly don't stake any original claim to this sometimes hackneyed

metaphor for aging. In Thomas Cole's (1992) book *The Journey of Life*, he notes that the aging-as-journey motif became very popular during the Middle Ages (along with the practice of pilgrimage) but can be easily traced back to the ancient philosophers. He cites Chapter 1 of *The Republic*, in which Socrates says, "I regard the aged as travelers who have gone on a journey [on] which we too may have to go, and of whom we ought to inquire whether the way is smooth and easy, or rugged and difficult" (1992:10).

12. Shield (1988:99) noticed the same phraseology used to describe this process. She likens it to the "stripping" of new inmates, observed by Goffman to be an elementary characteristic of total institutions.

13. Jackson explains in a footnote that he discovered sometime after this interaction that Nola's father did not, in fact, die against the tree but several hundred miles south. It made no difference. With naming practices and kinship relations tied so closely to the land, the spirit of Nola's father, and of many others, was intimately connected with the tree.

14. Beckett's remarkable text *The Unnamable*, as Gabriele Schwab (1986) argues, can be read as the narrative of a dying old man attempting to rid the self of the self. The narrator attempts to reduce language to its barest function and, hence, empty it of meaning. Semantic speech is reduced to guttural grunts and gasps, but he can't escape the reality that speech always refers back to the speaker, is a transitional object mediating self and world.

6

Alzheimer's Units and Special Care

A Soteriological Fantasy

J. Neil Henderson

Shady Hill has been created as a home-like and non-institutional environment, featuring state-of-the-art "sensory" design to better facilitate Alzheimer's patients. These features include soothing color schemes to prevent agitation....A wide variety of specifically tailored activities are available on a daily basis.

—Paraphrased from an actual promotional ad, 2003

Thomas Kuhn (1962) reminds academe that the firm foundations of scientific knowledge are actually quicksand in an hourglass. Kuhn's now-classic concept of ever-changing paradigm shifts has inspired many hours of philosophical discussion relating to state-of-the-art and best practice status in scientific endeavors. The quest for the ultimate fix for various problems, whether scientific or industrial, typically employs the most current buzzwords, such as *innovative, excellence,* and *best thinking.* The effort to be superlative is born of the American cultural value of excess, regardless of the cost. Yet, in the zeal to be the best (and first!), problem solvers' best thinking sometimes lacks an important characteristic—skepticism.

The concept of dementia-specific care units, or more popularly, Alzheimer's units (AUs), in nursing homes is a case of unquestioned best thinking promoting an intervention of (putative) therapeutic value. AUs masquerade as the prized tool of nursing home care for those with cognitive dysfunction, but are actually therapeutically impotent. AU characteristics were derived from extrapolating rationally derived facts about the nature of dementing disease and resulting problematic behavior and applying them to nursing home care. The result was the concept of "secure" segregated care, with special contrivances to compensate for the patients' cognitive impairments. Studies have cast doubt about the efficacy of AUs, yet AUs not only persist in the marketplace but also receive hearty endorsement from the nursing home industry. Moreover, general consumers of long-term care, on behalf of a loved one with dementia, still inquire about the availability of AUs and may even demand placement of their loved one in such a facility. Clearly, factors other than evidence-based scientific research underlie the rationalization of special care for persons with dementia. This paper explores some of the possible, nonobvious cultural underpinnings of the florescence of AUs. It also offers positive suggestions regarding good care that may be found within special care units, derived not from specialness as much as from ordinariness.

INSTITUTIONALIZATION: LOFTY AND MUNDANE VIEWS

Erving Goffman (1961) long ago noted that entering an institution constitutes an induction process designed to kill the prior social self and remake the person into another entity congenial to the goals of the new environment. This is not exactly a fix for the elderly dementia patient with impaired cognition. Nursing homes are not prisons, despite the analogy, although there may be a similarity of purpose strikingly close to mental institutions. Yet, when a person is institutionalized, he or she experiences a process of *mortification* (Goffman 1961). The root *mort,* as in *death,* is not accidental in Goffman's use of *mortification* to characterize the effect of placement.

Amplifying the concept of institutional mortification, Otto von Mering (personal communication 1975) noted that placement in a nursing home is contemporary American society's version of a "double burial." The steps are as follows. When a person is extracted from home because of dependencies that interrupt his or her ability, or his or her family's ability, to cope with the exigencies of life, the nursing home placement process becomes step one in a double burial ritual. A facsimile of real social life, called "long-term care patienthood" (Henderson 1995), replaces the person's status as a fully functioning member of society and family. That is, the now-institutionalized person's psychosocial self is slain at the nursing home door. At this point, the sometimes lengthy step two of the double burial ritual begins. Rather than lie supine on the burial scaffold, as in some cultures, the patient languishes in long-term care patienthood until biological functions cease, at which time the second, and final, burial occurs.

At some high level of philosophical abstraction, the preceding scenario is probably true and constitutes a type of "uncomfortable knowledge" for society (Stein 1988). Yet, the practical matter of failing health among older adults leads to dependencies so severe that ongoing supervision and care become imperative. Placement is often necessitated by a lack of resources to continue care at home. In any case, the fact is that some people with severe dependencies need a place where they can be cared for and cared about. Given the current American cultural attitudes about aging and the penchant for health care profits, older people are sometimes trapped in situations for which nursing home placement is the only available alternative. Nursing homes as currently conceived are not ideal environments for frail old people, yet they provide the mundane, practical functions of shelter and food. One test for the need for nursing homes is to imagine what would happen if, on a given day, all nursing homes were closed. Where would the elders go? What would they do? Who would feed them? Who would clean them?

Nursing homes cannot be so easily dismissed from the American landscape as some critics glibly seem to demand. Also, because they exist, nursing homes do have the burden of providing the best care possible to their customer base. This objective, although often promised, is not always delivered. Providing long-term care to vulnerable elder persons demands the best technical skills, built on a concrete foundation of ethical and moral direction, particularly when the elder has brain failure. Cognitive impairment makes an elder extremely vulnerable to the typical vicissitudes of an institutional environment.

The number of AUs has grown rapidly in the past fifteen years, but their utility as a therapeutic tool for behavior management and comfort is seldom realized. More often, the AU is a dualistic phenomenon, part myth and part monster. The *AU myth* is that residents with dementia receive better care in the confines of such units because some AUs tout slightly higher staffing ratios on the day shift, outdoor walking areas, and a serene physical environment. However, whether these factors are at the core of therapeutic care is questionable. The *AU monster* is its veiled use as a marketing device and a warehouse for difficult-to-manage residents—a response to a pent-up market demand and moving forward regardless of its unproven effectiveness (compare with Maslow 1994b).

The current disjunction between putative purpose and actual practice is disquieting because the large and growing target population is unable to speak for itself. Moreover, the families who are the agents for the afflicted person are often emotionally and physically exhausted from the demands of caregiving. They are nearly as vulnerable as the patient. In the marketplace of long-term care, the moral ambiguities of AUs become more obvious. Most nursing homes are unable to convert the putative therapeutic concept into practice. They experience institutional barriers to change in regulations favoring the status quo, such as a disproportionate number of regulations regarding physical care and not behavioral care. Moreover, the focus on behavior is outside the expertise of most nursing staff because their training is mainly an outgrowth of the medical model as filtered through nursing school curricula. Consequently, an AU model emphasizing *prevention* of behavioral problems is apparently difficult even to conceptualize. Currently, the effort aimed at reducing behavioral problems due to dementing disease is left to the diligent, ritualistic logging of such behavior without any analysis that might lead to the prevention of problems. Consequently, AUs become new ways to camouflage the warehousing of disease-specific elders.

This chapter seeks to unmask the underlying organizational and societal contradictions in which AUs are entrenched. Also, this examination is embedded in concepts of cultural construction of health and its related practices (Good 1994; Stein 1990). More specifically, the notion of dementia as a cultural construction draws from the work of Gubrium (1986), Henderson and Henderson (2002), Henderson (1981; 1987a, b, c; 1994a, b, c, d), Henderson and Vesperi (1995), Henderson and Whaley (1997), Herskovits (1995), Lyman (1989), and Stafford (1991). To delineate the issues involved in this case of cultural construction, a rationale for AUs and a sketch of them are presented. In addition, this paper uses as a point of reference a multi-site research program of AUs done by a National Institute on Aging initiative, reported in a special issue of *Alzheimer's Disease and Associated Disorders: An International Journal* (1994). Collectively, the findings from the multi-site study suggest limited levels of AU efficacy. Yet, AUs persist as the "rage" in long-term care.

To solve this persistent puzzle, a broad societal and organizational culture view is taken that drives us ultimately to see the Alzheimer's unit as a soteriological fantasy. *Soteria* means "the experiencing of a feeling of security and protection, apparently out of proportion to the stimulus, derived from some external object, which becomes a neurotic object-source of comfort" *(Dorlands Illustrated Medical Dictionary 1985)*. The nursing home industry offers the AU as the best care possible for a dementia patient; the family, anxious to find a solution, readily accepts the assertion. However, the actual value of the AU concept may be far less than the fantasized wish. Consequently, there is evidence that AUs fill a soteriological need much more than a therapeutic one.

THE ALZHEIMER'S UNIT RATIONALE

The eighty-plus population is the fastest-growing cohort worldwide and is exactly coincident with the age of highest risk for dementing disease (Jorm 1990). The response by institutions providing long-term care is a trend toward developing Alzheimer's units. Such units are really for patients with all kinds of dementia. AUs are proliferating, albeit without the guidance of exacting data. The purpose of AUs is to create a treatment environment that precisely meets the multiple, unique needs of residents experiencing brain failure and that maximizes the well-being of these and other residents (Cohen 1994; Coons 1991; Maslow 1994a and b; Office of Technology Assessment 1987; Sloane and Mathew 1991). The nature of what constitutes a maximally functioning AU is evolving under the pressure of demand but does rely on a growing body of research. Extrapolation from research on human response to institutional environments, combined with the great depth of research in the sequela of dementing disease, has produced a corpus of operational procedures upon which the logic of the AU is built.

Dementing disease produces permanent, progressively declining mental functioning. The loss of thinking, reasoning, and memory ability seldom occurs with other organ failure diseases. It is the hallmark of dementia. The resident has lost precisely the organ of greatest importance to maintenance of self-control, self-determination, and independence. Confusion, along with the likelihood of other medical disease or functional limitation, places the dementia resident in a unique and precarious life situation.

For treatment of this incurable, progressive disease, specific environments and staff capability are considered necessary to maximize remaining potentials and minimize confusing, detrimental stimuli. Such environments are restrictive, simplistic, and bland for cognitively intact residents. However, the resident with dementia is exquisitely sensitive to overstimulation and responds with worsened confusion, affect, and behavior problems in normal environments.

The purported benefit of AUs extends beyond the dementia resident. Cognitively intact residents become quite uncomfortable when mixed with cognitively impaired residents. Impaired communication, loss of privacy, and disrupted patterns of daily life impede normal social interaction. Likewise, the specific needs of the resident with dementing disease are difficult to manage in ordinary, general living environments.

OPERATIONAL ALZHEIMER'S UNIT CONCEPTS

The concept of culture is used here to identify the AUs as a specific environment in which staff members possess a set of beliefs, behaviors, and values characteristic of cultural groups (Baba 1986; Eisenberg and Kleinman 1980; Lepper 1983; Schein 1987; Silverman and McAllister 1995; Stein 1990). For example, AUs may have a work culture different from that in the other, non-AU parts of the nursing home. This unique culture may be unappreciated, though, because administrators and staff do not always understand intrafacility organizational diversity.

This chapter draws on multi-method inquiry into AU operations. Methods include self-report surveys (Henderson 1987a and c), interviews with staff (Henderson 1994a, b, c, d), and my own on-site participant observation as a trainer, behavior problem consultant, and AU implementation consultant in twenty-four facilities in three states, ending in 1998. This emic presentation of nursing home culture is offered from the perspective of AU staff, including facility administrators and directors of nursing. Findings across facilities and states are synthesized into an idealized culture construct. Commentary from the author is occasionally inserted. Resident and family perspectives are beyond the scope of this article.

Four cultural premises or themes regarding AU operations will be briefly delineated:

1. Resident placement strategies

2. "Specialness"

3. Human resources

4. Family involvement

These themes emerged from my observations of how nursing homes present the AU concept to prospective customers. As sales pitches, these themes are tied to what the nursing home considers useful, rational approaches to offering AU care. Also, these issues are tied to what has been accepted as appropriate "special" features of the AU, compared with the remainder of the nursing home.

Resident Placement Strategies

One operational element influencing residents' lives is their physical location or placement within the long-term care facility. In historical context, the new AU approach to long-term care for dementia patients is related to a type of frequently used placement plan that clusters residents according to common characteristic(s). *Resident placement strategies* refers to the practices governing the assignment of specific room locations for residents. Room location greatly influences resident well-being, depending on the desirability of matching basic resident-to-resident characteristics (Johnson and Grant 1985; O'Brien 1989). The location decisions regarding residents can vary by many dimensions, including functional status, disease diagnosis, religion, marital status, and the chance availability of specific rooms.

The placement issue is also connected to decisions about what degree of cognitive impairment warrants placement in the AU. Some patients present for admission with moderate levels of cognitive impairment and are considered obvious, immediate candidates for AU placement. Others enter the nursing home cognitively intact but develop dementia or become symptomatic during their stay. These become candidates for placement in the AU. There is no industry standard (or, in more scientific parlance, no *cut point*) for scoring on cognitive assessment instruments on which to base placement decisions. Consequently, AUs make placement decisions based on their own judgment concerning available space, location of that space, and informal assessment of the patient's cognitive status as it relates to presumed caregiving needs.

"Specialness"

The AU proposes to reduce excess disability to a true minimum as residents adapt to chronic, degenerative disease without the advantage of intact intellect. This calls for a new model of care, transcending standard bed-and-body care, to focus on behavioral symptom management. Such conceptual shifts in caregiving produce a sense of the unit's "specialness," contrasted with other units of the nursing home. Also, the physical environment considered necessary for AUs includes secured units with outdoor wandering areas from which no one can elope. The very act of specially designating space within the nursing home, demarcated by secured doors and specific names, automatically confers a "special case" concept.

Ironically, dementia is as likely to be seen outside the AU because early-stage cases and patients who are developing symptoms are assigned a room outside the AU. However, family and staff members perceive the AU as the special location of dementia within the facility. Because dementia is a slowly progressive condition, early stages produce symptoms that are mainly short-term memory interferences without behavioral agitation. Even if such people have a diagnosis of early-stage dementia, they are not necessarily recommended for the AU. Over time, such patients may become candidates for placement in the AU. Also, the specifics of the other issues noted in this brief roster foster the perception or construction of the AU as the location for dementia.

Human Resources

AU staff may well prove to be more crucial to the specialized care of dementia patients than the physical environment. However, the tangibility of the physical environment causes it to receive a disproportionate share of interest and research compared with the enormous resource potential represented by the staff.

Nursing homes attempting to operate an AU hold the belief that the staff should have training unique to the problems of dementia. It is generally considered appropriate for the AU staff to be trained in the organicity of the dementing diseases, the behavioral aberrations expected as a function of cerebral dysfunction, and behavioral management strategies with which to respond effectively to the needs of the patient population (Henderson 1987a, 1994a; Lawton 1980).

AU operators report that the nearly constant behavioral problems expressed by the patient population lead to stress on the part of the staff. The staff is constantly challenged to understand and respond effectively to the behavioral aberrations of the dementia patient. Therefore, the staff should be adequately trained in stress management techniques for use on the job, as well as during other hours (Ohta and Ohta 1988; Sand, Yeaworth, and McCabe 1992). Also, the staff should receive training in activities that are appropriate for dementia patients, many of whom are easily frustrated. Patients often express frustration through behavioral aberrations that further stress the staff (Hoffman and Platt 2000; Taira 1986).

In spite of the notion that staff need special training to conduct special care, all too often they feel that their work is exceedingly simple and, consequently, outside the bounds of therapeutic benefit (Henderson 1987c). The staff must be trained to acknowledge the philosophical approach, as well as a skills approach, in care of the dementia patient.

From one perspective, because dealing with the behavioral problems of dementia residents is exceedingly stressful, AU staff members are prone to burnout. However, another perspective exists. Some CNAs (Certified Nursing Assistants) not working in the AU consider AU assignment to be relatively easy. The perception may be that CNAs working in a secured unit, with relatively fewer incontinent or bedfast residents, have an easier eight-hour workload. (This perception may be restricted to AUs with discharge criteria, stipulating transfer of residents with end-stage dementia so that less "dirty work" is required.) Missing are the recognition and admonition that staff should also be expected to spend at least as much time communicating with patients as in properly making their beds, coordinating their attire, or showering them.

CNAs are trained to deal with bed and body care. Their training typically de-emphasizes psychosocial caregiving by relegating it to the cultural realm of politeness and congeniality. The reality is that the interaction of well-trained staff members with dementia residents is an enormously challenging form of clinical intervention. In an AU, it may be that CNA staff members well trained in behavioral symptom management can convert custodial care to therapeutic care by preventing further frustration, confusion, and fear on the part of the resident. However, CNA staff members must be trained in the requisite skills and be rewarded for using this "new" approach (Clark and Witte 1991; Henderson 1987c; Koury and Lubinski 1991).[1]

Similarly, activity coordinators must receive additional, specific training for activities appropriate to each resident's stage of dementia. AU staff must be sensitive to residents' constantly shifting level of frustration versus equilibrium throughout the course of social interaction and planned activities. Yet, this capability is rarely even discussed. Activities coordinators able to do this can function in a superior fashion compared with those who use activity models designed for general older-adult populations. The depth of training about cognitively appropriate activities and the acumen of the persons coordinating activities, however, are not always at the quality levels necessary for offering a therapeutic activity to older adults with an extremely complex neurological disease.

Family Involvement

For residents with cognitive dysfunction, the family member serves as a proxy for their history, patterns, and preferences regarding activities of daily living. Also, the family may become the target of care because of the occasional guilt that accompanies placing a relative in a nursing home. Some facilities develop a support group for families to help resolve anxieties, stresses, and grief responses.

SOURCES OF CONTRADICTION

Operating an AU produces a silent collision between the medical model and the behavioral model of care. Operation of an AU is an *implicit* desire to adopt the behavioral model that is undervalued by the biomedical model. However, operational policies and standards derived from the medical model continue to apply to the evaluation of the AU. The effect is to maintain the same physical-care approach common to the non-AU parts of the nursing home. This allegiance undermines the intended or wished-for effects of the AU.

In a recent case, Corporation X wanted to operate AUs in its facilities according to a behavioral model, but this did not materialize because of its failure to perceive the inherent contradictions between the behavioral and medical models. It perceived the way in which it operated the entire nursing home as simply the way that it is done. Without awareness of the various existing models, there is little chance of understanding this failure.

Ironically, specific staff members within Corporation X did understand the notion of models of care. In fact, the corporation identified an experienced staff member to be the corporatewide leader in the development of its AU program. The program was to include a very strong, behaviorally sensitive approach to patient care. Yet, unawareness of the full implications of the medical model in the AU, combined with the need to meet operational standards (also derived from the medical model), prevented the implementation of the behavioral model.

Other factors contribute to failure. These include staff turnover, cross staffing, and opening the unit during the late evening and night shifts to other staff. Staff turnover remains a ubiquitous problem in nursing homes. It is particularly problematic in AUs, in which consistent staff and protocols are necessary for maximal quality of care. Cross staffing occurs when CNAs are brought from other units within the nursing home or "pool" staff is called in on a temporary basis, for example, when a regular staff member is absent. A "floater" CNA does not know the full, explicit, and implicit details of working in a particular unit culture. The effect is to degrade the consistency of care and the logic of operation within the evolving AU culture. Variance in the boundaries of the AU occurs during evening and night shifts, when the unit is opened to allow the lower number of workers on all floors to migrate into the AU on an as needed basis. This breach in operational integrity further violates the cultural environment of the AU.

The issues identified in this deconstruction of the AU model contribute to the failure to convert intent into practice. Even when a nursing home discovers that AU operation is much more difficult than imagined, the AU continues to operate, but as a sham. The need for intraorganizational culture change is either unrecognized or considered unprofitable.

THE CULTURAL SHAPING OF ALZHEIMER'S UNITS

Cultural variables related to family patterns are connected to Alzheimer's disease care. These cultural variables include kinship structure, migration patterns, and values regarding division of labor and sex roles as these impinge on in-home caregiving and promote institutional placement (Henderson 1987b). The nuclear family organization in America concentrates human resources and financial resources in a relatively small number of people. As the family grows and ages, marriage and adulthood result not in the inclusion of new members into the residence but in a reduction of on-site human resources. This occurs because of the establishment of new and separate residences in which to start again the cycle of concentrated resources. The postmarital, neolocal residence pattern causes burden bearing to be placed on the intact spouse or, secondarily, another family member. The concentrated burden bearing is further intensified by postadolescent dispersion of kindred via geographic migration away from the nuclear family for educational opportunities, occupational opportunities, or other exigencies of life. In each of these cases, kinsmen physically distance themselves from the caregiving site and caregiving assistance potentials.

The nature and course of dementing disease specifically undermine the American values of independence and self-reliance. The stigmata associated with "crazy behavior" or "losing one's mind" derive from the failure to meet the sociocultural expectations of personhood. The nature of this disease not only disrupts one's normal life patterns but also invites the social penalties imposed for violation of cultural expectations. Such penalties may take the form of social distancing by friends and relatives and hostility on the part of caregivers.

Acute Care Medicine
The predominance of the medical model of care must be consid-

ered as a cultural product. For example, "senility" is still present as an operational construct in the minds of many practitioners who attempt diagnosis and treatment of Alzheimer's disease. The medical model further perpetuates an acute-care orientation emphasizing treatment with rapid cessation of symptoms. Acute-care orientations toward dementia fail. Also, they frustrate practitioners, who are trained to cure but are increasingly confronted with a chronic, incurable disease. In addition, a unidisciplinary treatment approach is employed in the presence of a bioculturally complex, lengthy disease process. The Alzheimer's patient and his or her family experience this disease in a medical culture oriented to in patient acute-care facilities staffed by practitioners with little medical education in geriatrics and interdisciplinary team management, using a health service system that is largely unarticulated in the provision of services, thereby leading to suboptimal care.

Many have suggested that the normal process of aging has been redefined in terms of the disease model (Arluke and Peterson 1981; Becker and Kaufman 1995; Estes and Binney 1989). Because the sick role is considered a deviant one, the medicalized process of aging is inherently penalizing. Viewed through the medical lens, even normal aging can be and is defined in terms of specific physiologic measurements, the absence of symptoms, and resulting social control of the elderly (Estes and Binney 1989).

The dramatic symptoms associated with dementing disease have produced an extremist view of aging as Alzheimer's disease (Gubrium 1986; Herskovits 1995; Lyman 1989; Stafford 1991). Some would charge that disproportionate amounts of funding go toward research on Alzheimer's disease at the expense of less dramatic diseases, such as osteoporosis. Osteoporosis, though, is much more manageable in terms of amelioration of risks and treatment and is much "quieter" in its manifestations and human costs.

Profit Motives

Health care is a for-profit business endeavor in American society. It is no mystery that Alzheimer's disease (and other dementias) has become the target of special attention in the economic arena. Drug companies have competed in heated races with one another to be the first to offer a pharmacologic treatment for managing the symptoms of Alzheimer's disease. Similarly, the nursing home industry has responded with specific or special approaches to the long-term care of individuals with dementia, notably AUs.

Getting a certificate of need (CON) for building additional beds in the long-term care market is now easier if the beds requested are designated as unique in some way. Alzheimer's disease and other dementias have served very nicely as a means to differentiate new beds in an area so that construction can begin.

Apparently, some in the nursing home industry have found that the use of Medicaid reimbursement for these beds does not make AUs profitable to the margin desired. On the other hand, private payers in such facilities are likely to be charged a higher rate for the "special" treatment. The actual differential cost of dementia patients compared with those who are cognitively intact is very difficult to measure (Holmes et al. 1994). However, the bed-getting ability of Alzheimer's disease CONs may offset any extra costs associated with AUs.

Also, the public is drawn to a facility that can offer a special case treatment, should the need arise. Those admitted who are cognitively lucid are told that special beds are available if there is a future need for one. This marketing agenda does not have to be pressed. The lay public now asks for the presence of AUs.

Soteria

Desperate people do desperate things. Yet, people want to be perceived as rational folks. This has created a window for duplicity. Alzheimer's disease and other dementias are death sentences, according to current discourse. Today, dementing diseases are well-known conditions to the public and have even taken on the folk term "Oldtimer's disease." The course of these diseases is played out on television dramas in great detail. One political figure, former President Ronald Reagan, and one celebrity, Charlton Heston, issued statements telling of their diagnosis, at a time in the progression of the disease that allowed lucid thought and communication. There is the anticipation of worsening cognition and, ultimately, death. Those around the dementia patient are aware of the long-term course of these conditions and cling to every lucid moment before there are none.

These increasingly common, brain-destroying diseases constitute a new dread on the roster of killer plagues that have attacked people through the years. They produce symptoms that slowly change people from their true personalities into people without a present and, finally, without a past. This metamorphosis occurs as the brain dies, but the body generally keeps its usual outward appearance. Only in the last years of brain loss does the body begin to show severe signs of decline. Initially, a person looks healthy but begins to show unusual forgetfulness and confusion. Eventually, the person may undergo personality changes and exhibit episodes of agitation and outbursts. Coping with the behavioral aberrations seems impossible sometimes. Those around them are confronted with a fully familiar-looking person who is totally unfamiliar in behavior, a person who looks normal but cannot communicate properly, behaves in unpredictable ways, and may not have full control of bodily functions.

Dementia and its behavioral aberrations evoke the seemingly deep-rooted "mentally ill person as witch" scenario. Bizarre behavior, the flexible definitions of such notwithstanding, produces bizarre reactions. When a normal-looking older adult is in the yard, naked, and flares with anger when caregivers try to remove him or her to shelter, the caregiver reaction is one of fear, pain, and sadness. Fear, born of years of normal life with a person who now manifests anger, hostility, and vicious looks very unlike the person they knew. Pain, from the anguish of not only seeing but also partly *experiencing* the degeneration of the person they knew. (Intensive caregiving can produce overidentification with the patient and self-projection onto the patient, resulting in a version of self-degeneration.) Sadness, from the daily confirmation that there will certainly be no return to life as it was.

What is the social response to the disease condition? In the past, families would call nursing home after nursing home, trying to place the demented one. Nursing homes declined. Eventually, the nursing home industry awakened to this pent-up market and started to accept demented patients into their facility, intermixed with lucid patients. Soon, the lucid patients and their families complained of the inappropriate intrusions into their rooms and bathrooms and of interrupted visits. A strategy was crafted to exploit the market and also keep the lucid customers. The AU was born.

Multiple forces are producing a duplicitous response. There is both a wish for care and a secret wish for storage. Families want care, of course. Yet, there is a burden factor that makes most cry out for respite. Nursing homes provide care for the patient and respite for the family—for a price. The AU provides the "best" of care, thus assuaging the guilt associated with the decision to "store."

In broad terms, other oppositional constructs are operating: the care-versus-storage and integration-versus-segregation views. The integration view is that people should be mixed together in nursing homes because that is the democratic thing to do. Some have come up with good reasons to do so. For example, the lucid patients can help the confused patients. However, the lucid patient is there, presumably, for dependencies due to medical conditions, not to be a surrogate caregiver. The segregation view prevails because of another opposition: acceptance versus stigma.

Dementia patients, with their behavioral aberrations, are not accepted as desirable buddies by other patients in the nursing home. They are, in fact, stigmatized because of their odd behavior. Dementing diseases provoke the notion of stereotypic "demented" monsters. In reality, the outbursts of dementia patients are most often fear-based reactions to being hurried or confused by staff or others around them. These outbursts can involve striking out, biting, screaming, or throwing things, which, obviously, can be upsetting to others not cognitively impaired.

Society has responded to the behavioral aberrations of dementia via the nursing home, in particular, the development of the AU. This also serves a dual purpose for the lucid patients. The lucid patients can salve their dementia fear by demonstrating, to themselves and others, that they are normal simply by being in the dementia-free part of the nursing home. Through the symbolic communication of the spatial psychogeography of location, they are comforted by the fact that their propriety is maintained, in contrast to the dementia patients, whose mis-propriety is quarantined.

In essence, the AU is contemporary America's mis-response to a chronic, noninfectious, disease-like condition. It is a response more often appropriate for uncontrollable infectious epidemics. For example, when tuberculosis was rampant, sanatoria in remote parts of rural

America were built. When HIV/AIDS was new, there were calls for quarantine and special institutions only for those patients, to minimize spread. Of course, these strategies also hide the afflicted and produce a pseudo-sense of confidence, that is, a type of soteria.

In summary, without implementing a truly behavioral model of long-term care, there is little way to overcome the therapeutically empty AU model, but the primitive psychocultural reasons for AUs will prevail. Those afflicted with a fatal disease that produces confused thought and severely impaired communication wish for a dramatic cure or reversal of circumstance. In the face of hopelessness, family members feel compelled to search for the very best for their loved one.

Nursing homes hold up their AUs as a place of special treatment precisely for those afflicted with a dementing disease. Even if there is not explicit language regarding the capacity of AUs to make improvements in this disease, implicit specialness of a designated place and physical plant is enticing, sometimes overly so, to family members. Yet, the offer of a special place for only those people meeting specific criteria should also hold the fulfillment of that promise. Unfortunately, this seldom happens, because of flaws in the concept of the AU and in its operational conduct. From the families' perspective, the AU seems to be a superior situation for their loved one, and they derive a sense of satisfaction from having done the best job possible for their loved one. The risk of emotional trauma is high when family members realize that such units have very little power to bring about the changes wished for. The combination of the family perspective and the facility perspective creates a classic "come-on" offer without fulfillment, the offer of salvation but with no heaven.

SUMMARY

The effectiveness of AUs was the subject of an Office of Technology Assessment (OTA) study by Maslow (1994a and b). Maslow reports, "The very limited positive findings in most of these evaluative studies are surprising and appear to contradict the conviction of special care unit operators and others that the units benefit residents, residents' families, and unit staff members" (1994a:S29). She goes on to discuss methodological problems that could account for such findings.

She points out that many special-care unit advocates cite the methodological problems in the studies as the source of negative findings. Yet, she notes that OTA concluded that six studies involving a comparison group constitute reasonable research and these studies produce very limited positive findings.

Nursing homes operate on the foundation of the biomedical model and its acute-care orientation. This inappropriate model for long-term care residents with chronic disease is foisted on the AU operation. Such practice constitutes a self-perpetuating error. As Howard Stein points out, regarding creeping medicalization, "by adding yet another 'corrective' epicycle to earlier failed solutions, the next solution removes us even further from the capacity to reformulate the problem itself" (1990:9). Chances for a truly new model for nursing home and AU care seem vanishingly small.

The combined issues of AU operation and soteriological fantasy collectively produce a cultural pressure toward the development and maintenance of AUs. In spite of lack of supporting scientific evidence of efficacy, AUs still proliferate. They are implicitly offered as soteriological havens for families of those afflicted with dementia.

EPILOGUE

Somewhere in a nursing home corridor, an administrator talks proudly but gently to potential customers as they approach the AU locked door.

ADMINISTRATOR: Rest assured that our "unit" provides the best care possible for your mother.

FAMILY: That's what we want, the best for Mama.

ADMINISTRATOR *(using the keypad to unlock the door):* Let's hurry in so that Mr. Smith won't get out. *[Laughing]* He always tries to get out. *[Then, a hurried explanation]* The aides are so busy giving good care in the showers and rooms— *[The silence is calculated to imply that Mr. Smith's constant efforts to escape the AU are of lesser priority than "real" care.]*

FAMILY: What will Mama be doing during the day in the AU?

ADMINISTRATOR *(with great enthusiasm):* Activities! Our activity program is the best feature of our AU. We will probably see some of the activities around this corner *[instructing the family to go ahead].* Just turn left, one more left. Now look through the windows on your right. *[In a small room, the AU residents, seated, are trying to bounce a beach ball around.]* This is one of the more popular activities. The residents just love it!

The administrator and family talk in place while the beach ball continues to be bounced, albeit most often assisted by the activity coordinator. Fifteen minutes pass with no change in the "therapy." The administrator moves the family back to the lobby.

FAMILY: Will Mama ever get outside? She just loves the outdoors.

ADMINISTRATOR: That's the best part of our AU! The residents can wander safely outside the AU and come back anytime. They just walk and walk....

Note

1. An evaluative study of the Eden Alternative (Thomas 1994) was done by Coleman et al. (2002). The Eden Alternative program seeks to improve quality of life by making a more home-like environment, bringing in pets, children, and plants to the nursing home. The Coleman et al. study noted that "anecdotal" reports of quality of life improvements included less drug use, fewer infections, fewer antibiotics, and a perceived improvement in residents' quality of life. To really test this array of benefits, the Coleman et al. study used data from the Minimum Data Set reporting cognition, survival, immune function, functional status, and cost of care after one year. Their conclusion was that there is no benefit from the Eden Alternative, but "qualitative observations" indicated that it was a positive experience for staff. In the same issue of the *Journal of Gerontology: Medical Sciences,* Morley and Flaherty (2002) comment on the Coleman et al. study and conclude that a home-like environment should be balanced with appropriate medical care by implementing a Continuous Quality Improvement program. In contrast to these approaches, which address quality of life by using indicators sterile of the lived experience of long-term care, one recent study examined the effect on agitation rates of patients with a pattern of agitation proneness

by measuring the benefit of training CNAs to use positive verbal prompts when communicating a needed change to a patient (Roth et al. 2002). Agitation was statistically significantly reduced simply by teaching CNAs to be positive in their verbal and nonverbal interactions with patients. In this study, the benefits came from how the care was delivered, something not found in "downstream" indicator data.

7

Family Involvement in Nursing Home Facilities

A Decision-Making Perspective

Graham D. Rowles and Dallas M. High

Efforts to enhance both the quality of care and the quality of life in nursing facilities have increasingly acknowledged that residents must be recognized and treated as "lives in process" instead of merely patients with functional disorders or persons to be managed. There is growing awareness that, first, an individual's life in a nursing facility should be framed within the context of his or her experienced world, with an understanding of his or her "horizons of meaning" and personal history (Gubrium 1993). Second, it is becoming increasingly accepted that each nursing facility engenders and sustains a distinctive culture, which determines whether, and to what degree, these horizons of meaning and personal histories are recognized (Gubrium 1975; Henderson and Vesperi 1995; Savishinsky 1991; Shield 1988; Thomas 1996). Third, there is growing recognition of the need to link the world within the nursing facility (the "inside") to the world beyond (the "outside") by increasing institutional permeability (the exchange of people, services, and communication) (Rowles, Concotelli, and High 1996). Fourth, maximizing resident autonomy, the degree to which residents are enabled and empowered to exercise choice, is increasingly accepted as essential for quality of life (Agich 1993; High and Rowles 1995; Kane et al. 1997; Kapp 1994; Lidz, Fischer, and Arnold 1992).

One outcome of this emergent consciousness has been an array of initiatives to humanize the nursing facility home experience: advocacy for pioneering strategies involving residents and families in the operation of facilities (Berdes 1987; Kari and Michels 1991; Thomas 1996), programs that encourage rather than deter reminiscence (Burnside 1996; Cook 1984; Haight, Michel, and Hendrix 1998; Taft and Nehrke 1990), design innovations that include the construction of shared facilities, such as swimming pools and restaurants, that can be entered both from the facility and from the community, enabling nursing facilities to interface directly with the communities in which they are located (Regnier 1994), and efforts to develop an ethos of individualized care (Burger and Williams 1996). All these reflect attempts to create an environment that sustains a sense of "being in the world" and a sense of continuity with the past and with the contemporary world beyond the facility.

Unfortunately, more than half of all nursing facility residents are cognitively impaired (Strahan and Burns 1991). They are unable to communicate effectively with staff. Cognitive incapacity often limits the value of innovative programmatic options as mechanisms for residents' sustaining and sharing the richness and meaning of their life. As a result, individuals may become "faces without stories," their personal histories, values, and preferences inaccessible to staff (Gubrium 1993:1). Yet, each nursing home resident has a personal history, each (to a greater or lesser degree) retains vestiges of a former identity, and each has values and preferences.

As already mentioned in this book, residents' family members often play a key role in ensuring that residents are treated in a manner consistent with their former lifestyle or a best estimate of what they would have wanted (High and Rowles 1995). We suggest that one approach to humanizing care lies in more explicitly recognizing and reinforcing the role of family members in processes of decision making in nursing facilities.[1] There are many possible definitions of family (Gubrium and Holstein 1990). In this context, family is considered to comprise primarily kin. Significant others are incorporated into this category when clear evidence of a family-like relationship exists (for example, two elderly widows who have resided together for many years). A family often involves subgroups or factions, each having a different viewpoint and level of involvement in the resident's life.

It is well known that families have an important role in the decision to admit frail, older adults to long-term care facilities (Groger 1994; McFall and Miller 1992). However, the continuing role of the family and the involvement of individual family members in decisions affecting the care and life experiences of residents have not been researched. Little is known about the natural history (the pattern of lived events over time) of family involvement in nursing facility decision making and the effects of this involvement on the quality of life of both the resident and his or her family members. This gap in knowledge is of concern, given continuing ambiguity regarding the appropriate role of family members in the lives of relatives in a nursing facility. There is the dilemma of deciding whether to defer to the authority and expertise of the facility or to maintain full involvement. Within the family, this dilemma may extend to determination of which family member assumes primary responsibility for liaison with the facility.

The purpose of the ethnographic research reported in this chapter was to investigate family involvement in the decision-making environment of the contemporary nursing facility, with particular emphasis on everyday decisions that profoundly affect the quality of life of residents. We describe an array of overlapping decision-making processes and roles assumed by family members. We argue that these manifest themselves in the nursing facility decision-making culture in ways that take into account the lifestyle and preferences of the resident before admission to the facility. Central to this thesis is a contextual understanding of the nursing facility as a decision-making environment.

THE NURSING FACILITY AS A DECISION-MAKING ENVIRONMENT

The contemporary nursing facility has evolved over the past 150 years as a response to the problem of caring for ever-growing numbers of frail elders who can no longer be looked after by their families or within community-based settings. (For review of the history of the nursing facility as a feature of American society, see Haber 1983; Johnson and Grant 1985.) As a socially created institution, the nursing facility reflects and projects cultural values and expectations regarding the role and treatment of frail elders in, or more frequently outside, society (Henderson and Vesperi 1995). As Stafford notes in his discussion of "double burial" (see the introduction and Chapter 5), the nursing facility has come to represent a netherworld, a kind of purgatory between life and death, in which discordant ambiguity and ambivalence exist in a tension between straining toward life (the Hippocratic obligation) and accepting the inevitability of death (the removal from society and palliative treatment of those soon to die).

As both a physical space and a social institution, the nursing facility has become a manifestation of these seemingly contradictory imperatives. Indeed, the designation *nursing home*—accepted terminology before passage of the Nursing Home Reform Act incorporated into the Omnibus Budget Reconciliation Act of 1987 (OBRA)—embraces the contradiction between a medical *(nursing)* facility and a residence *(home)*. In the past few years, new residential options for frail elders have included assisted living alternatives (Mitchell and Kemp 2000; Regnier 1994; Zimmerman, Sloane, and Eckert 2002) and public policy that focuses on keeping people out of institutional care and reducing long-term care costs. As a result, nursing facilities have become increasingly "medicalized" because they provide ever-higher levels of skilled care.

In spite of this intensifying medical focus, the nursing facility remains a place where people "live." It is especially important to understand those aspects of this environment that provide the best possible quality of life for residents. In this context, we seek to advance such understanding by considering the nursing facility as a decision-making environment. Our premise is that the institutional culture of each nursing facility is defined by a plethora of decisions—historical and contemporary, permanent and ephemeral—that, ultimately, determine each resident's daily lifestyle and quality of life. Decisions are made on many levels and are of many types. Some decisions are remote from the resident, even though they may significantly impinge on his or her quality of life. Federal and local government regulatory decisions, corporate policy decisions, architectural decisions made in designing the physical space, and other exogenous decisions are critical determinants of the resident's lifestyle because they define and place constraints on what is possible. Other decisions are more immediate and perhaps less immutable. The institutional routine and the rules and procedures (some explicit and some implicit) governing daily life characteristically reflect the working styles and preferences of the administrator and staff. Finally, myriad small but very important decisions are made every day in a facility. A nursing assistant decides to give a resident an extra helping of dessert. A social worker schedules a birthday party, or a family member decides to decorate a resident's room for the holiday season. The confluence of these multiple levels of decisions defines the milieu within which each resident lives out his or her life.

Within this rubric, it is useful to distinguish types of decisions: authoritative, given, negotiated, and reflexive. *Authoritative* decisions are relatively immutable decisions externally imposed by governmental or legal fiat or determined by corporate or facility administrative policy. An array of federal and state regulations impose de jure guidelines and constraints on the facility with respect to the nature and quality of care provided to each resident. Such decisions include regulations regarding staffing patterns, room assignments, access to a telephone, routine resident evaluation, and resident rights. Individual residents and their families generally have very little direct input into such decisions.

A set of taken-for-granted, or *given*, decisions defines the cultural environment of each nursing home and sustains norms and expectations regarding the conduct of everyday life in the facility. Evolving over the life history of each facility, these unspoken decisions set the parameters of life in the nursing facility. For example, our research has suggested that variation among facilities in the prevalence of room changes reflects different philosophies regarding the desirability of room changes and the process by which room change decisions are made (Everard, Rowles, and High 1994). Thus, a social worker with primary responsibility for room assignments in one facility may determine that disputes among roommates should be handled by mediation instead of separation of the protagonists through reassignment. In another facility, a room change may be the option first considered. The outcome may be one facility with a high level of internal residential stability and another where frequent room changes create an atmosphere of "musical chairs" and a more fragmented ambiance of institutional life. Similarly, each facility, over time, evolves its own pattern of use of space, time/space rhythm, and routine of activity, which imbues the nursing home with a given-ness as a behavior setting (Shawler, Rowles, and High 2001). New residents are required to adapt to essentially a priori decisions regarding the functioning of the facility. At the time residents enter the social world of the nursing home, they and their families have little input into such decisions.

A third type of decision is *negotiated*. These decisions result from interaction among various actors. Interaction between a nurse and a resident's physician results in a decision to increase a medication dosage. Conversation between a nursing assistant and a resident results in a decision to attend a concert to be given by local high school students in the dining room and to wear a favorite blue dress to this event. A more formal conference involving the social worker, the dietitian, and a family member results in a decision to reduce a resident's caffeine intake or to eat on a different time schedule. A decision may be made involving the night staff and a resident that will allow her to stay up later than usual to watch a favorite late night movie and to be awakened last the morning after. To a significant degree, these individualistic, negotiated decisions determine the ambiance of each nursing home environment, creating the mores and culture of the setting.

Finally, and perhaps most important from the perspective of this chapter, many decisions affecting the lives of individual residents in nursing homes are *reflexive*. These are autonomous decisions made by individuals through a process of self-deliberation. For example, a resident may decide to spend the morning in the solarium. A nursing assistant may decide to linger at the end of her shift with a resident whose family is unable to make its customary visit. A family member may decide to rearrange a resident's pictures, clean out her closet, or take her out to a restaurant. These decisions, too, become critical determinants of the social ambiance of the nursing home. They are particularly important for cognitively impaired residents because they help to define the level of expected resident autonomy that characterizes each facility. There is a delicate balance between sustaining the freedom of each resident to act in the manner he or she chooses—to wander around the facility at will, to move behind the nurses' station, to sing at the top of her lungs—and maintaining an environment wherein the needs and wishes of all participants are reconciled and respected.

The four types of decisions (authoritative, given, negotiated, and reflexive) are by no means mutually exclusive. Rather, they embrace an array of ways in which a nursing facility may be viewed as a decision-making environment. Into this setting, with established norms and rules of behavior, each new resident and his or her family enter at a time when they are particularly vulnerable. Generally, the resident is vulnerable because of the health condition that has necessitated nursing facility entry. Vulnerability from the perspective of the family results from entering an unfamiliar environment at a very stressful time. Family members must make numerous decisions. In this chapter, we explore how family members operate within the nursing home environment in their attempt to serve the best interests of their relative. They must assume various roles in a setting defined by authoritative and given decisions over which they have little say, and they must make negotiated and reflexive decisions that significantly affect their relative's quality of life.

THE STUDY

A three-year ethnographic study of family involvement in decision-making in four contrasting nursing facilities was undertaken. Facilities were chosen to represent a diversity of characteristics, including size, levels of care provided, proportion of private pay residents, nonprofit versus proprietary status, and location. Three of the facilities are located in an urban center (population 225,000).

Kensington Place is a spacious, 100-bed, proprietary facility.[2] The design is modern and the decor "plush." Approximately 85 percent of the residents are private pay. More than 95 percent of the residents have family members, many of whom live nearby in affluent neighborhoods. Residents' family members tend to visit frequently and to be actively involved in the life of the facility.

Greenhaven Manor is a single-story, modern, proprietary facility with 32 skilled nursing beds and 128 intermediate-care beds. The facility includes a 20-bed special care unit for Alzheimer's disease patients. Crowded corridors and constant activity characterize this more "institutional" setting, which during our fieldwork seemed to be perpetually undergoing redecoration. This busy facility is functioning at full capacity. Here, the presence of family members is less pervasive than at Kensington Place.

The atmosphere at the third facility seems less frenetic. Elizabeth Manor is a recently constructed, two-story, nonprofit nursing home located in a suburban area. There are two intermediate-care wings with 50 beds each and a skilled wing with 50 beds. In contrast to Greenhaven Manor, the design of this facility conveys a calm aura of spaciousness and light. The decor is simple and tasteful, incorporating carefully chosen and matched pastel blue, green, and plum color schemes. There are few private-pay residents at Elizabeth Manor, and the majority of residents are from modest- or low-income backgrounds. The level of family involvement ranges widely, with some residents receiving frequent visits and much family attention and others receiving limited family support.

The fourth facility, Mountain View, is a single-story building on the outskirts of a somewhat isolated, rural community of 2,795 persons, located in Baden County (population 11,700) in the foothills of southern Appalachia. The decor is utilitarian and institutional, in contrast to the attractive interior design at the other facilities. There are few private-pay residents in this proprietary facility. The majority of residents are from the county or adjacent counties, and the facility is strongly integrated into the local community—historically, economically, socially, and psychologically (Rowles, Concotelli, and High 1996). There is a high level of family involvement in this facility.

Considering the individual as the unit of analysis, *decision-making* was defined as an act of making a choice, reaching a conclusion, or making a judgment. The decision-making process was conceptualized as potentially involving a constellation of actors surrounding, and including, each resident. Operationally, this constellation was defined to include the resident (if cognitively capable), the nursing home administrator, the nursing staff member most closely involved with the individual's care, the nonmedical staff member (generally a nursing assistant) most closely involved with the resident's care, the resident's physician, other actors, such as lawyers and clergy with whom the resident might come into contact, and, most important, two significantly involved family members. Depending on the nature of the decision,

TABLE 7.1

A typology of resident-related nursing facility decisions

Type of Decision	Examples	Number of Subtypes
Daily living decisions	Timing of activities (breakfast, bedtime, etc.), food choices, bathing, access to a telephone, snacks, spending money	20
Physical environment decisions	Room arrangement, use of furniture, personal belongings, radio or TV	11
Social environment decisions	Room assignment, choice of roommates, where to sit at meals, social activities	10
Treatment and health care decisions	Medication, restraints, physical therapy, surgery, diet, wheelchair, geri-chair	16
Major financial decisions	Payment to nursing facility, spend down, Medicaid, selling of property, insurance	9
Transfer decisions	Hospitalization, discharge, transfer within facility, transfer to another facility	6
Competency decisions	Guardianship, durable power of attorney, confusion, decision-making capacity	7
Crisis or life-and-death decisions	CPR, DNR, Living Will, artificial nutrition and hydration, funeral arrangements	9

different individual actors or subsets of these actors were involved.

The research focused on a typology of eight decision-making categories developed during the pilot phase of the project: crisis or life-and-death decisions, decisions regarding competence, financial decisions, transfer decisions, treatment and health care decisions, decisions regarding the social environment, decisions about the physical environment, and daily living decisions. Within these categories, eighty-seven subtypes of decisions were identified. Table 7.1 provides examples.

Three principal methods of data collection were employed. First, extensive participant observation over the entire three-year period enabled us to develop a sense of the ambience and culture of decision-making in each facility. We learned about many of the authoritative decisions defining and constraining the operation of each environment. Participant observation also enabled us to experience, and thereby gain a firsthand understanding of, given decisions, the norms and expectations for particular behaviors in particular situations that defined the social ambiance and culture of each facility.

Second, a series of in-depth, semistructured interviews were conducted, centered around ten residents (per facility) who were seventy-five years of age or older. Participating in the interviews were the resident (if cognitively capable) and potential decision-makers for that resident. These interviews were repeated five times (once every three months), providing a longitudinal perspective over a fifteen-month period. Finally, event analysis, involving ongoing monitoring of individual decision situations as they were in progress, was undertaken. Data were gathered by four research assistants, one assigned to each nursing facility. The outcome included 1,084 tape-recorded, in-depth interviews (each was transcribed), extensive dossiers on the decision-making constellations of sixty-one nursing facility residents,[3] and more than 1,400 printed pages of single-spaced field notes.

An important finding emerged early in the fieldwork. Most families remain fully involved in the lives of their institutionalized relative throughout the relative's stay. Our interviews revealed a high level of reflexive decision making on the part of family members as, particularly in the case of cognitively impaired residents, they proactively took charge of many aspects of their relative's daily life and, within the constraints of the institutional environment, acted with a high level of decisional autonomy. Family members frequently play key roles in negotiated decision making pertaining to their relative. Family members provided information on 661 decisions during the course of the in-depth interviews. They had participated "fully" or "somewhat" in 90 percent of the 38 crisis decisions reported, 85 percent of the 34 financial decisions, 76 percent of the 136 daily living decisions, 67 percent of the 9 competency decisions, 65 percent of the 49 physical environment decisions, 61 percent of the 271 treatment decisions, 60 percent of the 52 transfer decisions, and 40 percent of the 67 social environment decisions they reported. As already stated, this high level of involvement persisted throughout the resident's stay. Family members were involved in 60 percent of the decisions they reported for residents with less than one year of residence, 70 percent for residents with one to two years of residence, and 63 percent for residents with two to four years of residence. Only for residents with length of residence in excess of four years does the level of family involvement appear to drop significantly (only six residents in the study population had resided in the nursing facility for more than four years).

CASE STUDIES

Acknowledging the consistently high level of family involvement in decision making, we now turn to the nature of this involvement and the way in which it manifests the propensity of family members to engage in various types of decisions and to assume an array of decision-making roles. We begin with three case studies, compiled from transcriptions of the in-depth interviews and from field notes.

Vicky Dorsey

Vicky Dorsey, an elegant, well-dressed woman with a silvery gray wig and tasteful jewelry, was ninety-six years old when she was admitted to Kensington Place. Her daughter, Andrea, visited her frequently and usually brought cookies (reflexive decision):[4]

> Well, I always bring her cookies. She has to have cookies.... She likes chocolate ones, chocolate chip usually, so she always has those...and I know she's getting heavy. Some of the summer clothes, I've had to take two home because they've just gotten too tight for her across the stomach. I think it's from all those cookies.... Used to be I'd buy her cookies once a week or once every ten to twelve days, but now it's twice a week. I try to let her go without them for a while, but she really complains about it if she doesn't have it. And she'd been without them for two or three days and say, "I haven't had any cookies for two weeks." So she really does like them. Who cares if she gets fat? She'll be ninety-eight next month.

Although she might acquiesce to Vicky's dietary wishes, Andrea was extremely vigilant regarding other aspects of her mother's well-being. She closely monitored her care and frequently intervened with staff when she perceived that something was amiss (negotiated decision). At one point, she became particularly concerned about her mother's foot care. A member of the nursing staff recounted this:

> Now, the decision has been made for her for Dr. Virgo to do her care—he is the podiatrist—to do her foot care every month because her toenails grow real fast and her daughter's real concerned about that. Well, she was, too. Mrs. Dorsey was too. Vicky was, too.... Okay, well, her daughter discussed it in Care Plan, and the charge nurse, you know, consulted with Dr. Virgo, who is our house podiatrist, and he agreed to do it. I wasn't here when that meeting went on, but she [Andrea] has approached me several times to find out when he was coming.

Andrea also initiated and mediated the decision-making process that resulted in her mother's going to the dining room for only one meal and taking the remainder of her meals in her room (negotiated decision). Andrea explained to the staff that her mother had always been something of a loner. In addition, Andrea played a major role in setting up her mother's room to make it home-like (reflexive decision). She arranged Vicky's pictures on the wall. She brought a radio and set it to her mother's favorite station so that Vicky could listen to classical music while she dined, something she had done at home.

As Vicky's stay at Kensington Place lengthened, Andrea came to know the staff better. She was able to share information on her mother's history and preferences. She educated the staff about "trigger" words that would involve her mother in conversation. As Vicky became increasingly confused, Andrea was able to explain some of her mother's behaviors to the staff. For example, when Vicky began to wander down to the nurses' station in the middle of the afternoon and ask to be put to bed, Andrea was able to explain that her mother's typical response to stress throughout her life had been to "take to her bed." As one of the nurses explained,

> You know, she was...just one of those people that couldn't stand for anything to be wrong. She had to go to bed. So it's nothing new to her daughter, but it's just showing up lately over here.

When Andrea was unable to visit for a few days, Vicky would sometimes become very upset. On these occasions, Andrea would inform the staff and work with them to minimize the trauma occasioned by her absence. She would make sure that she told her mother of her impending absence and arranged with the staff to be especially sensitive to Vicky's mood during the time she was away. On occasion, working with the staff involved benign collusion. A nurse reported:

> I did talk with her daughter last week about Mrs. Dorsey was complaining about her mattress being too hard, but her daughter said a month ago it was too soft and they put a hard one on it, so she just said leave it. That way, in a week from now she will forget it. (negotiated decision)

In some ways, Vicky's life in the nursing facility is controlled by her daughter. With respect to her influence on the arrangement of her mother's room, this can sometimes have unanticipated consequences. The administrator explained:

> We recently had all of the rooms, put new wallpaper...and when that was put in the room, we asked that they not hang pictures back on the new wallpaper [authoritative decision]. So, therefore, her daughter rearranged her pictures, and for about two weeks it threw her [Vicky] into an awful tizzy. I was called to her room by Carol Wilmore, the three-to-eleven nurse, who said that she was just very upset and kept saying, "Why did my daughter do this to me? Why did my daughter do this to me?" And after talking to her for a while, I finally figured out about the pictures being rearranged. We tried to talk to her and tell her about the new wallpaper, and she just wasn't processing what we were saying. She was just upset that her daughter had moved everything around without telling her.

Albert Fry

A similar level of devotion to enriching a resident's life is demonstrated by Eulalah, the seventy-five-year-old spouse of Albert Fry. A very thin, always well-dressed, seventy-five-year-old with both Parkinson's disease and Alzheimer's disease, Albert lives down the hallway from

Vicky Dorsey at Kensington Place. Eulalah visits every day and is often seen sitting with Albert, holding his hand.

> The first thing I do, I walk in and open his closet and start putting away his clothes that he had wore the day before [reflexive decision]. And then I get his clothes that he is to wear the next day, and then I get him an outfit put together, and then I take his dirty clothes, you know, find his dirty clothes. And I've been brushing his teeth, cut his toenails, his fingernails, and the hair in his nose and his ears. Honey, I do it all.

In addition, Eulalah diligently monitors his condition. During one span of a few weeks, she informed the nursing staff that the color and odor of his urine had changed (prompting a urine analysis), brought the deteriorating circulation in his feet to their attention (this had not been noticed previously), and intervened when he seemed to have been overmedicated (negotiated decision).

> He was agitated…. The third shift called the doctor at 4 a.m., and he was still out that afternoon when we arrived. My son and I took him to the bathroom, and, honey, he was just like somebody drugged, on this drug, and he couldn't put one foot in front of the other. Al is a small man, you know what I mean. He doesn't need a lot of medication. They overmedicated in giving him something that, you know, what they give a two-hundred-pound man. That's when I started calling the doctor, too…. And I didn't want them to give him any more. I don't care what the doctor said.

Eulalah's efforts transcend merely a concern with the quality of her husband's care. She explicitly tries to empathize with his experience. There is a gentle poignancy in her comments:

> Well, other than sleep, he just rattles. He don't know what he's saying. He's working. He's fired everybody and he [says], "That hole wasn't right!" I listen to him and then, finally, I [say], "Now Al, you're retired. You don't have to worry about things like that any more. Just forget it."

She also works assiduously to engage his mind. She brings photographs and family albums and encourages him to associate these pictures with the places and people in their life together (reflexive decision). She takes him outside the facility once or twice a week, often for lunch (reflexive decision).

> Now, Tuesday I picked him up, and I had an errand to run out on the beltline, to get some bags for my sweeper. And the weather, you know, halfway decent. So I picked him up, and we drove out there.... Things like that, you know, just to get him out and away.

Such excursions are no small feat for Eulalah: "Them wheelchairs is heavy to put in and out of the trunk of a car for a seventy-five-year-old woman." But the outings appear to rejuvenate Albert, as is apparent from her account of a trip to attend a family fiftieth wedding anniversary (reflexive decision):

> My intentions were, we would take Al to the dinner and then bring him back, and we would go...back to the party, dance—it was a dance. And so, after the dinner, we were lingering, talking with part of his family, and, uh, someone, and I can't think of who, someone came in and said, "There are some friends and that in the other room," where they were having the dance, "that heard that Al was here, and they want to see him. Bring him on in here." So we did. And everybody would just come over, his family and cousins... that he hadn't seen for some time. Of course, he couldn't remember it, but anyway we kept staying and staying.... Well, we were still staying, see, and we were sitting at this table, and it was about 9:30 and Al said, "I want to dance." Well, it kind of caught me, and I said, "Okay, let's go." So we got him out of the wheelchair, and everybody started hollering, "Oh, look, look, look!" And Al, poor thing, he was so weak—it looked like two drunks. And Grace, his sister, came over and I said, "Al wants to dance." She said, "I'll dance with you." And he said, "I'll dance with Eulalah, and then I'll dance with you." And I want you to know, we danced. It was

a slow dance, and then when it was over, he did dance with his sister.

Emma Wise

Eighty-four-year-old Emma Wise, a resident of Mountain View nursing home, does not speak, because of her advanced dementia. Her abundant gray-white hair is often matted to one side from leaning her head on the geri-chair, where she sits with her feet up and knees bent—but her hair is all that is disheveled. She is usually dressed in clean nightgowns or dresses that her daughter, Betty, brings from home, and her room is well decorated by an attentive family. Betty visits every other day for two or three hours, often arriving around lunchtime to help with feeding Emma.

> And then I always bring her something to eat. If I come in the afternoon, I bring her a strawberry sundae. I always bring her something to eat. I never come without bringing her something to eat.

Sometimes Betty stays for the evening meal. Like Andrea and Eulalah, she is involved in a variety of decisions and activities that serve to individualize her mother's care. She does her laundry, changes her bed when the CNAs are busy, and straightens up her room (reflexive decision). She also provides personal care, fixing her mother's hair, putting lotion on her dry skin, and cutting her nails (reflexive decision). She spends many hours holding her mother's hand, comforting her, and talking to her, even though her mother's only response is a pursing of the lips and utterance of guttural, sucking noises with her mouth and tongue.

Betty intervenes on her mother's behalf with the nursing home staff. As one of the nurses remarked, "Betty's really good about if there's any kind of problem. She always comes to the desk and talks to you about it." Thus, when she discovered that Emma was allergic to the soap the facility was using, she requested that they bathe her mother using a different soap, which she provided (negotiated decision). When the soap was changed, the rash disappeared. As Betty remarked on one occasion, "Yes, the longer you're here, the more you know what you can do" (given decision).

Betty spends the most time at the nursing home, but other family members also provide support and involve themselves in decisions that enhance her mother's care. Emma has four children (including a son who has durable power of attorney for her affairs), twelve grandchildren, and nine great-grandchildren. Remembering how she had always enjoyed her garden, Emma's son hung a bird feeder outside her window at the nursing home (reflexive decision). At Christmas, several family members decorated her room. Each year, the nursing home holds a contest to elect a Valentine King and Queen, and the winners are feted at a celebration. Votes for each resident are pennies placed in jars named for each candidate, with the proceeds donated to Alzheimer's disease research. Under normal circumstances, the nursing home administrator prefers that a cognitively capable, ambulatory resident win the competition (given decision). Indeed, generally, only cognitively capable residents are nominated. However, in Emma's case, the family was so enthusiastic about the contest that they made sure she was one of the nominees (negotiated decision). They saved pennies to donate all year, with the result that Emma won.

FAMILY ROLES IN DECISION MAKING

Andrea, Eulalah, and Betty provide examples of the way an individual family member's involvement in everyday decision making in a nursing home profoundly affects the quality of a resident's life. Family involvement personalizes and humanizes the life of a relative. It gives the resident a continuing link to his or her life history and the world outside that might otherwise be eliminated by the process of institutionalization. Similar scenarios could be presented for each of the sixty-one residents involved in this study, for all had family members who remained involved in decision making that affected the residents' lives to a greater or lesser extent.[5] In our review of the transcripts, consistent patterns emerged that enabled us to develop a typology of family decision-making roles:

- Caregiving
- Pampering
- Comforting
- Engaging
- Educating

- Monitoring
- Mediating
- Colluding
- Controlling

A major decision-making role involves direct *caregiving*. Family members frequently engage in reflexive decisions concerning their relative's activities, ranging from personal care, to determining daily attire and laundering clothes, to arranging the relative's room and daily activities. An essential feature of such caregiving is the ability to provide care in a manner consistent with the resident's former lifestyle. In all four facilities, it was apparent that reflexive decision making by family members with respect to caregiving was not only accepted but also appreciated by busy staff, who were relieved of time-consuming activities. In a number of cases, it was clear that family members had assumed a role of supplementary staff. As Betty remarked, regarding her mother, "I change her bed sometimes when the girls are busy," and on another occasion, "I try to stay and feed her supper.... I usually change her before I leave, and that gives the girls a [break], you know. They don't have to rush right on in and do it after supper." In a few cases, it appeared that by taking on such a caregiving role, conscientious family members experienced increased stress because staff essentially ceded responsibility for care during the times when the family member was in the facility.[6]

Beyond instrumental caregiving roles, family members make multiple reflexive decisions that personalize care by *pampering* residents. Family members often bring in residents' favorite foods: Vicky receives her chocolates, and Betty plies Emma with ice cream sundaes. In addition, family members facilitate the continuation of favorite activities, from listening to classical music to watching the birds outside the window.

The research also revealed a key socioemotional role in *comforting* residents, particularly those who were cognitively impaired, by sitting with them, talking with them, listening to their ramblings, and trying to re-establish or reaffirm connections to people and places in their past. This process often involved much hand holding, an indulgent empathy, and considerable patience. However, family members' decisions to sit with residents often reduced the residents' anxiety and agitation. Thus, Andrea's calming and reassuring presence was particularly missed when she was unable to visit Vicky for a few days. In many respects, assuming the comforter's role involves given decisions. There is generally no conscious decision to provide such comfort. Rather, such actions reflect implicit, taken-for-granted choices that are accepted, indeed, often expected, as part of the assumed responsibility of being a family member in our culture.

Efforts to comfort residents were complemented, in many cases, by conscious decisions of family members to introduce activities oriented toward *engaging* or reengaging their relatives in familiar aspects of their lives. By reviewing photographs and scrapbooks, taking them on trips to see former friends or familiar haunts, family members actively sought to sustain vestiges of their relative's identity and past. For Eulalah, such efforts, in addition to enriching her husband's life, served to affirm her own identity. Continual reminders of the meaning of the life they had shared provided a kind of catharsis.

A major family role in nursing-home decision making consists of representing the resident in interactions with nursing home staff. Family members may play a key role in *educating* staff to characteristics of residents—personal quirks, whims, and idiosyncrasies that could be gleaned from no other source but that explain seemingly incongruous behavior. In Gubrium's terminology, through active involvement in negotiated decision making, families are able to transform residents into "faces with stories" and, as in the case of Andrea's explanation of Vicky's afternoon wandering behavior, to make their behavior understandable to otherwise puzzled staff.

Such education often stems from vigilant *monitoring* of residents' status by family members. Knowledge of the resident and a keen, focused, caring family eye sometimes reveal critical concerns before they become apparent to staff members, whose attention may be diffused by their responsibility for multiple residents. Thus, Eulalah's vigilance resulted in a more timely response to the circulation problem in Albert's feet, hastened a needed urine analysis, and resulted in intervention when he had been overmedicated. Monitoring may also involve efforts to ensure that a resident's daily lifestyle is as consistent as possible with his or her past. Thus, Betty is especially concerned with her mother's clothing and closely monitors to ensure that Emma is dressed appropriately each day.

> The girls that really know me, they know that I like her clothes on.... Because my mother, the reason that I'm like that, because my mother was always a neat dresser, and I don't like to come in and see, now she doesn't have her gown on today, and it bothers me, I guess, mentally.... It's my personal feeling because my mother was always a neat dresser. My mother had everything to match. If she put on a dress, she had the shoes and pocketbook. It's not nothing to do with the nursing home about this. It's my personal feeling.... Yes. And I don't say nothing to them, you know. I just go ahead and do it because I like to sit there and look at her with her gowns on.

Because of their focused concern for a single individual, family members become especially important and effective in a *mediating* role regarding a wide range of decisions. Our data suggest that key family members often take their responsibilities very seriously and take charge of negotiated decision-making situations. Thus, Andrea intervened and followed up, with some persistence, to ensure that her mother received appropriate foot care. She also worked with the staff in arranging for her mother to take all but one of her daily meals in her room, a decision consistent with her mother's lifestyle before entering the facility. Betty effectively mediated a decision that resulted in the successful treatment of a mysterious rash her mother had developed. As a member of the nursing personnel explained,

> Emma had a rash. It was just a minor red rash, and her daughter was concerned about the rash and so she was trying to find out what they were using on Emma that might possibly have caused that. And the only thing we could figure out that was different was our periwash [anti-bacterial soap] solution. We'd gotten a new kind. So Betty looked at it

and smelled it, and she thought that maybe that might be what it was. So, at her request, we stopped using that, and we put up signs and we instructed our staff not to use that on Emma any more.

Although most aspects of the individualization of care by family members focus on satisfying the wishes, or presumed wishes, of residents, two decision-making roles emerged that did not fit neatly within this rubric. In some cases, we observed a propensity for family to become involved in *colluding* with staff in ways that appeared to contradict the stated preferences of residents. For example, collusion between Andrea and the nursing staff with respect to changing Vicky Dorsey's mattress resulted in a negotiated decision to take no action. In most cases, such collusion is benign, but on occasion, it may have more to do with the preferences of the family member. For example, Andrea was reluctant to take her mother to a recommended ophthalmologist because it meant transporting her to his office. As a member of the nursing staff explained,

> It wasn't because it was the doctor, per se. It's she did not want to take her out to an office visit to anyone, you know. And her reasons were that every time she takes her mother out that she has BMs all over the place.

Finally, we observed a propensity for some family members to be involved in the lives of their institutionalized relative to the point that they became *controlling*. For example, the nurse who worked most closely with Emma at Mountain View described how Emma's daughter had terminated her foot care:

> She brought these, whatever those bills are that they send out, and she came in and asked me what they were. And after I read them, it was, they specified some kind of surgery. And, at first, I couldn't figure it out. And then, it was from the podiatrist where he had trimmed her toenails. And she said she did not want him trimming her toenails, that she or we were capable of doing that. She saw no sense in paying taxpayers' money.

Again, in such cases, the intent was benign. However, on occasion, control of almost every aspect of the resident's lifestyle in the facility had negative consequences, illustrated by Vicky Dorsey's anxious response to her daughter's rearrangement of her pictures.

THE IMPORTANCE OF CONTEXT—LINKING INSIDE AND OUTSIDE, PAST AND PRESENT

Our data suggest that, in the majority of cases, family involvement in nursing-home decision making becomes coordinated through a single family member who assumes responsibility as a point person for the remainder of the family. Andrea, Eulalah, and Betty have assumed this primary family member role. At one time or another, each has engaged in most of the decision-making roles we have identified. Indeed, they have made or coordinated many decisions regarding the life of their relative, from the determination of competence, financing, and medical treatment, to seemingly mundane everyday decisions, such as the choice of clothes to wear or the provision of candy. In assuming these roles, individual family members become decision makers not only for those residents who are cognitively impaired and with residents who are intact but also, implicitly, for the entire family. Indeed, the primary family member often de facto assumes responsibility for most aspects of the resident's life. In this role, the primary family member provides a critical link between the worlds inside and outside the facility.

Under most circumstances, primary family members attempt to make decisions (either reflexive or negotiated) that involve the resident and respect the resident's continuing autonomy. Especially in the case of cognitively impaired relatives, they engage in surrogate decision making that reflects their best effort to reconcile what they perceive the relative's preferences would be with what they perceive to be in the relative's best interest. Within this rubric—adopting a kind of Janus stance, facing both inside and outside the facility—primary family members also attempt to represent the preferences of the entire family. Sometimes they consult with other family members regarding the appropriate course of action, but in many cases, particularly regarding everyday decisions, they act autonomously.

Generally, other family members are content to leave routine decisions to the on-site primary family member. However, intra-family tensions may arise when there is ambiguity or lack of consensus regarding the appropriate course of action. For example, there was some difference of opinion among Emma Wise's four children regarding Do Not Resuscitate (DNR) orders and use of cardiopulmonary resuscitation (CPR) on their mother. At the time of her admission, there was apparently consensus that extraordinary means should not be used to preserve their mother's life. Indeed, medical records revealed that Dr. Canter had provided a No Code order. Betty, who visited most frequently and had clearly taken on the primary family member role, assumed that this meant that her mother would not be "hooked up to machines." When she discovered that DNR orders would preclude the use of CPR, her opinion changed:

> Well, when I called my sister, she said, "Well, that's what I meant. Do nothing." I said, "Esther, you mean we don't do anything for Mother?" And I said, "Do you mean that if I'm sitting with her and she just doesn't breathe any more that the nurses are not, I mean, because they told me if we sign this, they don't do anything?" And I said, "How am I going to take that?" And she said, "Well, you," she said when Mother was in their home [Esther had lived with her before admission to Mountain View], that was what they decided that they would not do. And I said, "Well, if I'm not there, that's fine. But what am I going to do if I'm there? That's my mother, and how am I going to take it? I mean, just like right now if something happened to her, I'd want them to help her." And she said, "Well," then she said, "Well, call Ronald and see what he says." Well, then I called my other brother, Damon, and he said, "Well, Betty, you know we want them to do CPR." And I said, "Well, that's what I thought, but no machines." Of course, I didn't realize that the nursing home didn't have any machines now. I'm innocent in this deal, too. And I thought when they mentioned that, that meant that they had machines here that they put her on and bring her back, and I don't see no sense in that. I don't see no sense in the machines, but I do, I feel like they could try CPR. So I called my brother [Ronald] that's power of attorney, and I told him what she had told me, that he had to

send his papers in and they have to have it authorized by Dr. Canter. That's mother's doctor. So he said, "Well, wasn't that what we decided?" And I said, "Ronald, I have to say, I guess, that's what we decided, but I put my mother in there, I didn't think my mother would live but three months, if she lived that long." And I said, "Mother has lived for a year. I go see her every other day," and I said, "The more I think about it, how can...and I said it's fine if they don't do that if I'm not there. But when I call for those nurses or those aides and they do not come to Mother, if something happened to her, I don't know what I'm going to do?" See? I mean, I had never thought of it that way. So he told me, he said, "I'll tell you what I'll do." He says, "I won't send in my power of attorney paper," because it's not valid till he sends them in.[7] And he said, "Each of you children write me a letter and tell me how that you want it done." And then he says, "I'll go back and change them" [the DNR orders].

For several weeks, the issue was discussed via letters and telephone calls among family members before a final decision was reached and the appropriate documents forwarded to Mountain View to rescind the DNR order.

The primary family member as decision maker also acts within the larger context of the institutional setting. It is this individual who develops relationships with nursing home staff. He or she tends to establish a strong relationship with one or two members of the nursing home staff, who become key points of contact in discussions and negotiated decisions regarding most aspects of the resident's life. Indeed, many decisions affecting residents' lives are made on the basis of communication between the primary family member and a single member of the staff. Figure 7.1 best illustrates the contextualization of family involvement in the decision-making process.

Emma Wise is the focus of a decision-making constellation involving relationships among a variety of actors both inside and outside Mountain View. Within the facility, she is cared for by a series of actors, with differing levels of involvement and knowledge of her life. The administrator, Anne James, admits, "I don't think I know her well at

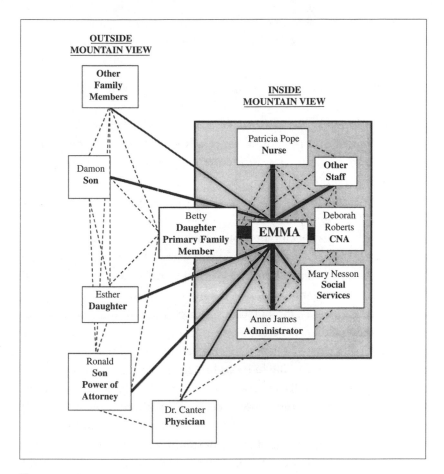

FIGURE 7.1

A decision-making constellation: Emma Wise

all." She perceptively notes, "I know what she is now, but I don't think I know what she used to be." Nonetheless, she provides some hands-on care: "I sit and talk, or I feed her sometimes." The majority of care is provided by nursing assistants. Deborah Roberts, a nursing assistant, has taken a special interest in Emma's care. It was Deborah who noticed that Emma, who had previously spent most of her time in bed or in a chair, had an inclination to walk:

> Well, when we were transferring her, she was putting her feet
> on the floor like she wanted to walk.... Well, then, from

> there we brought her...to the dining room and got under
> her arms and then tried to transfer her by ambulating her to
> the dining room.

As Patricia Pope, the nurse most fully involved with Emma's medical care, noted, "Yes, she got hold of a good aide taking care of her who's trying to get her up and take her out." Deborah was a primary point of contact with the family, especially with Betty, who appreciated the attention given to her mother. Commenting on the return of Deborah from temporary reassignment to another part of the nursing home, she commented, "But since we got Deborah back down on our end, it's a lot better."

It is within this specific network of institutional staff/resident relationships, involving a limited number of actors, that we must view the role of family. The family interfaces with the small cadre of staff directly responsible for Emma primarily through Betty. Although Betty is the liaison with the facility, the person who inserts herself into most negotiated decision-making situations, she is very conscious that she functions in this role primarily as her mother's representative. She also represents the entire family, especially her two brothers and her sister. Betty, her sister, who lives in an adjacent state, and her two brothers (one of whom lives fifty miles away) frequently exchange telephone calls. Such calls provide a means of sharing information on Emma's condition and a forum for family discussion of issues pertaining to her care.

As the primary point of family contact with the nursing home and as the on-site decision maker, Betty is careful to maintain a relationship with staff that stops short of meddling or what she perceives as unwelcome intrusion. She is aware of a delicate balance between assuming an active decision-making role in support of enhancing her mother's quality of life and maintaining a good relationship with staff (Foner 1994:110–119). On one occasion, after she had persisted in requiring of Patricia Pope that appropriate medical attention be devoted to a cough her mother had developed, she explained,

> I don't know if she was going to call that night or call the
> next morning, but then when I came back in two or three
> days, they told me she was on an antibiotic, so I just presumed that they had took care of it. Sometimes I don't like

to keep questioning them. I'm afraid that they'll think that I know more than they do, and I don't.

From the other side of the relationship, it is clear that most staff of the facilities in our study were fully aware that they did not know residents as well as did their family members. In most cases, they were very willing to receive decision-making input from family members and to adjust patterns of care accordingly. Some staff members felt that they served the families of residents as much as the residents themselves. In commenting on Emma's candidacy for selection as the Valentine's Day Queen, Anne James, the administrator of Mountain View, expressed this sentiment:

> I don't really think Emma knows or cares, you know, that she's running for Queen. And, you know, I would like for the person to win who, you know, realizes what's going on and either appreciates it or says, "I'm not being in your stupid contest!" But the family enjoys it, you know. We serve the families as much as we do the patient around here, sometimes more.

CONCLUSION

In the preceding pages, we have sought to integrate four needs of contemporary nursing home life—the need for sensitivity to individual residents' horizons of meaning and personal histories, the need for greater understanding of the distinctive culture of the nursing home, the need for deeper understanding of the ways in which nursing homes are separated from and, at the same time, a part of the community in which they are located, and the critical need for a focus on autonomy—within the framework of a study of the nursing home viewed as a decision-making environment. We have focused on the decision-making processes of family members and the roles they assume as they become part of the nursing home environment and, for the resident, the key point of contact between the facility and the family, the present and the past. In assuming this position, family members do their best to maintain their relative's autonomy against the backdrop of a decision-making environment within which they have only limited, ambiguous control. This chapter reveals the critical role of residents' families in the culture of nursing home life and enhancing their relative's quality of life. Our study represents an initial foray into a domain of research that should be pursued in more depth as we grapple with defining appropriate roles for residents' family members in nursing-home decision making. If the perspectives we have presented are confirmed in future research, it will become important to consider their implications for the reorganization of nursing home life and routine to maximize the ability of families to support the highest possible quality of life for their relative. We may be able to develop an entirely new perspective on the nursing home as a family-focused institution.

Notes

1. Research reported in this chapter was supported by a grant from the National Institute on Aging (AG08475). Some of the case study material incorporated in the chapter is reproduced from "Individualizing Care: Family Roles in Nursing Home Decision-Making," *Journal of Gerontological Nursing* 22:3, 1996: 20–25, with permission from the publisher, SLACK Incorporated. Views or opinions expressed in the chapter are those of the authors and do not necessarily represent the views or opinions of the funding agency. The assistance of Mary Doole and Evy Whitlatch in the review of transcripts and the development of case studies is gratefully acknowledged.

2. The names of all geographic locations, nursing homes, residents, family members, and nursing home personnel are pseudonyms.

3. This includes replacement of residents who died.

4. Throughout this section, the four types of decision—authoritative, given, negotiated, and reflexive—are identified in parentheses (or brackets, in quoted passages).

5. A focus on the nature of family involvement as the central concern of this project was such that only residents with family members were included in the study.

6. In fairness to staff, it should be pointed out that, in some cases, reliance on family to perform certain caregiving activities may provide the kind of assistance and temporary respite that enables staff to complete an excessive workload.

7. There was considerable ambiguity in this situation. From the staff's point of view, as revealed by the medical records, the physician had apparently approved a DNR order. However, Ronald, Emma's son with power of attorney, had not signed and submitted an Advance Directive. The complexity of the situa-

tion was described by a somewhat exasperated Patricia Pope, the nursing staff member with primary responsibility for Emma:

> She [Betty] noticed an old order on the chart that Mrs. Wise was not to be, was not to receive CPR, and she knew that we didn't have an Advance Directive from the family saying that she should not receive CPR. So she knew that there was a conflict, and she called Mary [the director of social services] and told her that, you know, we need to either get them to say, "No, we don't want her to have CPR," and we need to get Dr. Canter to say, "Yes, you can do the CPR," one or the other. So Mary called the family, and they had been, the daughter kept saying that she, that the son had legal power of attorney over here. And I think he was actually, did not want the CPR. And I think that's where Dr. Canter got that order. But you know, we did have that on the chart. So, you know, as long as there was a conflict, what we told the family was, until it was resolved, if they should walk in and she should be having trouble, they would do the CPR until it was straightened out. And she kept saying, "Well, we'll get it straightened out," but it kind of ran on for, like, three or four months, and they had never gotten it settled. So Mary called Betty and told her that we was going to have to get it straightened out.

8

Wary Partners

Family-Staff Relationships in Nursing Homes

Renée Rose Shield

This chapter examines how the family members of nursing home residents and the certified nursing assistants (CNAs) of two American nursing homes interact with and perceive each other.[1] It also reflects my perspective over time as a regular visitor to my mother's nursing home, trying to make sense of the quality of these relationships through ethnographic research and my own changing role in them. This chapter highlights how ethnography, with its emphasis on long-term personal involvement, can help clarify what nursing homes mean to their participants. I examine questions central to the School of American Research (SAR) seminar discussions of what a nursing home is, what home means, and how nursing homes can become more appealing places by nurturing the human connections within them.

The American nursing home is often considered a frightful place—the purgatory of old age. The SAR seminar entertained the idea that the nursing home removes a large group of old people from the public's consciousness, further extending the construction of old age as "other." Understanding individual nursing homes on their own terms is imperative, increasingly so as the population of the United

States ages and nursing homes undergo massive change. In some ways, the nursing home seems less cut off from the outside world than it used to be. Increasing numbers of aging Americans, various economic drivers, and attempts at nursing home reform have helped make the membranes separating these facilities from their communities more porous. Further, each nursing home has a distinct tone that strongly influences the quality of the relationships formed there, and broad generalizations may obscure rather than illuminate. For these reasons, one researcher's small, in-depth ethnography can help describe nuances of difference effectively.

In 1994–1995, I studied three floors in two very different nursing homes in the same city: one skilled/sub-acute care unit and one dementia unit in a nonprofit nursing home and one skilled unit in a newer, larger, for-profit, unionized nursing home. I hypothesized that the less "medicalized" dementia care unit would foster relationships that were more satisfying to the participants than those in the more medical, acute care units. However, other differences between the nursing homes proved to be salient, and those are discussed here, also. In 1996, my mother entered a small dementia unit of a private, for-profit nursing home. I have included my observations from this experience to provide yet another perspective.

THE BACKGROUND

Like all American nursing homes at this time, the two facilities were undergoing considerable change while I studied them. Both were struggling with higher costs of care, stricter accountability measures, and greater pressures from private and public payers (chiefly Medicare/Medicaid and HMOs) to reduce length of stay and provide more services and better-informed consumers. Fifteen percent of the residents of the nonprofit home paid private fees, whereas only 5 percent of the for-profit home's residents paid private fees. Nearly 7 percent of the residents in each home were Medicare-reimbursed patients.[2] The development of sub-acute and dementia care units in nursing homes results from financial pressures (Henderson, this volume, Chapter 6; Shield 1996) as nursing homes try to capture the higher Medicare and private-pay rates for skilled care and dementia patients in order to subsidize the Medicaid beds that lose money.

Further, increasing numbers of nursing homes, in general—and the nonprofit home of this study, in particular—strive for a more appealing, home-like ambiance as a way to signal better quality of life there.

Differences between the two nursing homes were important. The for-profit home was larger, had a greater patient-staff ratio, and paid higher staff wages. The smaller, nonprofit nursing home used *primary care assignment* (the practice of consistently assigning the same CNAs to the same patients), had smaller patient care loads (five residents to each CNA during the day shift, in contrast to an 8:1 day-shift ratio in the for-profit nursing home), held a daylong mandatory orientation for all employees, and was instituting total quality management (TQM) techniques for improved practices in the home. Finally, the nonprofit home was undergoing changes during the period of study. The skilled care floor was becoming a sub-acute care/skilled unit for patients requiring a high intensity of nursing care (as opposed to custodial care). This change required that CNAs receive extra training and that some patients be moved to new rooms and receive new roommates and CNAs.

Most of the CNAs were female and came from working-class United States and third-world countries, including Nigeria, Haiti, Thailand, Barbados, Mexico, Liberia, Cuba, Jamaica, and India. A few were African-American, and fewer were Caucasian. A significant minority of the CNAs were male and African-American, Caucasian, or Hispanic. Several CNAs were studying to become nurses. Others pointedly did not want to become nurses because they valued the resident contact their work entailed. Some worked two jobs. The CNAs ranged in age from twenties to forties. Most CNAs had children; many female CNAs were single mothers.

The families of residents in both nursing homes were quite similar in background: overwhelmingly white, of predominantly Italian, French-Canadian, and Eastern European ethnicity. Most visitors were daughters, sisters, or wives. Some were sons, husbands, and brothers, and the fewest were grandchildren, nieces, and nephews.

THE STUDY

I had been curious about the relationship between families and CNAs from previous research, when one particular resident's daughter joked with a nursing assistant about how vital their relationship was to her mother's care (Shield 1988). For this project, I gained approval from the nursing home administrators after ensuring confidentiality, explaining my consent procedures, and promising to share research results and recommendations with them. I also discussed the research with CNAs in both facilities in in-service sessions, stressing their voluntary choice to participate, the confidentiality promise, and the goal of making recommendations. Some CNAs, reluctant to sign the consent document, gave me their verbal agreement instead and directed me to write notes that reflected this. In general, they were eager that I validate their work. They saw the research as a way to teach family members about what CNAs do and how difficult their jobs are.

I met families at the nonprofit home through a family meeting. In both facilities, I met others when they were in the corridors, either going to visit a relative or leaving after a visit. Sometimes I knocked on a resident's open door when I observed that visitors were there. When I explained the research, they seemed positive about my describing their experiences, hoping that the nursing home staff would have a greater appreciation of their perspective. Most of what I observed occurred in corridors, the nurses' station areas, and the day rooms. When nursing home residents were present with CNAs and family members, I explained the research and welcomed their participation. I interviewed some family members at their homes as well.

Family members and CNAs sometimes speak about their vulnerability (Diamond 1992; Foner 1994), but this did not trouble the individuals in this study. One acknowledged her potential exposure yet blithely rejected a concern about consequences, saying, "If you put in three quotes from me, they'll know who it is."

I spent six months on the skilled floor of the nonprofit nursing home and an additional three months on both the dementia unit of the nonprofit home and a skilled floor of the for-profit home. I observed interactions, engaged in conversations, conducted interviews, and administered a questionnaire I had designed for this purpose. I spent approximately one to three hours at a time on each nursing home unit, usually during afternoons and evenings, when families were likely to be present. I spent time watching and talking as a participant-observer, and I conducted dozens of one-on-one, open-ended interviews with CNAs and family members, both on the units and off-site, in coffee shops, restaurants, and the homes of family members. In addition, I attended several family support group meetings and a day-long orientation session for new employees at the nonprofit nursing home. Eighteen family members and sixteen CNAs completed questionnaires with me. At both facilities, I interviewed the administrators, the people who hired and sometimes trained CNAs, and various nurses and social workers.

I relied on the spoken and observed experiences of family members and CNAs, which provide the essential authenticity of ethnographic research. I wrote notes and questionnaire responses publicly and kept (as closely as possible) to the words used by families and CNAs to describe their experiences, express their perspectives, and tell their stories. I wrote in the open in order to invite questions, believing that my notebook and pen signaled my willingness to talk. Many people responded accordingly. After each session in the nursing home, I transferred the notes to a word processor, resulting in approximately 150 pages of single-spaced narrative. Field notes and the material on the questionnaires were analyzed according to the patterns that emerged. As new themes arose, I explored them by asking families and CNAs to comment on them, and I oriented my observations accordingly (Luborsky 1987).

THE ETHNOGRAPHER'S SITUATION

The ethnographer, perhaps like the visiting family member, is less an outsider than an intermittent, expectable presence. To illustrate the "ethnographer's path" (Sanjek 1990), I describe details of the fieldwork situation and aspects of my changing perspective on it.

My stance toward the people I've studied, as well as my understanding of my own aging, has changed over time. My initial fieldwork in nursing homes took place in the early 1980s. At that time, I was a graduate student, had three children under the age of six, and reacted incredulously at my informants' hazy recollections of child rearing, contrasting vividly with the immediacy of my daily parenting (Shield 1988). These three children are now grown, and our fourth child is a teenager. Their early years blend together for us as their parents; they are irritated when we cannot competently remember who did what when, and their versions of their childhood compete with ours. I know now that raising children goes quickly, and much of it is a complicated blur.

Moreover, changes in my mother have given me another perspective on time. In my early research, nursing home residents were my metaphorical grandparents, each visiting daughter occupying a mother-like place in my personal geography. The old people were like trees in the landscape, offering little indication of the saplings they had been and seeming immutable. In contrast, during the research for this project, the residents were only parental distance from me, and the visiting daughters were my fictive sisters. As I was doing the research, I suspected that my mother might need a nursing home. In 1996, she was admitted to one, and regular visits to her are now part of my daily life.

As a result, nursing homes and the old people in them are less foreign to me than ever, and my research has become more complex and newly natural. In the course of these years, I have wondered whether it has been easy for us as ethnographers to distance ourselves from the knowledge that we will probably be old one day. Maybe some of us have done nursing home ethnography to inoculate ourselves from aging? I am beginning to understand how memories of children become a smudge. I understand better what loss over time means. I am implicated in nursing homes, and now I am a step closer to knowing that, one day, even I may live in one.

I now turn to a description of my findings, supplemented by more recent observations in my role as a nursing home daughter.

CNA VIEWS OF FAMILIES

CNAs in both facilities told me that they think families are beset with guilt, which makes them "act the way they do." This helped them understand that when family members are upset, they want things done perfectly and right away. "They all think that their mother is the only one I have. They don't see that I have all these others" was a typical statement by several CNAs. Some CNAs from other countries believed that the guilt was justified because they felt that families *should* provide the care. One said, "In my culture, we take care of our family. I can't imagine doing it [putting someone in a nursing home]."

Some CNAs insisted on respect and were indignant: "Some honestly put the *m* in front of *aide*," tersely commented an African-American CNA in the for-profit home," and we're not." A Haitian CNA in the same facility said, "I have no problem even if they're very rude to me. They're never satisfied." She added, "If they treat me like a maid, I tell them I don't have a license to be a maid, only to be a nursing assistant. I just want to be treated like a human being, not an animal or a domestic. Some talk to me with a mean face." Another Haitian CNA proclaimed, "Where I'm from, we treat people with respect." A white nurse in the nonprofit home noted that some families are unkind and others racist. A CNA appreciated how some families respect and treat her as a friend, in contrast to residents' harsher treatment of her. "Some [families] don't appreciate you. They look down on you," said another.

"Picky" is how many CNAs described certain family members. "You do everything you can for the resident, but it's not enough. Some want you to take vital signs—the whole bit—every half hour. It's too much," said one. Another from the nonprofit nursing home said that a son would come in early to pick up his mother: "He was bossy and acted like we're not capable. We would know to have her ready by 12, and he might come at 11. Another family was hard to please. We did her hair and they hated it. After she died, the family called to complain. They seemed good for her, but to us, they were hard to deal with."

The sensitivities between families and CNAs were sometimes exquisitely fine-tuned. Questions about the resident that CNAs sometimes found grating may or may not have been intended as criticism, but CNAs often took them that way: "Why does my father have this on?" "Why is she in bed? I want her to get up." "My father is wet" (when the person is not wet). "The second-guessing ticks me off," said one in the nonprofit home, "Like, 'How come you don't have the splint on right?' [when it is on right]." Staff and families picked up on nuances of behavior and language in each other and reacted accordingly. When right, communication flowed and good feelings followed, but when wrong, the missed signals sometimes led to compounded problems that remained uncorrected. One CNA in the nonprofit nursing home bristled at the implied (but veiled) urgency in the comment a family member made after returning with his mother: "My mother is really tired, and I think you should 'do her' [get her ready for bed]."

I had my own quandaries about making our wishes and preferences known when my mother was admitted to the nursing home.
After she had trouble settling in on her second day, I talked to staff
members about it. I told staff members that my mother had no hearing deficit and preferred a normal tone of voice. A few weeks later, a
nurse commented on my mother's good adjustment and said that she
appreciated that I had "backed off" after the first few days. That put me
in my place. It was one of the ways I realized that internal nursing
home parameters governed, and mine were likely perceived as intrusive and unwelcome.

In the nursing homes I studied, some CNAs appreciated and
admired family members, usually daughters, who were reliably present,
seemed to understand the role of the nursing home and the CNAs,
and were friendly, realistic, and helpful. Some of these families were
taken for granted (Foner 1994). Some families acted as brokers for
their nursing home relative, much as Hasselkus (1992) has described
in medical interview settings. One CNA in the nonprofit nursing home
appreciated that a daughter helped explain to her mother that the
CNA had to be with others, not just her: "She would smooth it out."
This daughter also interceded with her brother, who was suspicious
and afraid for his mother when the CNA walked her. Another family
member, who was a nurse, explained health care settings to the rest of
her family so that they would be more understanding of the nursing
home's routines and limitations. Sometimes it was the resident who did
the smoothing out between families and CNAs. One resident
explained the CNA's job to his wife and calmed her down when his
socks were missing.

Families can be helpful or in the way, and sometimes both. Family
members differ in what they are able and willing to do. CNAs seemed
to understand and tolerate these family differences and varying levels
of ability. They told me how family members might not want to do personal care tasks, such as toileting, because of generational notions of
privacy. On the other hand, when families tended their relative in the
most personal and private of tasks, they were respected for it. One said,
"They should. It's their mother." (Perkinson, Chapter 9, found that the
opposite was true in her study.)[3]

CNAs in both nursing homes had to counsel families about limitations but were often unsuccessful. They said that family members could rarely fathom the deficits in their loved ones. Families sometimes blamed the CNA for what the resident could no longer do. Blame often accompanied dying. Families sometimes become angry at CNAs "when they're upset that the person is dying." Another CNA hypothesized that families expect miracles to resurrect their relative. CNAs become the brunt for families' frustrations about their resident's mortality and limitations.

Families are often unrealistic about the amount of work CNAs do. A CNA and a certified medical technician (CMT) in the nonprofit home discussed with me how hard it was to deal with families who had unrealistic expectations of them. Regardless of whether family members *say* they understand that CNAs take care of several residents and work hard, these staffers believed that all family members focus only on their relative's care and think that CNAs do not work hard. Recognizing this belief and yet being on the other side of the divide, I make an effort to tell CNAs in my mother's nursing home that I appreciate their workload and am sympathetic. Families are, furthermore, in a good position to lobby on behalf of CNAs, and often they do. In our own way, we tell administrators when extra staffing is needed. Administrators listen, especially when families are private-paying customers.

Many CNAs described close relationships with residents' families. Some CNAs are genuinely liked and feel good about it. One from the nonprofit nursing home said, "I had a car accident. They care about me. They were sorry." CNAs felt appreciated by families and were gratified when families thanked and complimented them. Comments such as "Mother looks so nice today—thank you" were well received. One CNA in the nonprofit nursing home was gratified by the appreciation and commented that she would be crazy to do [the work] for the [minimal] money. She regularly visited a former resident of hers who went to another floor. This resident's granddaughter sought out the CNA every time she visited her grandmother, so that they could "catch up." She enjoyed exchanging cards with residents and family members. "This is what makes it worthwhile," she said, "I'm missed on the weekends." Some family members and CNAs maintained contact with each other after the resident died.

Some CNAs were angry with families who did not visit or, according to them, did not visit enough. A CNA in the nonprofit nursing home would tell family members to visit more often, explaining, "You see, they're very lonely." A CNA in my mother's nursing home lobbied at Thanksgiving for more families to take their relatives home. Seeing her efforts pay off, she whispered to me her reason for families resisting this: "They're lazy." Other staff members I studied seemed to understand the emotional difficulties of some family members that prevented them from visiting. A nurse told the story of a son who, because of his emotional distress, circled the nursing home countless times and could not actually come in.

The absence of family members was sometimes a relief to CNAs in both nursing homes, who believed that families brought complications. One CNA said that she could do more for the resident when the family was absent. A CNA summed up his view about "difficult" families: "This is business. If you don't like them [families], you go about your business and avoid them. It's your job. It's nothing special." Another in the for-profit home said, "I won't have conversations with them. I don't come your way. I just do for your mother or father." "If they're in that mood, I just avoid them," counseled one, who then reminded me, "The customer is always right!"

Many understood a certain time line along which family members progress. They saw families who were upset, worried, guilty, clingy, or suspicious at admission eventually become relaxed and trusting, with time and familiarity. At first, they may visit often and at odd times to check on their relative. Many CNAs understood how trust takes time, and they actively helped family members achieve the trust. Families need positive experience to learn that when they are not there, care and treatment are satisfactory. The thoughtful CNAs helped them reach that point.

FAMILY VIEWS OF CNAS

Families also understood trust as crucial to their relative's (and their own) equanimity toward the nursing home. The husband of a relatively new resident at the nonprofit home explained, "It's difficult to entrust care to someone else. The trust has to develop over a while before you feel they're doing a good job. I check my wife's ears and between her fingers to make sure they're doing okay. When they're consistently doing it all well, then I can trust them."

Like Duncan and Morgan (1994) and Savishinsky (1991), I found that many family members appreciated the supportive role that CNAs and other staff members played in helping them adjust to and live with their loved one's institutionalization. Housekeepers, as Henderson (1995) has noted, were also critical in this role. Families of skilled patients whose needs were more medically intense and of generally shorter duration, as well as families of dementia patients, developed close ties with CNAs and relied on their warmth, friendly concern, and enthusiasm over positive developments. CNAs scored higher than nurses in these behaviors and attitudes. Families in my study would have agreed with the informant in Duncan and Morgan's study who said,

> Now rarely do you get personalized observations out of a nurse…it's the aides…and I sometimes think why aren't the nurses more this way? But the aides do the hard work and you see the difference and you have so much respect for them because this is the person you care about and this is the person who is dressing them, undressing them, taking them to the bathroom, feeding them, bathing them. The most intimate things are being done by these people. (1994:238–239)

CNAs were often appreciated as especially caring. Comments about them were touching. The wife of a resident on the nonprofit skilled unit said to me that she liked her relationships with most of the CNAs. She and others felt that CNAs cared, and they reciprocated the feeling. One family member emphasized, "They listen." Another said that a CNA sat and talked with her when she was feeling depressed one day. Another family member from the nonprofit nursing home believed that the staff took care of *her*, not just her father. She said that she would sometimes sneak onto the unit when she was feeling out of sorts, hoping that no one would see her, so that she could visit and leave unnoticed. The CNAs and other staff, however, invariably read her mood and tried to cheer her up. One would ask whether she wanted to talk about what was bothering her. She learned from their friendly manner with her father how to do the same with him. Chatting and joking with him lightened everyone's mood. Another family member praised the nursing home unit when she described it as "a family." She appreciated the personal touch, especially when she herself needed it.

Many welcomed the help offered by CNAs. "They wanted us to have ice cream and coffee when they were giving it to the residents. If I'm upset, they give a hug. The day we brought [my mother in], we were upset, and they were so nice. They took us outside. The little extras..." said one grateful daughter who was still adjusting to her mother's admission to the nonprofit nursing home. She said other nursing homes made her feel that she was in the way. Here, she said, "You're never in the way. You're never a problem. They'll assist you. Even the sweepers and cleaners have a relationship." Now that I am a daughter in a nursing home, I know something of that feeling, too.

Family members maintained a vigilant stance, trust notwithstanding. Some defended urgent requests and their right to be "picky." A resident's son remembered that without the proper accompanying liquid, a medication his mother had taken in a different nursing home had left a horrible aftertaste. He tried to snare a CNA, but the response he received was "We're sorry, but we have thirty-two other people that we are feeding right now." "Well, *I'm* sorry," he told me, "but they had to take care of *her* right now." He was weary in the telling. Families hearing a story like this often gave assenting nods.

One daughter at the nonprofit nursing home wanted the caregiving to be worth what it cost. As "manager" of her parent's care, she devised strategies to deal with ongoing problems, coordinated her visits with other family members, and organized meetings with the social worker or charge nurse to discuss problems. As time went on, she trusted them more, although her continued scrutiny remained essential to ensuring that the care stayed at the level she could trust.

Although some families may come down too hard on minor matters, a nurse noted, they have legitimate grievances when simple preferences are repeatedly thwarted. When one resident of the nonprofit nursing home, for example, asked the staff at the nurses' station for her cigarette lighter, it was usually missing. The family had brought in several new lighters as replacements. "There should be no excuse for the lighter not being available when it's needed," this nurse commented, irritable about the persistent problem.

Family members feel a terrific powerlessness in the nursing home, especially at admission. The perceived lack of power spurs family members' attempts to exert control, be continually informed, and otherwise be intimately involved with the resident's care and routines. This contradicts the leverage family members often do have, however. One daughter described how she was "petrified" at first, "didn't believe in nursing homes," had heard terrifying stories about them, and was mortified that here they were. She could not manage her father at home with Alzheimer's disease, and she felt that she was losing control of him and the situation. When he was admitted, she visited all the time to reassure herself that her father was all right. Finally, she was able to decrease her visits when she realized that he was being well cared for.

Families know that they don't understand the interior world of the nursing home and how they and the new resident fit in. When my mother was admitted, the words from interviews I had conducted came flooding back to me. Everything was difficult for us. I feared that the staff members would not like or accept her or me and that she or I would not fit. Like the people I had interviewed, I found that talking with staff members—and the passage of time—helped, but I newly understood families' fears now that I was experiencing them.

Effective staff members helped families trust the caregiving that occurs when they are not present. Families also learned from observing how CNAs treated the other residents when their relatives were not there. Over time, they, too, developed relationships with certain CNAs. As their comfort level increased, they found it easier to visit and also easier not to be there. Sometimes, both CNAs and family members agreed, the focus on a less-than-clean floor is the family's attempt to increase control over what is an emotionally overwhelming situation.

Family members in each nursing home said that they were confused by the situation and unsure of their place. They said that they could not always distinguish CNAs from nurses on the units, and some blamed themselves for not knowing the distinction. They felt that a larger name tag would help, so that they would not have to strain for a look at the name or status. Some were unsure of how and when to ask questions, and of whom. They saw the rushing around, constantly heard about understaffing, felt timid about adding to the burden, and were generally uncertain how to make their wishes known.

As many family members worked to get the best care for their relative, some coached their relatives to speak up for themselves. One daughter described a misunderstanding between a CNA and her mother. The daughter urged her mother to talk to the CNA but backed off when the mother did not want to do it. The situation was not resolved, but everyone managed with the status quo nonetheless.

Families of both nursing homes helped their relatives and maintained contact and continuity with them in varied ways. Families brought in favorite foods, did laundry, read, assisted in the bathroom, washed the relative's face, attended activities, went on walks and outings, helped with positioning, got snacks or drinks, and assisted in feeding, shaving, nail cutting, mouth care, dressing, straightening and cleaning up belongings, and folding and putting away clothes. Some relatives changed diapers when they considered it necessary and believed that it would ease the immediate situation.

Families told me how hard CNAs worked, how short-staffed they usually were, and how much they were valued. They frequently presented little gifts to staff members and were appreciated for these. Food meant a lot to the resident and the CNAs. It was understood as a symbol of love and generated conversation and recipe sharing (see Savishinsky, Chapter 4, for multiple meanings of food). A family member brought in a large cake for his father's birthday and shared it with staff members of the for-profit nursing home. One visitor knitted a sweater for a CNA's new baby. Although tips were prohibited, cards and gift giving were common at the Christmas holiday, and food was always welcome.

SEPARATE TOGETHER

CNAs and family members often expressed how separate they felt from each other, yet they also seemed joined together by the shared resident. CNA statements that they "got along great" with many families because they kept their distance from families demonstrated separateness. When I asked CNAs whether they thought family members knew much about them, some said that they did. However, one CNA at the nonprofit nursing home answered, "They never ask me something like this [about their families or what they do on their days off], and it's private." When asked whether CNAs knew anything about residents' families, she replied, "They won't waste their time to tell me, and we don't want them to anyhow." Another answered, "It's none of their business." The CNAs deliberately fostered a certain distance. For some, it meant professionalism.

One CNA at the nonprofit home stated, "I never really get close to anyone in particular. I have to 'be even.'" Some said that they liked all family members equally and did not want to show favoritism. At least one saw the danger of manipulation: "Some try to get on your good side as if trying to get better care. You can see it. They keep saying, 'You're so good to my mother,' repeatedly, as if they're putting the other [CNAs] down."

Physical separation between the CNAs and the families and residents was maintained frequently. Many families visiting both facilities did not have contact with staff members. One family member at the for-profit home said that she did not like staff members to sit sequestered by themselves at the nurses' station or elsewhere. Several objected that during visits, no one would ask whether everything was all right or whether something needed to be done. For their part, CNAs mentioned that they did not want to intrude on families and residents during visits because it was the family's private time. One staff person suggested that CNAs should say hello to families and ask specifically whether everything is all right during visits. I watched an experienced CNA at the nonprofit nursing home do just that when she was assigned a new resident after a room change. She introduced herself and asked the family member to call her if she was needed. This gesture conveyed professionalism and warmth to that particular family member.

There was also joining. "Families are a part of the resident," said a nurse simply, "It is impossible to separate them." She taught the CNAs the futility of trying to keep families out of their picture of the resident. A nurse in my mother's nursing home told us flatly that we could never visit "too much." Some CNAs spoke with feeling about residents and families with whom they felt close. Even though their primary allegiance was to the residents, they considered the family so connected as to be a part of the caregiving the CNA was providing. Some CNAs' closeness to residents made them critical of family behavior, for example, when families did not visit frequently.

The families often took their cue about the CNA from the resident's response. When the resident seemed content with the CNA, the family member followed suit. I observed easy-going, affectionate inter-actions among a resident, relative, and CNA who had known one another for a time. I watched family members enjoy the nursing home setting with their loved one. One particular woman said that her hus-band thought that the two of them lived there. When she had to go home, she would tell him that she was going "downstairs." She thought that he believed she was downstairs doing the laundry and would soon reappear. To a large extent, she did live there. She had taken on her husband's community as her own. In my mother's nursing home, staff, residents, and families often sit in the same large room, comfy in rock-ing chairs. Individuals comment on one another's conversations, they add jokes, they sing with the music. Private conversations are held in the resident's room.

EXPECTATIONS

Family members held varied expectations of care. Some family members contrasted the CNAs in the facility with those in other nurs-ing homes. For example, one man complained of theft, an unpleasant attitude, and nonEnglish speaking CNAs in another nursing home he had visited. One noted a nursing home where residents lay in bed day after day.

Some terrified family members expected the worst and were vastly reassured to find that this nursing home was significantly better than what they had imagined. Family members who were nurses generally knew more than nonmedical visitors. Although they demanded high standards, they took some of the routine glitches in stride. Some fami-lies at the for-profit nursing home seemed to expect little from the nursing home and were pleasantly surprised when CNAs or other staff were friendly or exhibited caring behavior. One family member at the for-profit home displayed his low expectations when he told me how happy he was with his mother-in-law's care. Specifically, he was grateful that when she was given the wrong meal tray, CNAs were willing to cor-rect the error!

Other family expectations included an insistence on shiny floors and immaculate rooms. The wet diaper should be changed as soon as it is discovered. The resident should be up, should have her hair done differently, or needs to go to bed "right now." A few wanted the care to be worth what it cost. Others, in contrast, valued caring and competency over cosmetic cleanliness. This appreciation helped families learn to understand the work from the CNAs' point of view. When families were sympathetic toward CNAs, CNAs often became more approachable.

Family expectations often clashed with those of CNAs. Ironically, some family caregivers who had reluctantly transferred their caregiving to the institution expected better care than they were able to provide at home. This contradicted the nursing home perspective illustrated in the CNA protest from the nonprofit nursing home: "What does she expect? The care cannot possibly be as good as what there was at home!"

That this protest came from the nonprofit nursing home is especially ironic because it deliberately strived to emulate home-like caregiving. An idealized notion of home is a goal for some nursing homes to replicate, but others seem to use the unattainability of home as an excuse to avoid this effort altogether. My mother's nursing home embodies a notion of comfort that staff, residents, and families seem to value. I didn't expect it, and I welcomed the experience of it (see Stafford, Chapter 5, and the conclusion of this chapter for related notions of home).

CONFLICT, COLLABORATION, AND STRATEGIES

Most conflicts related to me were about frustrating details of daily life whose solutions were self-evident to families. They found the frequent recurrence of these situations difficult to take. Conflicts occurred because CNAs performed tasks in ways the resident or family member found objectionable. When requests were made of staff to handle situations in a certain way, families were dismayed when there was no follow-through, there were lapses, or promises were not honored. They did not like to see CNAs rushing, unable to explain, and unwilling or unable to take time to provide proper care. A daughter was exasperated when her mother did not have on the right underwear and there was ample in the drawer. Here, too, families expressed how intimidated they often felt. A staff member told me that I needed to buy my mother more underwear, but when I reorganized the drawer, I found plenty.

CNAs and families often had to work hard to create good relationships despite the irritations. One family member at the nonprofit home said that her rapport with the CNAs was very good but that she had to initiate it and continuously work at it. This was especially difficult in the beginning, when she was afraid. The accommodations that families and CNAs made with each other were individual and dependent on openness and good will. Even with everyone's good will, toes are occasionally stepped on in this delicate dance.

I heard the wife of a patient appealing to her husband's evening CNA about how his diaper had been uncomfortably positioned during the day shift. At the start of the next shift, she asked helpfully, "What are we going to do about this?" She had been there since 1 p.m., and no CNA had asked about it. She did not bring it up then because the CNAs would have had to use a special lift. To avoid this, they probably would have put him to bed. However, because her husband wanted to stay up longer, the dilemma caused him discomfort. She tried to find nonconfrontational ways to bring up problems. She knew that staff members tried to devise solutions but was dismayed when problems persisted.

The wife of a resident explained how she had learned to assert herself as she acclimated to the dementia unit. She did not like that her husband wore slippers instead of shoes, and she wanted him more involved in activities he enjoyed. She made her wishes known, her requests were generally honored, and she thus established an ongoing, working collaboration with staff.

Some wives spent large amounts of time in the nonprofit nursing home and became enmeshed in the daily goings-on with the other residents, family members, and staff. They became accustomed to the nursing routines and seemed to understand how the place worked. They observed the other residents and their visitors and were regularly involved and helpful. They created an informal support group among themselves, sharing information about one another and their relatives, commiserating about developments, and discovering common points of interest. They were ombudsmen for the residents who did not receive regular visitors, and they provided information to one another to tide one another over from one visit to the next. The knowledge making these visitors created with one another helped them make sense of the nursing home and seemed to make this environment tamer and more predictable. Because they were respectful of and knowledgeable about the routines and necessities of the nursing home, they were trusted by staff members and could actively collaborate with CNAs.

OWNERSHIP OF EXPERTISE—SHIFTING CARE

Family members often felt frustrated when staff did not consider their expertise about the resident relevant. Medical priorities take center stage and relegate the family's knowledge of the resident to secondary status. Some nursing home staff use family knowledge of the resident's preferences and habits at admission when the resident is unknown to them, but it perplexes many families that their knowledge is little valued thereafter. We were dismayed, when my mother entered the nursing home, that no one asked her or us about her preferences, abilities, and routines. Staff members began routines she didn't like and then pulled back when she resisted. It was as if she didn't count as an individual, that her self-awareness and our knowledge of her had no relevance. The lapse—so significant to my mother and the family because of the timing, at admission—as well as the symbolic message it conveyed about the insignificance of this knowledge, was eventually rectified. We were shook up by it, it put us on guard, and it seemed needless. After an equilibrium was reached in which the staff felt that they knew my mother and were able to care for her properly, they became receptive to new information about her and her past. Too bad this sensitivity was not apparent at the vulnerable time of admission.[4]

In caring for those with dementia, staff members may initially value family knowledge of the resident, but the value of this information decreases with time. This progression probably varies, depending on whether the dementia unit follows a more medical than social model and whether staff believes that behaviors are attributable more to the disease than the person. The relevance of the family's knowledge may become less apparent as the staff members get to know the resident, the resident becomes more comfortable in the nursing home, and the family's importance to the resident recedes as the dementia progresses.

Through persistent involvement, a wife of a dementia patient made her knowledge of him relevant to his care. He still knew her, and she seemed amenable to his growing attachment to staff members. Other family members could not make this shift, seeing it as a question of loyalties, a kind of competition. During a family support group meeting, many expressed sadness that their importance to their loved ones was receding. One family member wanted to take her mother "home" for her birthday, but others gently counseled her that the nursing home was now more familiar and reassuring to her mother than home. When a new family member protested, "I can't let go of the closeness we had," seasoned family members described how they had weathered this shift and were now reconciled because their relative was receiving loving care at the nursing home. The development of these relationships in the nursing home seemed to help create a sense of community there.

STAFF WITH INSTITUTIONALIZED FAMILY— BRIDGES OF MEANING

Staff members whose family members are in nursing home have special dilemmas and insights. A male CNA related how his grandfather sent his first home-health aide away because the aide inappropriately started with personal care before establishing a relationship. As a result, the CNA understood the families he dealt with daily in the nursing home. Now he felt protective and suspicious. "You have to build up trust, after all," he explained.

A nurse's experience provided a related insight. She was upset that she could not continue to care for her mother-in-law at home. Then she relaxed when she saw her mother-in-law bond with a few CNAs. "I think families don't mean to be distrustful, but their hands are tied. I was picky, looking back. I was watching out for other residents, too." Some aspects of her mother-in-law's care were troubling. Her mother-in-law liked tea every evening, but the family saw that the tea was always placed just out of reach. Because this nurse frequently had to remind the staff to put the tea closer, she began to question whether basic nursing tasks were also being done. Was her mother-in-law really getting her Coumadin? How would the nurse know? She believes that her experience has helped her be more sympathetic with families.

A few staff members had relatives in the same nursing home where they worked, but they were not their relative's direct caregiver. Each helped the family member in the nursing home be his or her own advocate and resisted taking over for him or her. One staff member found having the relative there "emotionally draining." She checked her often, was gratified to find the care very good, and felt more empathic with the CNAs as a result. Another staff person worried that her relative might receive (undesired) VIP treatment because of her.

DIFFERENCES BETWEEN THE NURSING HOMES

Beyond numerous qualities of organization—such as number of beds, percentage of private-paying residents, ownership, staffing ratios, presence of union, and services provided—intangible factors, such as culture or "climate," also characterize a nursing home (Farmer 1996). For example, some posh nursing homes that provide gracious amenities seem cold, whereas some spartan nursing homes project warmth. The importance of these differences in tone among nursing homes cannot be overestimated.

Several factors differentiated the nonprofit from the for-profit nursing home of this study. These differences had a profound influence on the character of the interactions between family members and CNAs on the individual units.

The Nonprofit Nursing Home

The nonprofit facility deliberately attempted to project qualities of warmth, family feeling, and community teamwork. Staff members and visitors commented that these qualities were genuine. Nursing home management explicitly taught these values. All new employees underwent a daylong orientation to learn the values of this immutable doctrine: The nursing home is a family, cooperation and shared responsibility are necessary, individuality of residents is vital, and this is their home. The doctrine seemed to be accepted, and it persisted on the units. Occasionally, nurses or CNAs told me about taking each other to task if one of them did not work to these standards.

"The nursing home is the resident's home" was one of the repeated messages. "The resident is not a child" was another. Residents suffer numerous losses before they enter a nursing home, they were taught. New staff members were challenged to imagine what a series of losses would feel like to them. What if they had to give up job, home, spouse, car, furniture, daily routines? How would they prioritize, if they could? They were taught to empathize with the residents, to penetrate the "otherness" in the attitude that non-old people implicitly hold toward old people.

The values included respect for the individual—in life and in death. Honoring residents' and family wishes about treatment decisions was a high priority at this nursing home. Family members remarked how staff members sat with them when the resident was dying. Memorial services for residents were considered meaningful and helped generate a community spirit.

Affection, humor, and gentleness were prominent features of the interactions between staff members and residents on both units of the nonprofit home. Staff members—including CNAs, housekeepers, nurses, and others—often hugged Alzheimer patients, held their hands, and regularly said loving words of endearment to them. CNAs often asked solitary dementia patients to "keep me company" during routine tasks. Attention was paid to the atmosphere of each unit, not just to the treatments and tasks being carried out. Patients on the skilled unit were also the objects of caring words and gestures and, universally, seemed to appreciate this. Affectionate touching was common. Family members often commented on how they felt that the residents were "loved" and that this helped them trust the facility.

Divisions among people and between staff and residents were mitigated in some ways. On the dementia unit, residents often walked into one another's room, often napped on one another's bed, lingered at the nurses' station, interacted with staff members in various ways (including being hugged and kissed), and were eventually and gently coaxed to other destinations. During music sessions, the floor secretary, housekeepers, and other staff members spontaneously danced with residents and stimulated participation with cheerful encouragement. The quality of easy interaction and free movement bolstered the warm feeling that family members often noted to me and to one another. Teamwork principles of total quality management (TQM) also seemed to have a positive effect. Although the hierarchy of the medical model remains highly impervious to such efforts and staff members were not fully convinced, the administrator believed in TQM's promise to improve productivity, worker empowerment, morale, problem solving, and a sense of community. His twice-daily walks through every unit and department of the nursing home signaled his accessibility and watchfulness. CNAs appeared aware of the TQM effort, although some were cynical. They already knew how important their observations of residents are and how much teamwork helps.

Families said that they appreciated the support group sessions. Problems about daily care of individuals or changes in the nursing home (such as the transition of the skilled unit to a sub-acute/skilled unit) were discussed there. Periodically, a meeting of the dementia support group was devoted to teaching families the particulars of CNA work in order to facilitate family understanding of staff perspective. The dementia certification course for CNAs similarly included a session designed to teach CNAs about the family perspective.

Finally, assigning the same CNA to the same resident (primary assignment) positively affected the quality of the relationships between CNAs and family members. The stability of primary assignment allowed the participants time to develop collaborative relationships. Original CNA fears about being "stuck with" difficult residents in primary assignment were less significant in practice because those residents became less difficult with familiarity and other residents became more rewarding in the context of the relationships that were fostered. In my mother's nursing home, however, an alternative seems to work well. One CNA is assigned to one resident for a month; then the assignment is switched. The staff explained that the change provided continuity while also allowing for relief, recognizing that some residents are harder to manage than others. This method also ensures that all staff members know the routines of all the residents.

The For-Profit Nursing Home

This facility illustrated several opposing characteristics, sharp divisions among people being the most apparent. Exaggerating the classic marker of dehumanization in hospitals, where a person may be labeled "the gallbladder," CNAs in this nursing home referred to residents by their room numbers. Sometimes the families did likewise. Did this reveal how quickly they adapted to nursing home ways or the extent to which they wanted to communicate? Also, CNAs teased the residents and sometimes sharply reprimanded or scolded them.

The corridors usually stretched empty of visitors, and the day room had few visitors, too. These long, dull corridors contrasted with the shorter corridors and more intimate scale of the nonprofit nursing home. (The layout of my mother's nursing home unit consists of a dining room/kitchen area next to the living room, with rocking chairs, and bedrooms off the central two rooms. Most residents spend their days in the two central rooms.) When visitors came to the for-profit home, they usually remained sequestered in the residents' rooms and did not mingle with other families, residents, or staff. There was little activity in the unit other than the movement of CNAs. I did not see informal visitor groups in the for-profit nursing home.

Few support meetings for staff or visitors existed. Family support meetings had been organized in the past but were phased out because of dwindling attendance. Administrators said that staff members responded adequately to individual resident and visitor needs. Orientation for new CNAs consisted of reviewing official policies of the nursing home and checking CNA mastery of techniques and procedures. Staff in-services similarly concentrated on technical tasks. A monthly meeting of CNAs, called "Let's Talk," was organized to discuss various problems on the units, including staff conflicts and difficulties with resident families. This meeting was popular among staff. Advice given to CNAs about families was summarized to me as "Tell them what they want to hear," meaning, give family members information, such as their relative's mood, meals, and other behaviors of the day. She added that if the CNA did not volunteer such information, families would not believe that activities, such as taking the resident for a walk, were done.

The staff, especially the CNAs, were usually physically distant from both residents and families in the unit. They often sat by themselves in the day room. A family member criticized this separation. As we talked in the day room at change of shift, we observed a cluster of several CNAs charting and chatting. Residents were positioned at tables at the other end of the room, and the television was on. A few residents talked with one another. Occasionally, one called out because another was bothering her. With each protest, a seated CNA verbally reprimanded the resident not to tease the woman. The CNAs seemed amused by the incident. This visitor criticized the CNAs' separation and remarked that the unit was not friendly, in contrast to the hospital his relative had just come from. One new family member felt suspicions of the staff because they did not make an effort to talk to her. This relative guessed that the CNAs were overworked. They seemed "stressed," and she thought that their smiles looked forced. While we were talking, however, a CNA came over to us and introduced herself, immensely pleasing the relative.

Sometimes I observed playful interactions between the CNAs and some of the residents and family members in the day room. All the participants enjoyed these interactions. They were witty and sometimes affectionate. Most of the spontaneous fun occurred among staff, however. The CNAs and nurses seemed to enjoy one another. They teased, playfully hit each other, joked, and laughed easily. One CNA said that one of the best things about working in this facility was how well the workers got along. The collegial camaraderie among the nursing assistants was buoyant and happy, contrasting sharply with the communication gulf between them and the residents and family members.

The clear distinction among CNAs, residents, and family members generally exists in any nursing home as a total institution (Goffman 1961). How rigid the division is, however, can be mitigated or exacerbated by other factors. The presence of a union, for example, sharpens the barrier between union and nonunion persons at all levels and permeates the facility. An underlying adversarial tone was hard to ignore at the for-profit nursing home. Management insisted on adherence to tasks. The huge policy book of dos and don'ts revealed attention to rules as opposed to relationships: "To 11–7 shift: The practice of putting your legs up on two chairs together and covering them with a sheet ceases now."

At both nursing homes, the nurses who hired new CNAs insisted on attracting good people. It's not just money. Although the for-profit home paid higher wages, its higher patient-staff ratios were burdensome and possibly contributed to the division between staff and residents. Each spoke of the difficulties inherent in hiring and stressed how important the traits of competence and consideration are. Each discussed her strategies for eliminating individuals she thought were unsuitable. How an applicant talked or behaved toward her child in an interview, for example, revealed important information. The nurse at the nonprofit nursing home said that she sought gentleness. If an applicant indicated that he or she thought that nursing home residents were similar to children, "I file it right here" [the application goes in the waste basket]. There is no dilemma between competence and caring, she insisted.

The contrast between the two nursing homes was more significant than the differences among the three units. The basic tone in the two facilities differed. The quality of the relationships between CNAs and families on both the skilled/sub-acute unit and the dementia unit of the nonprofit nursing home was of a similar warm character—even though the CNAs and families had known each other longer on the dementia unit and the dementia unit was a less medicalized setting. The skilled unit of the for-profit nursing home was remarkable in its contrast. (My mother's small [twenty-bed] unit in a for-profit nursing home provides another example. The tone is warm and comfortable.)

Further inquiry on the dementia unit in the for-profit home might reveal whether the nursing home characteristics described there persist in that setting, whether that unit has a uniquely constructed ambiance as a separate and sheltered community, or whether the qualities that distinguish the for-profit nursing home from the nonprofit home persist in that unit, too.

CONCLUSIONS

Small-scale ethnography provides the opportunity to discover salient factors that might be missed in larger, more quantitative research. In attempting to understand certain elements that create satisfying nursing home care, the present study examines relationships between family members and CNAs within nursing homes through participant-observation and open-ended interviewing. The researcher's frequent, prolonged contact with both nursing home staff members and the residents and their families has led to several basic conclusions.

Beyond the Idea of Home

We need to clarify the distinguishing characteristics of home that would constitute good care in nursing homes. Because the reality of many homes is often harsher than the idealized construct, we tend to refer to only positive qualities when signifying the idea of home, as Stafford has also noted in this volume (Chapter 5). The distinction a social worker made during our search for the right nursing home for my mother was clarifying and a relief to hear: "Of course, our nursing home won't be 'home' for your mother/wife, but we attempt to make it as home-like as possible." Because we were mourning her leaving her home, these words were reassuring in their simple acknowledgment of the loss.

Home versus hospital is not the only choice of caregiving in nursing homes. In this study, the nonprofit nursing home attempted to be home-like, and the for-profit home had no such aspirations. My mother's for-profit nursing home has distinct home-like attributes. Even though no institution can be home, the nonprofit nursing home seemed to offer more humane caregiving, derived from its explicit philosophy respecting residents' unique preferences and needs.

A "good" nursing home offers excellent care and also comfortable surroundings, yet the ambiguities remain profound. I have been impressed by my mother's nursing home unit, but I have also seen the atmosphere turn indifferent with a change in personnel. Then the pleasantries and interactions seem hollow. When staff members take time to sit among residents and visitors and make genuine conversation, it "works." Their idle chatter enhances the small snippets of talk of which the residents are capable. Released from the ordinary, reality-based strictures governing talk and behavior outside these walls, residents, staff, and visitors seem to construct talk for its own sake and enjoy the comforts of communion that these conversation fragments confer. Sometimes, within these constricted walls, staff members help create a good feeling.

Perhaps certain qualities we think of as *home,* with its balm of domesticity, include a sense of being known and accepted, a feeling of comfort, a measure of sensory satisfaction, and continuity with caring people in a familiar and safe setting.

Ethnography and the Aging Ethnographer
Small-scale ethnography allows an intimate appraisal of relationship and the nuances of difference. Further, anthropologists who study aging and old people must recognize the basic reflexivity of this work and our embedded position within it. Ethnography and reflexivity are linked, especially in studies of age. Unlike our treatment of other

subjects, we cannot hide behind otherness in the study of old people. Whether or not acknowledged, aging is the one process we study in which we actively participate. It is ironic that the ethnographer's aging is rarely considered in this endeavor, although some (such as Moody 1988 and Ray 1996) have called for its inclusion. In this spirit, I offer certain reflections.

One value of a single ethnographer doing the research is that a consistent, attentive observer selects and sorts the data over time. This is also a limitation. A large-scale study would observe more reliable patterns, perhaps, but might lose sight of the telling detail within the two nursing homes. My interactions with the people who were studied—as well as my ongoing preoccupation with my mother's situation and its effect on our family and me—were aspects of this study that require description.

A related limitation—or perhaps an enrichment—is that as the ethnographer ages, her senses sort and select differently. This given is rarely acknowledged. I have included my changing perspective to try to own up to it. The CNAs and the visitors also have changing perspectives, depending on their age and their situation. I didn't explore this dimension; another study should attempt to understand some of these nuances. In my mother's nursing home, I have the feeling that the gentle caring provided by the mostly middle-aged staff members comes from their professional interest and also, perhaps, how they themselves would like to be cared for in old age. I have been able to share stories with staff members because we all find ourselves aging and undergoing similar experiences with parents and children.

As a daughter in the nursing home setting, I am increasingly cognizant of myself as an aging self. As a daughter, I have felt vulnerable for my mother to the routines of the nursing home. As a daughter, I have felt automatically "on the other side" from staff members. As a daughter, I am automatically "not old" because she is my contrast—but I see my children viewing me as potentially "her." I see their reflected concern about me as I bustle about for her. Their concern implicates me, and as I think about it, I turn it back to them. Reflexivity continues.

The situated ethnographer may privilege the experiences that resonate with selected observations and reports. I have tried to guess how my situation has affected these aspects of my work. I know that when my experiences seemed similar to those reported to me, the resonance was strong. I wonder whether I am listening and observing well or have replaced old blinders with new ones. I hope that these thoughts will help initiate discussion among readers and other ethnographers of aging.

Toward Relationship and Community

The basic macro-structure of the nursing home facility remains in place—with the relatively unempowered CNA (and resident and family member) at the bottom of the hierarchy and the imperatives of the bureaucratic medical model burdening the care of frail old people. However, individual nursing homes are distinct from one another. In this medicalized environment, the "psychosocial stuff" (Diamond 1992) and relationships tend to be undervalued and relatively unnoticed. Treatments often replace kindness (Thomas 1994). Family members in this environment have often been viewed as interlopers, whose intrusions are tolerated to varying degrees. A unionized staff adds another layer of complexity that tends to impede trust and collaboration.

The traditional management of the medical bureaucracy has perpetuated the rotating assignment of CNAs to nursing home residents. There may be a belief that this method saves money, is efficient, and provides control; the scheduling is easier, and the "difficult" residents are shared equally. Some nursing homes have instituted primary assignment, instead. With consistency and over time, relationships result that are personal and humane, instead of mechanistic and task-centered. As a result, turnover rates of staff are lower. The individualized care that the nonprofit nursing home prided itself on had a consistently positive pay-off in the resulting quality of collaboration between CNAs and family members.

Flexibility and scale may be key. The implementation of both primary assignment and TQM principles is more successful when not rigidly applied. TQM is an empty promise unless a genuine teamwork spirit flourishes. When nurses pass trays at mealtimes or assist in toilet care, CNAs witness firsthand what authentic teamwork means. Similarly, if the assignment of CNA to resident is stymied by a personality clash on a particular day, improvising and working together with other staff members can remedy the situation.

Small numbers help. People are better known, and solutions can be personalized. An environment that tries to replicate positive features of home helps. Sensory effects, such as the smell of baking cookies (and then the cookies!), are wonderfully inviting to staff, family members, and residents alike. Idle conversation, the small chitchat of everyday, fosters a feeling of well-being and a sense of domesticity that relaxes and nurtures. Staff members in my mother's nursing home unit sit periodically among the residents. They talk, ask interested questions, and follow the ambling route of the conversation in its unexpected turns.

When a nursing home administration—or even the nurse on the unit—can transmit an attitude of respect and affection for the individual person (staff, resident, and family member), the rigidity of the medical model, its numbing hierarchies, and its overwhelming rules can be ameliorated. Nursing homes that shift from task-centered to person-centered care (Williams 1990) make a commitment to individuals and relationships. Shared responsibilities and relationships among nursing home residents, staff members, and families that are encouraged to flourish are vital factors mitigating the harshness of the institutional setting. They help to create a sense of community and enable us to transcend the "other" of their aging and ours. Nurturing and valuing the individuals in these settings enhances the quality of life for all.

Notes

1. This continues the discussion about family-CNA relationships by Bowers (1988) and others (such as Bowers and Becker 1992, Duncan and Morgan 1994, Heiselman and Noelker 1991, Rubin and Shuttlesworth 1983, Ryan and Scullion 2000, and Schwartz and Vogel 1990).

2. Extra costs in the unionized facility may have been due to the layer of nonunion supervisors of union employees and to additional policies and documentation in place there.

3. CNAs, nurses, my mother, and I have now collaborated on several intimate tasks that my mother and I never anticipated but have found relatively easy. I find that I can appeal to them for help, which is comforting. On the other hand, when my mother had to have surgery, I naively expected more assistance from the

nursing home staff than I received. Taking my mother out of the facility for the consultation and the outpatient procedure meant absolving them of legal responsibility. I was on my own.

4. A measure of how staff members came to know my mother and our family is illustrated in the following vignette: I recently asked that her hair be done before a family event. When I visited the nursing home the next day, the staff members were embarrassed and rushed to tell me that I was going to hate my mother's hair-do. The hairdresser had flipped her hair up, and although the staff members thought that it looked nice, they knew that it wasn't at all in keeping with who my mother is and what she prefers. She would like it sedately turned under, and they knew it. I was happy that they understood our point of view.

9

Defining Family Roles
within a Nursing Home Setting

Margaret A. Perkinson

The move to a nursing home is commonly regarded as a major life transition for a frail older adult, but few realize that it also represents a significant transition for his or her family caregiver (Aneshensel et al. 1995). Even though nursing home placement typically occurs after a period of burden, when a family's ability to provide care has been pushed to its limits (Morycz 1985; Tobin and Kulys 1981), many family members are reluctant to relinquish their caregiving role (Perkinson 1995). While desiring continued involvement in their relative's care, they are unsure of what they can do or are allowed to do within an institutional setting. In many ways, the social world of the nursing home represents a foreign culture for uninitiated family members, one which they must learn to negotiate through trial and error.

As Rowles and High also note in this volume (Chapter 7), there is growing evidence that many families maintain contact with their nursing home relatives and continue to assist with various tasks (Dempsey and Pruchno 1993; Duncan and Morgan 1994; High and Rowles 1995; Karr 1991; Linsk et al. 1988; Litwak 1985; Moss and Kurland 1979;

Nalippa 1996; Smith and Bengtson 1979; Stephens, Kinney, and Ogrocki 1991; Stull et al. 1997; Tilse 1997; Yamamoto-Mitani, Aneshensel, and Levy-Storms 2002; York and Calsyn 1977). Family involvement can greatly enhance the well-being of nursing home residents (Bowers 1988; Brody 1985; Cohn and Jay 1988; Montgomery 1982; Tobin and Lieberman 1976) and results in lower levels of depression for family caregivers (Brody, Dempsey, and Pruchno 1990; Townsend 1990). Frequency of family visits is a key predictor of staff knowledge about the resident, which, in turn, predicts staff feelings toward the resident. That is, the greater the staff's knowledge of the resident and his or her background, the more likely staff members will have positive feelings toward that resident (Retsinas 1986). As outside observers, scholars have recommended that family caregivers be integrated into nursing home programs and become partners with nursing home staff (Bowers 1988; Brody 1986; Brody, Dempsey, and Pruchno 1990; Buckwalter and Hall 1987; Cohn 1988; Pillemer et al. 1998; Pratt et al. 1987; Solomon 1983; Townsend 1990).

In spite of this unanimous and unambiguous conclusion, families continue to represent a "neglected resource" within nursing home settings (Buckwalter and Hall 1987). Family members may desire continued involvement in the care of their relative but often lack an understanding of the nursing home system and their place within it. In an attempt to remedy this, the Family Roles in Nursing Homes project used ethnographic techniques to identify and convey to families the basics of nursing home culture and to elicit input from both families and nursing home staff in defining family caregiving roles that were productive and workable within that culture.

As already noted, many families are unfamiliar with the culture of the nursing home—the expectations, assumptions, values, and norms shared to varying degrees by its members—and the complicated bureaucratic restrictions that influence the actions and interactions occurring within its confines. Family members are faced with the challenge of redefining and negotiating former domestic roles of family caregiving within a medicalized institutional environment that is decidedly nondomestic in nature. In attempting to define their niche in the nursing home, family members must negotiate their roles with countless members of the nursing home staff, whose composition changes from shift to shift and from weekday to weekends. It is a confusing and often overwhelming place that typically offers few guidelines to outsiders other than a vague expectation to stand clear of the many mandated routines structuring daily life.

The Family Roles in Nursing Homes project was designed to assist families in understanding nursing home culture and assuming a meaningful, satisfying role within it. With a community development philosophy of empowerment as a guiding framework (Perkinson 1992), family members of nursing home residents were enlisted as active participants in the development of the intervention, that is, a family guide to the nursing home. In an approach similar to that employed by various social gerontologists involved in public health and community action programs (Weschler 1986; Weschler and Minkler 1986), family caregivers were invited to share their perspectives on the issue of family involvement in the nursing home.

The negotiation of meaningful family roles within an institutional context affects the entire system and implies changes in the attitudes and relationships of all involved, not just family members. Therefore, the input of nursing home staff and nursing home residents also was solicited in the development of the intervention.

Family members, residents, and all levels of staff in a large, urban, long-term care facility were invited to participate in a series of focus groups and individual interviews to elicit their views on the desired levels and nature of family involvement and to identify problems that family members typically confronted within the nursing home. This chapter reports the results of these discussions. It describes the families' perspectives, what they typically did and hoped to do within the nursing home, and the problems they encountered. It also describes the nursing home staff's perceptions of family involvement and suggestions for developing meaningful family roles within the institution and a more collaborative relationship between family and staff.

SETTING

The research was conducted in a nonprofit, 550-bed nursing home located in a large city in northeastern United States. This facility contained twelve units and a hospital wing for emergency medical care. The nursing home was part of a geriatric complex that included congregate housing, an adult day care center, a diagnostic and assessment unit, a research institute, and various community health services.

Two floors within the nursing home were selected for the study. The dementia floor contained fifty-two beds for residents who exhibited moderate levels of dementia. It was a "gated unit" (a wooden gate, which buzzed when opened, barred entry to and exit from the unit). In contrast, residents on the second floor were generally free to go where they pleased within the facility or on the campus grounds. This unit housed thirty-six residents with various levels of physical, not cognitive, impairments. Residents on both floors were predominantly Jewish; staff, for the most part, was not. The majority of the nursing assistants were women of color.

METHODS

A total of eleven focus groups were conducted: four with family members, one with residents of the nondementia unit, and the remaining six with nursing home staff. To keep the focus groups as homogeneous as possible, separate groups were held for the family members of each floor. Also, an attempt was made to have separate groups for adult children and older family caregivers, such as spouses or siblings.

All family members designated as the primary family contact with the nursing home for residents on the two floors were invited to participate in the project. Although many family members expressed interest, a large number were employed, making it extremely difficult to find convenient time slots for their focus groups. Family members who did participate in the groups were those whose schedules allowed them to attend a lunchtime weekday meeting.

Staff focus groups were homogeneous by approximate rank in the nursing home hierarchy. Three groups were composed solely of nursing assistants. One group consisted of the social workers and activity therapists assigned to the two floors and the substitute nurse manager from the nondementia unit. Another group was composed of the nutritionist assigned to both floors, the director of physical therapy, the occupational therapist, the director of the clinical psychology department, and the nurse manager from the dementia unit. The final staff focus group consisted of the entire clinical psychology department.

Other than the clinical psychology focus group, which convened in their department building and consisted of approximately fifteen people, all family and most staff groups were held in a small conference room within the nursing home and ranged from two to eight participants. The nursing assistant groups were held in a private room on the dementia unit, and the resident focus group was held in the small (mostly vacant) activity room on the nondementia floor.

The focus groups lasted an average of ninety minutes and were conducted by an anthropological linguist with many years of experience as a professional focus group convener for various market research companies. The author attended the groups as an observer and interjected questions at the end of the sessions.

The groups were structured by separate sets of questions specifically designed for the family members, residents, staff, and clinical psychologists. The focus group leader covered all designated topics but was flexible in pursuing unanticipated issues and comments of interest.

The focus groups were supplemented by individual interviews with the rabbi of the facility, various social workers, and the nursing assistants from the nondementia unit. (Focus groups were precluded for these nursing assistants. Because only four were assigned to the unit, only one could leave the floor at any given time.)

All focus groups were tape-recorded and transcribed. Transcripts were analyzed using the *grounded theory approach* (Schatzman and Strauss 1973; Strauss 1987), in which data are initially sorted by relevant codes and then analyzed for underlying patterns and themes. The following illustrates the perceptions of both the nursing home staff and the family members of residents regarding the role of families in the nursing home.

INITIAL ENCOUNTERS WITH THE NURSING HOME— NEGOTIATING FAMILY ROLES WITHIN MULTIPLE REALITIES OF CARE

Defining their niche in the world of the nursing home was the last thing on most family members' minds during the placement process. Families were preoccupied with their elder's medical condition (especially if he or she were admitted in a crisis situation, for example, after a hospitalization) and financial issues. They put all else on hold. As the son of a resident on the dementia unit explained,

> My original concerns were my mother's health and finances.
> I was worried about affording this, and what to do when we
> ran out of money, and her health. Beyond that, I figured I'd
> deal with the rest of it.... From minute one, that's all I cared
> about. And then, as I got into it...then I was interested in
> social kinds of relationships and personal care and all of
> that. In the beginning, I wanted her to be healthy, and I
> wanted to know whether I was going to have to get a second
> mortgage to make this happen. As soon as the crisis was
> over...when I realized, here are nurses, here are doctors,
> and here's a bed, and here's where she'll be, and here's the
> medicine...and here are the bills...I dealt with all of that,
> and in a week or so I was ready to settle into "My mother is in
> a nursing home, and now what?"

Echoing the above comments, the wife of a man on the dementia unit agreed that her attention focused completely on her husband's health crisis during the placement period, but "once the patient is here, then we begin to notice other things, of course. You know, everything widens considerably."

Staff psychologists confirmed that families typically entered the nursing home in a crisis mode, ignoring their own feelings and personal needs:

> The decision is being made...in crisis or made at a point
> where they feel that they have no choice whatsoever, and
> they're driven by that, so that they ignore their own feelings,
> reactions, or concerns, or hesitations about it. Once the
> family member is here and the crisis has been alleviated,
> then all of their own emotions come out about it, dealing
> with it.

Family members, as well as residents, experienced a period of adjustment and orientation to this initially foreign setting. One psychologist (whose family member resided in another nursing home) described the difficulties that families experienced in their attempts to decipher the social world of the nursing home:

> The adjustment period is for the families as well as for the residents. When I've had contact with families, they're terribly confused....It is very confusing trying to figure out who do you talk to about what, how do you get something done, who do you complain to about which issues? And who's who? If you visit at different times, the number of different people you come in contact with, when you figure three shifts, weekends and weekdays, you might come in contact with thirty to forty different nursing people, and trying to sort out who they all are is very confusing.

Lack of knowledge of nursing home hierarchies and designated roles doomed initial attempts by new families to gain information on their relative's status or to convey concerns. Asking questions of the wrong staff was clearly counterproductive and a source of irritation for all involved. In frustration, some families either focused on one staff person they trusted, funneling all questions and requests to her, or engaged in what staff termed "scatter-shooting," complaining to everyone within reach. The latter strategy was especially self-destructive and set those families on a downward spiral in their relationships with nursing home staff. One staff psychologist explained:

> Things only get worse when you have a family member telling everyone their complaints, and what happens is, they're telling it to people that have no decision-making ability to change anything. And so what happens is, the family member just gets worse at it and just keeps doing it more and more and more, and the danger of that is that staff will start shutting down and not listening to anything. I mean, there's no way that you can discriminate what the person is saying, because they're just going around.

To add to the confusion, many families did not anticipate the very significant differences between institutional and familial caregiving and entered with major misconceptions regarding the care their relative would receive. These misconceptions were not always corrected by information offered at admission. As one therapist described the situation,

> I think people think when you admit someone to a nursing home setting that they're going to have twenty-four-hour supervision, care around the clock. Someone's always going to be there at their beck and call to take over the very specific caregiving duties that this person received in the community and the home setting on a familial-type basis. And we just go along with that sleigh ride, that they're going to get as much therapy as they would want, not explaining Medicare regs, what our criteria are to go in and treat them, the regulations that drag us and help us to get paid.... Because they still see it as a family member. "Why can't he have all the care he needs? And individualized treatment?" Because they moved from a community setting where it's one on one or five on one, to forty-two to five, something of that nature.

Another staff member elaborated this point:

> The input for the person coming into the nursing home is, somebody says to the family, "Your family member needs more care." And so the expectation is, "Well, the reason I'm putting Mom here is because she needs more care." Therefore, she's going to have all these things. The expectation is that there's going to be somebody there at all times to care for Mom, where, in reality, they're probably getting more care in the community if they had companion care and home health aides and home health PT and home health nursing and everybody else coming in to support the care of that patient. They're getting a lot of care on that one person, whereas here you get forty-two people using whatever number of staff happens to be on the floor on any given day, depending on who's pulled and who's not pulled.

In a later focus group, one of the staff admitted that many family members of newly admitted residents did not understand what ordinary life was like in a nursing home (for example, that items are lost, residents often lose weight, not all roommates get along). The nursing home has a culture of its own and operates under certain restrictions and limitations that many family members did not anticipate. As noted before, staff could do more to inform them:

> At intake, there should be some kind of statement to families that, "Yeah, we'll help. You don't have to worry about washing them and all that kind of stuff. We'll do it here, but are we going to do it like you do it at home? No."

Another staff added, "We don't always say, 'This is how it's going to be,' right from the up-front. We wait until someone gets upset about it, and then we talk about it."

In hindsight, a son of a resident on the nondementia unit described the families' need for a more thorough orientation to the nursing home, including advice on helping residents adjust to this major life transition:

> FAMILY MEMBER: I would like to have them point out those main subjects that you should discuss with the parent...what your responsibility will be in preparing your relative in coming here, so that you can discuss this prior to being here, and what they should look for on a one-to-one basis. They don't do this.... Let them prepare you pre-admission what your responsibilities should be with that person.
>
> MODERATOR: The main subjects that are going to be relevant to you would be what?
>
> FAMILY MEMBER: Roommate would be one. Environment is going to be another. What you're entitled to. What you should do when you get there. And then basically, you're going to be living in another place now. How do you want to conduct yourself, and what do you want to do, and what do you want?

Eventually, most families did establish a routine of visits and various caregiving activities within the nursing home. Nursing home staff perceived family involvement as fitting into three categories: basic care, advocacy, and interpersonal/connective activities.

WHAT FAMILIES DO—BASIC CARE

Maintaining the resident's personal appearance, especially his or her clothes, was a frequently mentioned caregiving activity. Although the nursing home furnished laundry service, many family members chose to do their relative's laundry, hoping to avoid the hassle of missing or mutilated garments. They also mended old clothes and furnished and tagged new items as needed.

Attuned to their relative's preferences, many brought special supplies to help maintain continuity of past daily routines and, in some cases, a sense of personal dignity. The son of a resident on the non-dementia floor explained:

> She has an idiosyncrasy with mouthwash. She has to have a certain mouthwash.... She uses a diaper type, like Depends. I supply her with bags. She puts these pads in a bag. She's very conscious of this.

Family members often brought snacks or favorite foods, such as take-out Chinese dinners or deli feasts, to break the monotony of institutional cooking and to share and bond with other residents on the floor. Staff encouraged this practice, especially if the resident was losing weight, provided that the foods were appropriate for the resident's diet. Staff acknowledged the importance of food in the nursing home routine and speculated on its significance to families:

> PHYSICAL THERAPIST: You know, the food is a sort of focus of how they move in their world every day.

> PSYCHOLOGIST: The feeding thing, I think, is really tricky because for a lot of family members...they're carrying this whole burden of guilt that they're not caring for their family member, that they're not taking care of them. Well, you know, feeding them...carries this tremendous symbolic weight. So in terms of maintaining function and that sort of stuff, I mean, the basic symbolism of feeding somebody is so heavy for people. They probably can't help themselves.

In addition to feeding, families helped with a few other activities of daily living (ADLs), such as grooming (brushing hair or doing nails) and walking. Few family members helped with the more intimate ADLs, such as bathing or toileting. As one staff member explained,

> I think family members, what they're giving up, I think, is the physical, hands-on. But not even, that's not quite the right word because I think they still retain the feeding, which is physical, but I think in terms of bathing, toileting. But I think they'll retain grooming. We get a lot of hair brushing.... I think there are certain elements of caregiving they want to give up, which are the more, maybe, intimate body functions—may be the way to distinguish it. And they want that given up, and to some extent maybe ambulation and transferring. So it's intimate body functions and heavy, physical, body functions. But they retain some of the nurturing caregiving—feeding, grooming

Often, the reason for nursing home placement was rooted in an inability to do the more physical tasks (for example, the spouse caregiver was too frail) or an unwillingness and sense of discomfort (on the part of both the adult child *and* the impaired parent). As one adult son explained,

> All her personal care needs are being beautifully taken care of...and they're things that I can't do as a son or am not comfortable doing...toileting. I'm letting the staff do that. When I'm there, if there's a problem, I ask for help because I don't think either my mom or I are comfortable with that kind of involvement.

The few family members who did assist in more personal ADL tasks tended to be spouses who were dissatisfied with the staff's less-than-immediate responses to residents' requests. These family caregivers were usually perceived as problems for the staff because they were often frail and unable to accomplish tasks safely, such as transferring the resident when toileting.

WHAT FAMILIES DO—ADVOCACY
Some family members described themselves as "care watchers" instead of caregivers. With intimate knowledge of their parent or

spouse's eating habits, coloring, mode of interaction, and general energy level, family members sometimes noticed changes in habits or appearance that staff did not. Alerting staff to these changes prompted medical attention that may have otherwise been delayed.

Family members also informed staff of residents' preferences in activities and foods. The dietitian noted, "The family is very verbal about the food, which, in some cases, definitely helps because sometimes the resident can't tell me if they like something or if they don't like something."

However, family members may not always be correct in identifying the resident's preferences. As one nursing assistant reported,

> We have one that comes in who picks out her father's menu, and she keeps ordering this man sardines. Mind you, she's not here when the sardines arrive, to see this uproar that her father makes over these sardines that they want him to eat. And we keep telling her, "Your father doesn't like sardines." But she argues with us, "Yes, he do like sardines!"

Sometimes attempts to act as advocate for the resident did more harm than good, if the family member was out of touch with or refused to recognize the resident's potential to improve. Another nursing assistant from the dementia floor noted,

> But a lot of times when they place them here, they come with all these demands, you know. "You should do this for Mother," or "Mother likes to do this," and "Mother shouldn't do this," or "She can't feed herself." I mean, we have a program where we do restorative care. In other words, we're trying to teach them maybe to eat again, and a lot of times we have residents here that does well. They can sit and feed themselves. You have a family member come in and they'll say, "She can't feed herself," or "He can't feed himself." "Well, Ma'am, he's been eating all the time. He can feed himself." "No, no. And he doesn't like this."

On the other hand, a family member may be unrealistic in assessing the resident's abilities. Hoping to restore his mother's ability to walk, one son pushed adamantly for physical therapy and other exercise programs. He recalled the eventual outcome:

> She couldn't do it. And she had some valve problems. It was my effort that I was considering, not hers. And somebody finally said to me that she's physiologically incapable of doing this kind of activity. She, no matter, even if she really tried, she doesn't have the capabilities.

Central to the role of advocate, especially when there were conflicting perceptions of residents' preferences, abilities, and needs, was the issue of who is the authority. Who knows the resident best? The family member(s), most of whom have a long and intimate knowledge of this person's past history, or the staff member who is in close daily contact with the resident? Who is the complete authority is rarely a clear-cut matter, so occasional differences of perceptions and opinions did arise.

In their push to obtain the best of care for their relative and tend to his or her needs, family members at times erred in being overprotective, inadvertently denying their relative the opportunity of maintaining a degree of autonomy. Adult children of cognitively intact residents seemed especially torn between the desire to encourage and preserve a sense of independence and self-efficacy in their parent and the desire to ensure that their parent received sufficient care. Many perceived their parent as too proud to ask for help, especially with personal care. One adult son stated,

> My only concern is for her welfare, that she is taken care of. And, being independent, she doesn't ask. And that bothers me, that she will not ask for help. Now, she can't dress herself that well, and you can't tell me that she is getting undressed, because I'm almost positive she's not.

Nevertheless, he limited his involvement in her care:

> No, I don't want to be any more involved, because she deserves some independence, and if I did everything for her and I was hovering over her all the time, I don't think she would like it. She has told me numerous times, "What's the matter? I've got a mind of my own. I'll do this." "You're right, Mom. Whatever you feel you want to do, do it!"

WHAT FAMILIES DO—THE INTERPERSONAL AND CONNECTIVE ASPECTS OF FAMILY INVOLVEMENT

Family visits represented emotional high points for most residents. As one resident told us, "I'm only happiest when I'm with my family." Family members structured visiting time in various ways. Some timed visits to coincide with activities or religious services that both the resident and family member would enjoy. Others identified and encouraged favorite activities of the resident, providing magazines to leaf through, greeting cards to inspect, or napkins to fold and unfold. Two sisters found that joint visits enhanced their interaction with their mother: "Usually, my sister and I come together. We find that since Mother doesn't talk that much about what's going on here, we bring things to talk to her about, or we'll talk to each other with her, to stimulate her somewhat."

When family members were asked to describe a recent good visit, it often involved sharing family photos or videos with the resident, bringing grandchildren or pets to the nursing home, or taking the resident off the floor, either to the cafeteria, the main lobby area, or outside.

Visits were, nevertheless, sometimes frustrating for family members. Communication, especially with residents with dementia, was a major issue. Several adult children questioned the value of shared activities during visits, admitting an inability to assess their parent's reactions. One daughter described a recent visit:

> I'm not sure whether it was more for me or for her. I mean, I got her out of that floor. I don't know if she really and truly enjoyed it.... They had a piano player, and Mother used to play the piano, and I thought she'd love that. I moved her around so she could see the back and watch him play, and I'm not sure it really meant that much to her. She kept waving to him. She waves to everybody.

Some longed for more satisfying modes of interaction with their parent. When asked if there were anything else he would like to do for his mother, one son confessed,

> I would like to find a way where I could spend time with her

in a more satisfying way, and I'm not sure what that is. When she and I talk, she can hold a conversation as long as you carry two-thirds of it, which is okay. I don't mind. I would love to find things that we could do that were more interesting for her, and more interesting for me.

Later in the focus group discussion, after talking about the proposed intervention, this same son came to the realization that, indeed, his visits could involve more than a struggle to converse:

If there were things, say, you're talking about games and stuff, you know, it never occurred to me that I could do more than sit there and talk. And now that you've even got me thinking about it, I will come up with some of my own things that I can do. But, oh, I would love it if there were something we could do. A package of stuff....

Some family members seemed better able than others to relate to their impaired relative. One brother explained his strategy for helping his sister overcome lapses into confusion:

When she seems confused, I try to talk to her about things that would be familiar to her. Usually, I can get her to come out of it. It's a strange thing. She'll be very confused, and I'll say, for instance, "What do you know about the Freed Hospital?" Well, she knows the Freed Hospital because she knew the Freeds. So she doesn't seem as confused after that.... I feel that I know her that well that I can always think of something, and even if it's something that I told her last week, chances are she won't remember that I even discussed it with her, and I can bring the same thing up again.

Past patterns of relationships between the family member and the resident often carried over into the nursing home. This was especially evident when patterns of mutual support continued, as in the case of two never-married siblings. The sister, who lived in the adjacent congregate housing, was advised for health reasons to engage in a regular walking program. Her older brother, who lived in the nursing home, was concerned for her safety and immediately volunteered to accompany her on her daily walks, after he received clearance from the nursing home physician.

Certain spousal caregivers became overinvolved in the care of their husband or wife. As one staff member described it,

> And what it typically is, is a spouse who can't let go and the spouse is basically living on the floor. Shows up at 8 a.m. Doesn't leave until 10 p.m. Is in nursing's hair, like, all day long…and the behavior is sometimes really bizarre…. So I would say in those cases, typically, we just find that it's when certain family members can't *not* be there. They really don't have a life other than being in the nursing home. That's their role.

The issue of overprotection discussed earlier resurfaced in other forms. Some family members chose to shield the resident from bad news, especially news of a family illness or death. When her brother was hospitalized for bypass surgery, one daughter explained his prolonged absence by telling her mother that he was away on vacation. Although the mother did not question this, she wondered why the son did not send postcards.

Disclosing bad news to persons with dementia was a particularly difficult issue. These residents continually relived experiences of intense shock and grief after repeatedly forgetting and being re-informed of a relative's death. Both families and staff struggled with this issue, as one psychologist related:

> A gentleman who was very demented…his wife died quite suddenly. He would ask where she was. He would be told that she had passed away, initially was told that she had passed away. The family decided that he would not go to the funeral, would not sit shiva with the family—and all of which, in retrospect, I think, would have been extremely helpful for him. Even though he was demented, it would have reinforced the grieving process in going through it. But they decided not to do that. He would constantly question the staff in a very distressed manner, "Where is my wife?" But the problem is that the tack those chose to take

was to say, "She's off doing the laundry. She'll be back." "She's going to the grocery store. She'll be back." And just enough got through to him about realizing that she was dead that in periods of lucidity he would come up and he'd say, "She really is dead, isn't she?" And so then the staff would be in this tremendous bind between "How do I, when do I, tell him a distracting thing, and when do I tell him the truth?"

With strikingly few exceptions, nursing home staff welcomed appropriate family involvement in the care of their relative. Staff had various ideas and suggestions to help family members deal with several issues mentioned above, develop legitimate roles in the nursing home, and establish collaborative working relations with nursing home staff.

STAFF PERSPECTIVES ON FAMILY INVOLVEMENT IN BASIC CARE

Staff acknowledged that families could provide critical assistance to them in providing basic care. They welcomed family help in persuading residents to cooperate with various routines or therapies. As one nurse manager explained,

Sometimes somebody can't be convinced to do something unless their daughter's there or their son's there. So things like maybe going to the hairdresser or going to certain appointments, if somebody won't go down for an X-ray, I may call and say, "Well, the daughter will be in tomorrow morning. Could we bring her down tomorrow?" Because they sometimes have the way with them that we don't.

Staff agreed that family members could interact with residents in ways that staff could not. In explaining how one family motivated their relative to participate in physical therapy, one therapist related, "They yelled at him. They said, 'If you don't get up, I'm going to knock you on your —.' But essentially this is what the patient needed."

Competent family members who were willing to learn and execute their relative's exercise program augmented staff's efforts and represented true collaborators in the provision of care. The physical therapist described such situations: "I'll go over an exercise program with them and explain to them how often it should be done, and they'll learn it along with their family member and often encourage them to do it. And that works out really well."

The occupational therapist agreed:

> The advantage of working through the family member, if they're appropriate and able to do it, is that there's a better chance of carryover of what's done in the clinic up on the unit, because people might be put on a floor program and you might have two CNAs [certified nursing assistants] pulled. So that floor program isn't performed that day or whatever. So that you have this extra link or safety net to carry over things.

The occupational therapist emphasized the importance of family involvement for dementia patients:

> With dementias, you take a real systems approach. You can't just treat the patient…but you really have to see who impacts this patient, because there is no carry-over with them. There is no trainable element. So you're training the people that impact this person's world.

STAFF'S PERSPECTIVES ON ADVOCACY ROLES

One CNA appreciatively dubbed attentive family members his "third eye," assisting him and the other CNAs in their attempt to monitor the actions of the fifty-two moderately demented residents on his floor. Staff agreed that family members could also play a critical role in alerting them to changes in the resident, especially in regard to mental status. As the charge nurse for the dementia unit explained,

> We are going to notice a lot of times a physical change in a person, from doing their ADLs, feeding them, lifting them, you know. We're going to notice when they actually can't get out of bed by themselves anymore, but there's not always the time to be able to sit and talk with them and really get their orientation. And a lot of times I'll have family members that'll come to me and say, "You know, I just noticed that

Mom's a little more confused than she used to be," and I really rely on those family members to let me know those kinds of things, because I don't have the time every day or every week.

However, families who monitored residents and patient care too closely sometimes interfered with that care:

Sometimes I've heard on our floor that there's a problem with family members coming into the bedroom when the nursing assistants are trying to provide real dressing and bathing and washing, grooming care. And it gets to be a tense situation when the family member's in there with the nursing assistants, because the family member wants the nursing assistant to do all the little details that they did for their relative at home, and it's just really tense. So the family members, I guess I could say, they get in the way at times during that interaction.

Nursing staff added that such intrusive behavior often made residents uncomfortable: "Of course, you have the privacy issue, too.... A lot of them are very proud people and they don't want their children to see them in that state."

Families who were especially aggressive in their advocacy role sometimes embarrassed their relative. As one staff member commented,

We wonder about the reaction of one resident to his wife when she gets hostile and when she starts giving the staff a really hard time. He gets embarrassed because he knows it's all about him, you know. And she does it right in front of him, and then there's this big discussion. He's sitting in the wheelchair, and there's these two people bantering above his head, and it's just humiliating for him.

STAFF'S PERSPECTIVES ON INTERPERSONAL AND CONNECTIVE FAMILY ROLES

Staff recognized families' potential to act as partners in care by providing cognitive stimulation and psychological uplifts to residents in need of intensive, one-on-one interaction:

> I find if a family member, say, has been visiting for an hour and they are prompting verbal responses and they're trying to do reminiscence and stimulating the resident cognitively, it does affect the resident in that maybe for the rest of the day they're a little bit more verbal and they're more apt to just talk to staff because they've already got that stimulation going.

The nutritionist acknowledged families' potential effect on the morale of their relative:

> Sometimes the family members help to bring them over if they're going through some sort of slump. Maybe they are losing weight, or they're a little bit more depressed, or something has changed. Maybe they just came out of the hospital or something like that. When the family sort of picks up that little, like, slack, the part that's missing, sometimes it helps them to get out of whatever it is they're getting into.

Both the psychologists and nursing staff felt that family members could play an important role in helping to preserve the resident's sense of dignity and personhood and of continued involvement in the outside world. Several staff expressed strong reactions against those who shielded the resident from news of family misfortune:

> My feeling is unless somebody's really demented and can't make sense of it, they're still human beings. They have a right to know what's going on in the life of their family.... I think it's really terribly disrespectful and infantilizing not to be honest and let people know what's going on.

The staff rabbi observed,

> Families feel they should spare their relative sorrows that are going on in the family, but what they're doing is treating that person like they're no longer alive or like they're a child...not respectful of the humanity of this person, no matter how impaired they might be.

The effect of sharing family misfortunes was illustrated in the resident focus group. One resident, clearly saddened by his son's marital problems, nevertheless expressed pride and a sense of affirmation that the son confided in him and sought his advice in this matter.

One psychologist made an additional recommendation for preserving or enhancing residents' self-concept, suggesting that adult children continue to place their parent in a parental-teaching role:

> It's worked very well, but with more intact residents. The idea where, no matter how old you are, your children are still your children, no matter how old they are, and that they're still looking to you for answers. And you can show them how to deal with the problems of old age, because they're looking at you and they're saying, when they get older, they think, "I remember when Mom went to the nursing home when she was eighty, and now I'm eighty." And it's sort of empowering for the resident to put them back in the sort of teaching-parental role.

In her suggestions regarding family contributions to the spiritual needs of the resident, the nursing home's rabbi urged family members to encourage and attend to the resident's discussions of issues of profound concern, such as death, the significance of his or her own life, and the moral legacy or "ethical will" he or she may wish to leave for future generations:

> In terms of spiritual needs, I think that thing about continuing to treat the person as a whole person and being willing to listen to them about what's really on their mind, and I'm not talking about the food. But I think a lot of people have a need to a life review, and the family members need to really hang in and to listen to that. And…listen to the verbal ethical will, and that's when people want to say their piece about what it is that they believe in and what they hope that their kids have gotten from them and whatever. And the last thing is to let people talk about death. A lot of people are thinking about it ninety-nine percent of the time, and a lot of families have a very difficult time broaching the subject.

Families can help to maintain the resident's past identity and convey that identity to staff and others by sharing information on the resident's past achievements, roles, and characteristics. The rabbi suggested that family members could make collages, assembling images of the resident's past, to create a visual representation that would give staff and other residents greater insight into that parent or spouse's personal identity and past life:

> In some homes, they've done this thing where somebody comes in and they make a poster about a person, with pictures, some information about who they've been in their life, members of their family, or whatever.... If there could be a way of doing that, to have a family involved in creating a representation of who their person is in the world.... You know, one of the saddest things is people feel like, "You don't really know my Mom. You have no idea who this woman is. You're calling her 'dear,' and she was a pharmacist," or whatever.

Regarding the resident's emotional status, especially if the resident was depressed, the rabbi felt that the family members' role was to empathize, not necessarily to cheer up:

> I would think in some way the most important thing is to talk to someone who's depressed. I mean, you don't have to make them feel better.... When someone's depressed, just be with them, and listen to them. Diversion is sometimes an appropriate tactic; sometimes it's not. I can think of one very depressed lady who does nails. You have to find the thing that's meaningful to that person. But you don't have to cheer them up, in the sense that, like, "Come on, Grams, it's okay. Buck up! Keep a stiff upper lip." You don't have to do that, you know. And I think people don't know that. Reminiscence can be an enormously helpful thing. They may feel really rotten about their life, living here now, but maybe it would be meaningful to review some other times in life that were positive.

Staff pointed out that even severely demented residents could relate on some level and benefit from family visits. Two CNAs described the situation of a resident with dementia on their floor:

FIRST CNA: You can't get any sense out of Martha. You really can't. Martha reacts to one-on-one. She likes company. She likes smiles. So you can walk down to Martha, walk down the hall, one end of the hall to the other with Martha, and she'll just be talking about "Yeah, the plants," and whatever, and it makes no sense at all, but she just enjoys that company…but I haven't met any of her family since I've been over here on this unit. I haven't met any of her family, but they take very good care of her clothes, and that's not Martha. Her clothes are not her. So, you know, in her instance, even with the mental status that she is…

SECOND CNA: They could take some time and try to understand her.

FIRST CNA: Yeah. She needs company.

One nursing assistant wondered whether family members realized the full effect of their visits and their importance as a link to the past:

They don't understand that sometimes that one visit, just seeing that one person, means a whole lot, just to see somebody they know besides us that don't even know them from what they used to do, who they used to be. You now, what they're all about. You know, because I know, when some of them get a visit, every time their daughter come, and I met her twenty times, "Hi, Kay, this is my daughter. This is my daughter." You know, they're excited. They're happy. Or they get a phone call. Like Lydia's daughter, she phoned up, and we say, "Lydia, your daughter says she loves you." Oh, her face just lights up.

Another nursing assistant acknowledged the unique and irreplaceable contribution of family visits in maintaining residents' sense of well-being:

I think, if they visited more, and I think it would make a big difference in a lot of them. I think they feel forgotten, you know. And their spirit's gone. You know, there's not a whole lot we can do. I mean, we're here every day, but we're not family. We're family in a sense, but we're not the family that they're used to. So I think it makes a difference. They may not even be able to verbalize it, but you can sometimes see in a face.

SUMMARY AND CONCLUSION

The perspective of the nursing home as a "contested cultural domain" offers insight into the relationships, roles, and interactions of its various members. We have seen that family members and nursing home staff employ divergent frameworks of meaning to inform what they do and how they interpret and evaluate daily events surrounding the care of nursing home residents. There are, indeed, multiple realities of care. This was most evident in the description, earlier in the chapter, of families' initial encounters with the nursing home. Family members entered with expectations of care carried over from their experiences as caregivers in the community. These expectations were incorporated into a nebulous model of the nursing home that, for most families, lacked clear notions of the ideology and roles of those who worked there and of the general nature of daily life within the nursing home. Institutional caregiving was assumed to represent a more intensive version of the care their relative had received in the community prior to placement. This assumption led to misunderstandings and, at times, tensions between families and nursing home staff.

As noted earlier in this chapter, many staff were aware of this situation, acknowledging the discrepancy between families' expectations and what actually took place. Staff's observations of families coincided with focus group families' disclosures that the initial encounter with the nursing home was a time of confusion. While still reeling from the stress of their relative's hospitalization and nursing home placement, family members were forced to decipher what was, to them, essentially a foreign culture—the culture of the nursing home. Most were unaware of the hierarchies of authority, the duties of specific staff, or the norms governing communication within the facility. Many were unclear as to where they fit in and how they should conduct themselves. Not knowing the "rules of the game" as defined by the nursing home, family members sometimes inadvertently interacted in ways deemed inappropriate by nursing home staff (for example, the "funneling" or "scatter-shooting" styles of help seeking, described earlier), resulting in frustration for all involved.

Over time, most families established routines of visiting and caregiving activities, as documented in this chapter. Families who could not develop constructive and meaningful roles within the nursing home were sometimes reduced to looking for inadequacies in the system and in the care their relative received. Filled with guilt for placing their relative in the nursing home, some families may attempt to prove to both the staff and themselves that they still care. This may be accomplished in a dysfunctional manner (for example, being overly critical of nursing care or overprotective of the resident) if there are no apparent avenues for constructively channeling their energies and desires to continue their roles as family caregivers. Such a situation may result in the pitting of family against staff in confrontational relationships. Staff who are unaccustomed to regarding families as potential partners in caregiving may be tempted to view the family member as another client to soothe and reassure (or, in extreme cases, to avoid).

As noted before, the divergent frameworks of meaning evoked by families and staff to interpret and assess each other's actions made day-to-day interactions and attempts to establish legitimate roles within the institution problematic for family members. Many families desired to maintain involvement in the care of their relative. The constraints of life in the nursing home (for example, the regulations, the group setting) required that the nature of that involvement be negotiated with nursing home staff (and, to a certain extent, the resident).

The Family Roles in Nursing Homes project assumed that families could become partners in care with nursing home staff, that they could complement staff care and provide significant additional assistance to their relative. The contrasting frameworks of meaning held by families and staff posed a potential barrier to such an endeavor. Nevertheless, meaning making is an ongoing process. One basic assumption of the project was that social realities and roles are open to negotiation and revision. The ultimate goal of the intervention resulting from this project (the *Family Guide to Nursing Homes* manual) was to help develop a collaborative relationship between family and staff and assist families in identifying and negotiating meaningful roles or modes of involvement in nursing home care. Working within an empowerment model, in which participants are encouraged to assume an active role in resolving their problems and needs (Perkinson 1992; Rappaport 1981, 1983), input was enlisted from all sides (families, residents, and staff) in identifying barriers to family involvement and suggesting ways to overcome those barriers. The research process itself was used as a "tool for empowerment" (Moller 1995). As focus group participants, the families, residents, and staff were given the opportunity to voice their perceptions of, concerns about, and suggestions for family involvement in the nursing home, becoming active partners in the research on which the intervention was based.

As described in this chapter, members of the focus groups gave examples of and suggestions for family involvement in basic care, advocacy roles, and interpersonal/interconnective roles. Families expressed interest in new forms of involvement. Staff participants seemed open to the possibility of family members becoming caregiving partners, provided that families did not inadvertently harm the resident or themselves (for example, in attempting basic care, such as toileting or transferring) or interfere with care as staff defined it. Many of the staff's observations of family involvement and suggestions for extension of that involvement reflected an appreciation of actual and potential contributions of families to the psychosocial well-being of the residents and to the potential to make the institution a more home-like environment.

In conclusion, we have seen that multiple realities of care, stemming from the contrasting models of the nursing home held by families and staff, can result in misunderstandings and potential conflict. These models are not set in stone, however. Meanings are open to negotiation and modification. Anthropologists conversant with nursing homes are in a position to intervene in the process of negotiation of meaning, acting as "culture brokers" (Press 1969; Schwab, Drake, and Burghardt 1988; Van Willigen 1986), by making explicit areas of potential misunderstanding and helping those involved to discover alternative ways of interacting and relating. It is clear that there are many areas in which family members can significantly contribute to the care and well-being of residents, thus redefining their caregiving roles within the nursing home. By negotiating collaborative partnerships in care with nursing home staff, the families participating in these new roles may help to transform nursing homes into homes of nurturing that address all levels of residents' needs.

ACKNOWLEDGMENT

The author gratefully acknowledges support for this project from a three-year Action Demonstration Project grant, "Family Roles in Nursing Homes," funded by the AARP Andrus Foundation. Thanks, also, to Robert Rubinstein and Miriam Moss for their helpful suggestions in developing this project, Anne Bower for her assistance in running the focus groups, and the families, staff, and residents who so generously shared their experiences and insights in these groups.

10

The Social World of Assisted Living[1]

Paula C. Carder

INTRODUCTION

This article is based on an ethnographic study of Oregon's assisted living facility (ALF) program, a type of housing for persons, primarily elderly, with physical and cognitive impairments. It presents the world of assisted living as seen through the eyes of assisted living practitioners, direct care staff, and nurses. It is about the collective action of people involved in the daily practice of ALFs. Their actions and beliefs construct the social world of assisted living, including vocabulary terms, boundaries, legitimacy strategies, and practice standards.

Oregon Administrative Rules (OAR) define a set of six abstract principles that providers at ALFs are expected to implement—resident independence, individuality, dignity, privacy, choice, and a home-like setting. These principles, defined as elements of the social model approach to long-term care (Kane and Wilson 1993; Mollica et al. 1995), led me to question whether it is possible to govern such abstract concepts as independence, individuality, and choice in the daily practice of commercial long-term care facilities. Thus, this research began with a broad question: What difference do the assisted living values make in daily practice?

This article is both seminal and descriptive. It describes the creation and maintenance of the social world of assisted living. By examining the current legitimacy processes of this world, I explain the central features they seek to project to others outside this world. With this foundation, I suggest that researchers interested in assisted living can evaluate (1) whether the projected approach is likely to be a useful one and (2) whether the reality of assisted living corresponds to the image it attempts to project. Defining assisted living as a unique social world became the organizing framework for this study (Becker 1982; Clarke 1997; Fujimura 1996; Pratt 1982; Shibutani 1955; Strauss 1982). From a popular culture standpoint, to describe a group as a "different world" is to recognize that the behaviors and values of one group are unique, possibly different from others. To use the phrase *a different world* to describe a particular set of people—say, airline pilots, political pundits, or soccer moms—allows one to summarize the unique characteristics of the group without going into specifics. From a theoretical perspective, it is not enough to recognize assisted living as a different world. Instead, a social world is defined as "a set of common or joint activities or concerns, bound together by a network of communication" (Strauss 1982:172). This communication network helps proponents and providers to both define and defend their world from similar others.

BACKGROUND AND KEY TERMS

The term *assisted living* is so straightforward, it would seem to define itself. Yet, the very breadth of the term means that it can be applied to nearly any type of assistance with living. Thus, both policy makers and researchers, especially those who rely on a quantitative approach, are frustrated with the lack of a standard definition. However, it is this lack of a uniform definition that makes ethnographic research in this setting both compelling and appropriate. For the purposes of this project, the focus is on ALFs licensed to operate in the state of Oregon. However, because Oregon's rules have served as a model for other states (Mollica et al. 1995), this study has implications beyond that state. OAR define assisted living as

> [A] program approach, within a prescribed physical structure, which provides or coordinates a range of supportive personal and health services, available on a 24-hour basis,

for support of resident independence in a residential setting. Assisted living promotes resident self-direction and
participation in decisions that emphasize choice, dignity,
privacy, individuality, independence, and home-like surroundings. (OAR 411-056-0005)

Nationally, definitions vary, but most states refer to a residential
setting where individuals contract to receive assistance with personal
and health care needs. In a comparison of assisted living and nursing
facilities, Kapp and Wilson (1995) include residential character, consumer autonomy, and service capacity as three important characteristics of assisted living settings. People move into ALFs because they have
health and personal care needs, not because they are looking for
leisure amenities common to retirement housing (that is, golf, tennis,
or swimming). ALF residents are said to include two types. The first
group includes those who have relatively few physical impairments but
have mild confusion, memory loss, or judgment problems; the second
includes residents with one or more chronic health conditions requiring physical assistance with daily activities, but not ongoing skilled
nursing care (Regnier, Hamilton, and Yatabe 1991).

As mentioned, the heart of Oregon's administrative rules includes
a set of six values that are described as necessary components of the
social model of care and the appropriate approach for all ALFs
(Regnier, Hamilton, and Yatabe 1991; Wilson 1990, 1991, 1996). In
1989, the agency that manages senior services for the state of Oregon,
the Senior and Disabled Services Division (SDSD), produced a white
paper titled "Assisted Living: A Social Model Approach to Services,"
which described the model this way:

We are developing educational modules that can assist developers in the marketplace as well as the Senior and Disabled
Services Division and Area Agency on Aging staff to understand how the social model is different from the medical
model. Assisted Living demonstrates this difference in physical structure and support services for the residents. The
outcome of the residents is better: they have more independence, more choices in living, more dignity, and they live in a
homelike environment that continuously treats them with
respect and keeps their privacy in mind. (SDSD 1989:5)

In 1993, the American Association of Retired Persons supported a national study of ALFs (Kane and Wilson 1993). The title of this report asked a question: "Assisted Living in the United States: A New Paradigm for Residential Care for Frail Older Persons?" The authors, possibly intending this as a rhetorical question, do not specifically answer it. When Kuhn (1970) introduced the concept of paradigm shifts, he highlighted major changes in the ways that physical scientists think and practice. This concept helps explain why assisted living proponents behave in the ways described in this manuscript. Using Kuhn's terms, in times of change, group members share "symbolic generalizations," commitments, values, and exemplary behaviors that guide their behavior. In the world of assisted living, the social model may be considered a symbolic generalization that annotates the appropriate approach to long-term care. The social model became a subject of gerontological discussions in the late 1970s with the development of community-based care options for frail elders, especially adult day care centers for individuals with physical disabilities and cognitive impairments. In the United States, the On Lok Senior Health Services Center in San Francisco, California, set the standard for the social model approach (Ansak 1983). The social model literature typically presents the concept in relation to the preexisting "medical model" approach to long-term care. For example, the latter treats the individual as "someone with a medical dysfunction requiring treatment," while the social model considers medical diagnosis as only one of several needs, including psychosocial, housing, transportation, and financial needs (Smith and Eggleston 1991:34). The way that Oregon's assisted living proponents define their actions in contrast to nursing homes is informed by this dichotomous view of the social and medical models. The social model ideology provides the framework for the six assisted living values that drive daily practice. (For additional readings about the social model, see Havens 1995; Malmberg and Zarit 1993; Mann et al. 1984; Miller and Wilson 1991; and Monohan 1993.)

METHOD OF INQUIRY

I approached ALFs as a cultural anthropologist might approach a rural community or urban neighborhood, intending to study the daily practices, the language, and the laws governing those who work in assisted living, especially managers and direct care staff members. This approach emphasizes "the direct observation of the activity of the members of a particular social group, and the description and evaluation of such activity" (LeCompte and Goetz 1982:32). Because of my focus on a specific public policy, I describe this research as "an ethnographic policy study." Ethnography provides a means of exploring a group's culture—the beliefs, values, and practices of members. The fact that the group I studied is organized by a state policy definition of six organizational values served as a guiding principle for both observation and analysis. Participant observation and semistructured interviews provided the tools for studying the daily practices of ALF providers. Because the ethnographer is interested in the meanings behind the activities, language, and interactions of culture-sharing groups, these standard ethnographic tools are valuable for examining the lived and local realities of a public program.

Primary data collection included twenty-two months of participant observation in three ALFs and analysis of the state administrative rules that define ALFs. I also participated in six manager training programs (for a total of 144 hours), each approved by Oregon's SDSD. Three sessions were cosponsored by the Oregon Assisted Living Facilities Association (OALFA), and three were run by proprietary organizations. In addition, I conducted both formal and informal interviews with residents, family members, and ALF employees. The three facilities are called, for the purposes of this study, Timber Heights, Spring Hollow, and Valley View. Each is licensed for assisted living in Oregon, located in the same metropolitan county, and owned by a different for-profit company. At the time of data collection, Timber Heights and Valley View were newly opened facilities, and Spring Hollow had been operating for five years. At the new facilities, I could observe how various participants (staff, residents, family members) experienced the facility for the first time, including new staff members and both new and prospective residents. Spring Hollow, the older facility, was included so that I could observe a facility with established policies and procedures. However, differences among the three facilities were minimal and did not factor into this analysis. During the months of participant observation, I assisted with administrative duties, took prospective residents and their families on marketing tours, cooked and served meals, cleaned resident apartments, did laundry, coordinated the admission of Medicaid clients, transported residents to doctor appointments, bought groceries, and helped with social events.

Several precursors for this study provided instruction both substantively and methodologically (Diamond 1992; Gubrium 1975, 1993; Hochschild 1973; Lyman 1993; Ross 1977; Rowles 1978; Rubinstein, Kilbride, and Nagy 1992; Shield 1988). In particular, Gubrium described three worlds that coexisted within a nursing facility, including administration, staff, and residents:

> Each world provides its participants a way of looking at and understanding social life at the Manor. And each has its own logic: its own ideals, sense of justice and fair treatment, method of expedience, prescribed duties, rhetorical style, and proper mode of making decisions. (1975:37)

The present analysis is based largely on observations of interactions between staff members and residents. Although residents and families are the target of the various activities of providers and proponents, they are not necessarily active participants in the creation and maintenance of this social world. In this document, the term *provider* generically describes both managers and direct care staff; *resident* describes people who live in these facilities; and *proponent* describes all persons or groups who promote assisted living, including owners, developers, state employees, and marketing professionals.

The Social Worlds Framework

Shibutani defined the *social worlds* concept as "a culture area, the boundaries of which are set neither by territory nor formal group membership, but by the limits of effective communication" (1955:566). Examples of social worlds include the arts (Becker 1982), medicine (Strauss et al. 1985), neighborhoods (Pratt 1982), science (Clarke 1997; Fujimura 1996), and social movements (Lofland 1996). Any individual might orient toward one or many different social worlds, and social worlds themselves are considered dynamic (Shibutani 1955). Ultimately, the social worlds approach allows one the flexibility to study a social whole through the words and actions of individual members and group activities.

Social Worlds Terms

Two social worlds concepts of particular importance to this analysis include commitment and legitimacy. Becker (1982) identified *commitment* as a basis for social action, and a *social world* as a group with a shared commitment. A social world provides the "meanings, commitments, and perspective in knowledge making both to practices and to the people practicing them" (Fujimura 1996:12). In order to commit to an idea, organization, or movement, individuals must believe in the legitimacy of doing so. What makes an idea, a group, or a social movement legitimate? How believable are proponents' claims? Social worlds, especially new ones, require legitimacy to succeed. Individuals, or groups, compare themselves to others in order to define and legitimize their own behaviors and to ascertain that their actions are appropriate.

In a historical case study of cancer research, Fujimura (1996, 1997) uses social worlds theory to describe how scientists became committed to a particular model that evolved as the dominant (read *legitimate*) approach. I borrow two concepts from her work—the "bandwagon" and "package." In the world of science, "a bandwagon exists when large numbers of people, laboratories, and organizations commit their resources to one approach to a problem" (Fujimura 1997:97). In the present case, assisted living advocates both join and promote the social model bandwagon as the basis for legitimate practice. People, or groups, may join a bandwagon because it offers a compelling "package" of tools, methods, values, or ideologies. These concepts are described below in the context of assisted living.

The Social Model Bandwagon of Assisted Living

A bandwagon describes a rapidly expanding, group-level commitment to one approach to a defined problem. In the present case, the "problem" of interest is that of long-term care: how to respond to the varied needs of chronically ill and disabled elderly persons who can no longer live in their own homes. Risk, as will be described below, is a central concern. The social world of assisted living provides a package of tools, including a common vocabulary, practice standards, and practice techniques. This is not to suggest that all members of this world, including private developers, policy makers, providers, and residents, share the same motives. For some, the motive might be profit, for others, a less costly alternative to institutional care, and for others, a safe place to live. However, most of the groups described here do have an interest in seeing assisted living succeed, regardless of personal motives. Strauss (1982) provides several strategies that social worlds members use to establish and maintain their world. In varying degrees, each of these legitimacy processes is evident in the social world of assisted living, as summarized in the second column of Table 10.1.

The social model provides the ideology for this compelling package. Joining the social model bandwagon can be justified when such tools exist. The package helps to establish and support the social world of assisted living by making the enterprise legitimate. The assisted living vocabulary is an important component of the package, as detailed below.

THE ASSISTED LIVING VOCABULARY

Assisted living proponents have established a unique vocabulary that differs from the terms they attribute to nursing facility employees. Defining how "we're different" also explains that our ways may be "even more legitimate than those of another, earlier, established, or more powerful" social world (Strauss 1982:175). Assisted living proponents emphasize that they are part of a revolution in long-term care, and revolutions require new terms. Ball (1970) uses the phrase "rhetoric of legitimization" to describe the adoption of new vocabularies by specific groups. The social model terms evoke images of places where clients are treated with dignity and respect for their individuality, independence, and privacy. That place is home-like, not institutional. Because assisted living proponents seek to distance themselves from nursing facility practices, converting medical model terms into social model terms affords a foundation for setting legitimate practice standards.

Assisted living managers learn that for the assisted living model to succeed, residents, their families, and health care and social service providers, in addition to facility staff members, must be socialized to the assisted living values. Thus, a culture of assisted living must be established. Through their words and actions, managers and staff teach residents, families, and others what is expected of them. This

TABLE 10.1

Legitimacy strategies of social worlds

Social Worlds Concept	Application in Assisted Living
Claiming worth "A collective definition that certain activities are worth doing, and 'we' are doing them."	Assisted living proponents believe that their social model approach is what seniors demand as consumers and that it will improve the quality of frail elders' lives.
Distancing Social world may form out of an existing world and "gain distance merely by distinctions being readily made between both what others do, and how differently they now talk and even think."	Proponents assert that ALFs differ from new nursing home facilities and make comparisons when explaining what assisted living is. Nursing facilities are institutional, hospital-like settings that do not respect the individual's need for independence, dignity, and choice. In contrast, ALFs provide home-like environments where respect for the "resident's" independence, dignity, and choice are the primary concerns.
Theorizing and conceptualizing "Building an ideological base for defense and attack" and "legitimating conceptualizations."	The "social model of care" serves as the conceptual model that drives and lends credibility to members' actions. Managers can use this model to explain why certain behaviors are not in keeping with the social model focus on resident dignity, choice, and independence.
Standard setting "Questions of authenticity" and "guides for properly performing, collecting, selling, appreciating, making products, improving technology."	Various groups have authority in this arena: State agency staff members act as consultants to ALF managers, monitor facilities for rule compliance, and sponsor educational forums. Professional associations provide training events for managers, nurses , and direct care staff in addition to political activities like lobbying the state legislature.
Boundary setting "What lies definitely within, what without, and what placements are ambiguous? How is all this to be determined or ratified, and by whom?" [Based on Strauss 1982: 174–185.]	In art worlds (Becker, 1982), where boundary lines are less clear, questions about who counts as an artist are more complex. Because ALFs are licensed, who is in and who is not is more obvious. However, state rules leave room for interpretation, leading to complaints that some fcilities provide only "assisted living lite" rather than the more intensive care services originally intended.

culture is reinforced through the adoption of a common vocabulary.

The social model sets the tone for most of what ALF providers say and do. The ways that nursing facilities are represented by and to members of this world provide important lessons for understanding how the social model bandwagon was established and maintained. In an elementary way, the difference between assisted living and nursing facilities can be defined as a simple dichotomy: good–bad or normal–abnormal. The adoption of the new language begins, for managers, with the formal training, but ultimately everyone, from residents to nurses, is expected to use the appropriate terms, listed in Table 10.2. The medical model terms, presented in the first column of Table 10.2, evoke hospital imagery. The first three rows include the terms used to describe various staff members. Those from the medical model, including *Aide, Administrator,* and *Charge, Floor,* or *Ward Nurse,* sound like types who run programs, enforce rules, possibly even enforce care. In comparison, the corresponding social model terms have a corporate flair. To those outside the world of assisted living, a *Personal Service Assistant* might sound like one who is more likely to take a memo than to give a bath. Most of these terms evoke a business atmosphere in which the individual consumer has control and choice over what products or services he or she desires. For example, in nursing homes, *Patients* are either *Admitted* or *Discharged* (rows 12–13), seemingly with very little choice in the matter. Assisted living *Tenants,* on the other hand, presumably either *Move-in* or *Move-out,* according to personal preference. Similarly, the *Charge* or *Floor Nurse* (row 3) sounds like an ever-present force, while the term *Nurse Consultant* suggests an individual who is generally available on the unlikely chance that an ALF tenant should experience a medical need. Nursing facility staff may well take issue with this presentation of terms; however, this information was presented to new managers who were expected to adopt it. From a symbolic interactionist perspective (Blumer 1969), if a manager believes that this difference between assisted living and nursing facilities is real, it will influence his or her behavior.

Over the course of almost two years, I observed many instances of the assisted living vocabulary in practice. For example, within the first few minutes of a resident care staff training at a newly opened facility, the manager offered the following information after two new

TABLE 10.2

Assisted living vocabulary

	"Medical Model" *terms to avoid*	"Social Model" *terms to adopt*
1	Adminsitrator	Manager or Director
2	Aide	Resident Care Assistant, Caregiver, Personal Services Assistant
3	Charge, Floor, or Ward Nurse	Health Care Coordinator or Nurse Consultant
4	Patient	Resident, Tenant, Consumer, or Client
5	Care Plan	Service Plan
6	Patient Chart	Resident Record
7	Chart	Document
8	Bed or Room	Apartment or Unit
9	Facility or Institution	Residence, Community, or Setting
10	Physical Therapy Room	Exercise Studio or Wellness Center
11	Diaper	Incontinence Product or Undergarment
12	Admission	Move-in
13	Discharge	Move-out

employees described their prior nursing home work experience: "Assisted living and nursing facilities are different things. We're more home-like, less institutional, and we emphasize respect, independence, individuality, and choice. We do not have 'patients'; we have 'residents' or 'tenants.' Think of this as an apartment building. It's a new philosophy that we need to start ingraining."

This manager emphasized that the training would cover "walking the talk, no matter what." With these comments, she not only informed the new employees of the "new philosophy" but also suggested that "we" all needed to adopt and "ingrain" it in others. She informed her new employees that they needed to memorize the six values of assisted living, and she provided a mnemonic to help them: HIPDIC. She said to the new employees, "Remember, every morning, chant HIPDIC" (home-like, independence, privacy, dignity, individuality, choice).

Each course instructor in the six training sessions that I observed emphasized that students were about to engage in something completely different, a revolution in long-term care. They described the concepts of the "social model of care" as representing a "paradigm shift" in aging services. Each explained that this shift evolved in direct response to "consumer" rejection of nursing homes that operate under the "medical model." The assisted living industry strives to be something completely different. One instructor said that comparing nursing homes and ALFs is "comparing apples and oranges." He described the development of assisted living as an effort to provide an option for people who are "in between—not totally independent but not bedbound." Another said, "Our goal—I sound like a broken record—is to promote independence. In the medical model, they create dependencies." A final example comes from the marketing director of one company who spoke to participants in a new manager training course:

> I went through assisted living manager training, and at the end, the company director came in and gave this great speech and said, "We're on a mission and journey together" and that "our tenants will die under your care." I came from the hospitality industry where I was just worrying about wine and whether someone found a hair in their salad. Now I'm hoping that somebody I care for is going to die in my care. That five minutes was the most important of the whole week. If I hear a new manager say they have a hard time marketing assisted living, I say, "Go sit in the lobby of a nursing home for one and a half hours. It's a living hell," and that's the alternative.

The above speech sets the tone for how some members in the social world of assisted living are socialized to social model terms and concepts, and the total departure from nursing home practices.

Not only managers and staff members but also residents are expected to learn and use the assisted living terminology. Residents may begin hearing about the differences between assisted living and the more familiar nursing home during their initial visit to a facility. I observed a new resident asking the Timber Heights manager, "How many patients do you have here?" She was told, "We don't have patients here. We have residents." At Valley View, the receptionist told an elderly woman who wanted to tour the facility, "We have a social model here. It's not a medical model." The receptionist did not offer an explanation for her terms, nor did the older woman ask for one. The manager of Timber Heights frequently reminded residents that the women who assisted them with their showers and medications were not "nurses" but "personal service assistants." When some residents complained that the staff members should wear name tags, the manager explained that name tags are not "home-like" and, therefore, not done. Although I observed that most staff members adopted the assisted living vocabulary, there were occasional complaints and jokes about a manager's insistence on particular terms. For example, during a coffee break at Timber Heights, two staff members discussed their take on the need to use specific words. Lucy, a registered nurse with hospital and home health experience, stated that she was "programmed" to use the word *patient* and that she was always "catching" herself before saying "tenant," the preferred term at this facility. She said,

> *Tenant* implies a different kind of relationship, a tenant-landlord relationship, and this is how they get away with having only one person on at night, because in a normal apartment building you don't have people on at night.

She went on to joke about how it is "criminal" to use the word *patient* in assisted living and complained that she had been admonished by the manager several times for her infractions. For the members of social worlds, "perspectives are continually subjected to the test of reality" (Shibutani 1955:569). This hospital-trained nurse attempted to resolve her existing knowledge base with the new reality of assisted living practice.

To the first-time observer, the distinction between the social and the medical models may not be as obvious. For example, state rules require a handicapped-accessible environment. Each apartment must include a bathroom equipped with grab bars, an appropriate turning radius for wheelchair access, a threshold-free shower, and an emergency pull cord. During a resident assessment that I observed, a new tenant asked the nurse consultant whether her new unit had a "raised toilet seat." The nurse explained, "No, we're a social model, not a medical model, and so we don't provide things like that because not everyone needs it." This reference to the social model went without comment from this new assisted living resident. However, the nurse's identification of a raised toilet seat as an object belonging to the medical model provides another example of how assisted living staff legitimize some things as social while treating other similar objects as medical. The nurse had been trained to define only those objects required by state rules as legitimate elements of the social model. A raised toilet seat somehow crossed an invisible line into the medical model. ALFs are not required to purchase durable medical equipment; however, this nurse could have referred this resident to local medical equipment providers. The fact that she did not suggests that either she was unaware of such providers or she believed that she had done her job by keeping to the social model paradigm. However, in this case, a raised seat would have served as an important prosthetic to a woman afflicted with severe rheumatoid arthritis.

ASSISTED LIVING PRACTICES

The second part of the social model–inspired package includes practice standards and techniques, both those required by state rules and others that have been developed by the organizations that provide new manager training. Social worlds require standards for action and ways of evaluating whether members have met these standards. Questions of authenticity may be raised. Is this member performing by the standards? Do the staff members at that facility embody the commitment to the social model of care we all share? If so, they might be used as an example for others to emulate. If not, do their practices threaten the stability of this social world?

As mentioned, state rules define minimum standards, but these standards leave room for interpretation. During ALF manager training workshops, the instructors define the principles that future managers must follow. The specific standards and techniques used by assisted living providers revolve around a resident assessment process driven by the social model bandwagon. Within the social model, this assessment is intended not to emphasize functional limitations, a practice attributed to nursing facilities, but rather to identify resident strengths, choice, privacy needs, and potential risks. An important distinction between nursing facility and ALF practices concerns the issue of risk. Assisted living practitioners do not attempt to prevent all possible risks, because risk is defined as a normal part of adult life. Instead, assisted living practices are designed to negotiate and manage risks associated with impaired physical and cognitive function, as discussed in more detail in the following section.

Case studies are the featured instructional tool in both the initial manager training and continuing education seminars. The challenge of balancing independence with risk is a major concern. For example, should a staff person monitor each resident to verify that medications are taken? Should staff members check on individuals who do not attend a meal? How do you encourage a person who does not want to take a shower to do so anyway? What are the responsibilities to the son who assumes that his mother is safe and not lying on her apartment floor for six hours before being discovered? One instructor noted that assisted living is not a "safe deposit box" and that "we can't monitor people all the time." We have to balance "concern versus monitoring."

Within the discussion of how to incorporate the values are examples of what not to do. One instructor referred to the "recent proliferation of 'assisted living lite,'" which she described as providers who merely want to "provide a little help with bathing." Other examples of what not to do include "do not knock and walk" into a resident's apartment, do not close the dining room between meals because that is an important part of each individual's home, do not require residents to come to the medications storage area for their medications, and do not use a public address system to announce resident needs.

Negotiated Services and Managed Risk

Risk is an important concept in the social model of care as explained by the instructor of one manager training course: "Risk defines who you are. Why would you think you can define a risk for someone in your community? That's defining that person, and we have no right to define these people. In the medical model, doctors' orders define the person. Things have changed." Two specific ALF techniques for managing problems posed by risky behaviors include the Negotiated Service Agreement (NSA) and the Managed Risk Agreement (MRA) (Kapp and Wilson 1995). For a detailed discussion of these strategies, see Carder (1999). Both practices represent organizational efforts to implement the state rules requiring resident choice, privacy, independence, individuality, and dignity. An NSA is the outcome of a resident assessment; it is a formalized process in which the provider and the resident negotiate what personal services will be provided, when, how often, and by whom. A reasonable comparison is to the Minimum Data Set (MDS) used by nursing homes. While the MDS documents that a given patient requires, for example, bathing assistance, the NSA documents that the resident prefers to take showers on Tuesday and Friday mornings between seven and eight, that she requires stand-by assist only but needs help applying skin lotion, and who will provide that care.

The MRA describes a process by which a resident who engages in risky practices, as identified by a staff member, family member, or health care provider, signs an agreement whereby he or she indicates understanding of risks and agrees to accept responsibility for negative results. This process might be initiated when an NSA breaks down. These tools are an important part of the social model package because they further distinguish assisted living from nursing facilities by offering organizational strategies for managing risk, a common problem in long-term care (Kane, Kane, and Ladd 1998; Kapp and Wilson 1995). Based on my observations of manager training programs and daily practice in three facilities, I summarize two categories of risk that providers must address in training and practice: risks to residents' health and safety and the risks particular to operating an ALF.

The first category includes two types, risks the individual poses to himself or herself and risks that person poses to others. The first type is exemplified by what I call "the case of the diabetic who ate cake," presented at each of the training sessions I attended. The following is an abstraction of the various training representations:

Mrs. Wilson is an eighty-six-year old tenant with insulin-dependent diabetes and a physician-recommended diabetic diet. Yet, Mrs. Wilson insists on eating cake, cookies, and other sugary deserts. What should you and your staff members do? In a nursing facility, Mrs. Wilson would not be given the option of eating cake. In the ALF, the provider must balance respect for the individual's autonomy and rights as an adult to make choices, even risky ones, with the institutional responsibility to see that this individual does not cause harm to herself or others. Should the staff prohibit her from eating cake? How can staff control what food items she has in her apartment or while on social outings? What if she has dementia? Participants in the manager training sessions consider such dilemmas in preparation for work as an assisted living manager. Responses include targeting family members and other health care professionals to support Mrs. Wilson's independence but also preserve her health. An MRA might be implemented in order to define the rights and responsibilities of the resident and her care-givers. Not all ALF staff members, especially those with a medical background, agree that diabetic residents should be permitted to eat inappropriate foods. For example, the Spring Hollow nurse complained to me that it made her very uncomfortable to see residents with diabetes eating pie for dessert.

In addition to risks that the individual might face because of his or her own actions are risks that one resident's behaviors present to others. The example of Ralph, a former resident at Timber Heights, will be familiar to readers who have spent time in a long-term care facility. Ralph was physically capable but cognitively impaired. He entered other residents' apartments and was sexually suggestive, verbally abusive, and intimidating. He struck one staff member and stomped on the foot of another. Several of the female residents feared Ralph, but a few either chose not to or could not remember to lock their apartment doors. A week spent in a gero-psychiatric ward did not alleviate Ralph's behaviors, and the manager asked his family to relocate him. In this case, an MRA was not possible because of Ralph's cognitive impairment. Examples like this one, and others involving potentially risky behaviors such as smoking, cooking, and burning candles, were discussed during manager training. Providers must think of ways to balance the rights of the individual against the well-being of the others.

The final risk category, operating a facility, also includes two types—traditional liability concerns and the more subtle risks associated with maintaining balance in a community of disparate individuals. Liability issues were a topic of concern during manager training programs. The MRA responds to matters such as "the diabetic who ate cake," although it is not a tested legal document (Kapp and Wilson 1995). Providers must consider the rights of the individual to make even foolish choices against the need of the organization to avoid liability. The second type of risk, also discussed during training, requires achieving a balance between the business goal of maintaining full occupancy against retaining residents whose behaviors are offensive to others. The following text is from a manager training document:

"What would you do if a resident ate in such a way as to gross other residents out so badly that they wanted to leave?" This example portrays the delicate balance between responding to one resident's needs without disrupting the community or even losing other paying clients. While a resident's "gross" eating style might not pose a health or safety risk, it does represent a risk to both the business and the community if some residents choose to move. In such cases, managers are instructed to consider the values. Because the facility represents "home" to the residents, individuals should have the choice of not inviting offensive guests to the table. However, providers are caught in a bind because, in this case, the offensive guest also considers this place home.

Examples from Spring Hollow and Timber Heights highlight the complexity of this issue. At Spring Hollow, residents complained about two women, both with some form of cognitive impairment, who made a "mess" during meals. These women poured water and ketchup onto their dinner plates, removed flatware from their dining companions, and put food in their coffee cups. The dining room staff members moved these women to different tables, and each time they were rejected by the other residents. Eventually, they installed a TV tray in Mrs. Hines apartment and served her meals there. At Timber Heights, Mrs. Reese's record indicated a diagnosis of "dementia," although my conversations with her case worker and son indicated a lifetime of mental illness. Over time, she came to experience what assisted living providers call "problem incontinence." She was willing to bathe, but Mrs. Reese emitted an aroma offensive to several residents who complained to the manager. Over several months, the staff members attempted several strategies, including increased frequency of showers and laundering, and the use of various incontinence products. Finally, the manager asked Mrs. Reese to move, complaining that the facility furnishings and carpets were being ruined.

Although it is not defined in the state rules, Oregon's SDSD, like many state agencies, expects ALFs to allow residents to "age in place" (Kane and Wilson 1993; Mollica et al. 1995). Providers must weigh the risks of accepting or retaining residents who might exhibit behaviors that current or prospective residents find intolerable. They must balance the need to fill an apartment versus leaving it empty, and they must consider their staffing levels—do they employ enough personnel to care for an individual who is severely disabled? In contrast to the earlier risk types, providers do not have clear strategies such as the MRA available for managing such dilemmas.

DISCUSSION

What are the benefits of a social world of assisted living to members of this world? What are the implications of depending on a social model ideology? These questions must be pursued in relation to providers, residents, and the broader long-term care arena. First, what are the benefits? In Oregon, providers act on the basis that the social model is the method that works best for disabled and chronically ill seniors, adopting a vocabulary and practices designed to meet the ideals attributed to the social model. Because of the commitment that current members have to this model, those new to this world simply join the bandwagon. Thus, the social model, along with its package of values and practice techniques, becomes a phenomenon with its own structure and force. A bandwagon has been created and is now sustained by the very activities that created it in the first place. What difference does this make in daily practice?

Assisted living providers benefit from the products of a stable social world. They may legitimately claim worth to what they do, as opposed to what, for example, nursing home providers do. In the package of values and practice techniques, they have a strong ideological basis for defining and defending most of their actions. However, it is possible that they face frustrations in their daily efforts to implement the social model, as the examples of the nurse who was "programmed" to saying "patient" and the nurse who could not accept the risk of persons with diabetes eating sugary desserts. Some providers have difficulty resolving such incongruent situations. In such cases, a nursing background may be a liability rather than a strength in this world.

What are the benefits of a defined social world of assisted living to residents? Possibly, the greatest benefit to residents is the viable alternative to institutional care. The social model values have, in many cases, been translated into products that consumers prefer. For example, the value of privacy has resulted in private apartments with individual bathrooms, temperature controls, and locking doors. However, the strong commitment of ALF proponents to the social model ideology spells an uncertain future for residents whose needs progress into the medical realm.

What are the benefits to the long-term care arena? Based on this research, it is clear that public policy goals will be adopted by private industry if clear legitimacy strategies are provided. The social model bandwagon, with its package of values and tools, makes it easy for those new to senior housing to enter this industry. Of course, this might be a double-edged sword as increasing numbers of hospitality and real estate corporations enter and then abandon the long-term care arena. Understanding this bandwagon and the associated package is critical to understanding assisted living practices. Future efforts to evaluate, regulate, and research assisted living practices should be informed by an appreciation of these foundational principles. From a phenomenological standpoint, one could say that the social model, with its six values, represents the essence of assisted living. Evaluators accustomed to outcomes that can be quantified and measured will need to seek other tools to ascertain whether assisted living residents are receiving the appropriate amounts of independence, dignity, and choice.

What are the implications of employing the social model in this world of assisted living? Defining some elements as *social* and others as *medical* has implications for both providers and residents. As Kane, Kane, and Ladd (1998) note, once a legislative and organizational commitment has been made to principles such as the six assisted living values, programs may then face resistance to change or problems implementing other important goals that might conflict with the values. For example, do larger public policy goals of improving functioning and supporting aging in place conflict with the social model? Is there room for medical model practices within a social model ideology? Kane and Wilson (1993) found that many public officials cannot accept the idea that disabled older persons will be at risk in facilities supported, in part, by public monies. Public officials tend to err on the side of caution by eliminating as many risks as possible, even at the expense of resident independence and autonomy. Based on my research, these issues remain central to the people doing the work of assisted living. At this point, individuals who represent key groups internal and external to each ALF are still actively interpreting and constructing this social world.

The implications for residents are, at this point, relatively uncertain. Clearly some residents "fit" better into the social model than do others. But what determines the degree of *fit?* As the above examples indicate, some residents do not fit into the social model, and providers currently lack the tools for making decisions about residents whose behaviors are offensive, but not dangerous, to the larger community. The tendency of assisted living proponents to define elements of the medical model as negative, in relation to the social model ideology, implies that people who require medical care have failed in some way. It feeds into gerontophobic views held by either residents or staff members. Finally, of additional interest is whether or not the social model values (privacy, independence) are culturally appropriate to people who do not hold such Western beliefs.

This article provides a brief lesson in continuity and change in long-term care. Since the 1960s, nursing homes have served as the primary provider for very old and disabled persons who can no longer remain in the community, and ALFs represent a significant departure from nursing homes practice. Although residential housing for disabled seniors is not a new concept in the past century, the package offered by assisted living proponents is new. Assisted living represents a shift in thinking about how to approach long-term care. It is a world in transition, and participants are actively engaged in sorting out dilemmas such as the ones presented by the "diabetic who ate cake." Assisted living proponents continue to seek legitimacy, perfect methods, and market their concepts to a larger audience. The social worlds perspective tells us that as more ALFs are developed and as other states and countries establish public policies and rules, legitimacy claims will be called into question, boundaries may not remain stable, and the allegiances of subgroups may waiver. ALFs developed in the next decades may include "lite" versions, as well as extended care models that meet the needs of all but the most medically unstable individuals. Challenges to a stable social world boundary may come from within or outside. Although the values provide strong symbols for members of this social world of assisted living, the stability of this package over time remains to be seen.

Finally, a number of research questions are raised by this exploration. One set of questions should be pursued that addresses the resident perspective. How involved are residents in the NSA and MRA process? What is the role of family? In what ways are ancillary health care providers involved? How do residents with cognitive impairment take part in these processes? A second set of policy questions may be asked. What is the legal responsibility of the assisted living provider when an MRA fails? What level of risk can be tolerated? A third set of questions might pursue practice concerns such as the training of managers and direct care staff. Do these individuals adopt, adapt, or subvert the social model principles? Finally, evaluative research should assess whether ALF providers are actually achieving their stated goals of implementing a social model of long-term care.

ACKNOWLEDGMENTS

This research was funded by a grant from the Agency for Healthcare Research and Quality (No. R03HS09886) to the author. Preparation of this manuscript was supported by a fellowship through the AHRQ-sponsored National Research Service Award to Oregon Health Sciences University. I would like to thank David L. Morgan of Portland State University for his editorial and conceptual assistance on this and earlier drafts.

Note

1. Reprinted from *Journal of Aging Studies,* Vol. 16, 2002: 1–18, copyright 2002, with permission from Elsevier Science.

References

Agich, G. J.

1993   *Autonomy and Long-Term Care.* New York: Oxford University Press.

Aneshensel, C. S., L. I. Pearlin, J. T. Mullan, S. H. Zant, and C. J. Whitlatch

1995   *Profiles in Caregiving: The Unexpected Career.* San Diego, Cal.: Academic Press.

Ansak, M. L.

1983   On Lok Senior Health Services—A Community Care Organization for Dependent Adults. *Pride Institute Journal of Long-Term Home Health Care* 2 (7):12.

Anspach, R.

1993   *Deciding Who Lives: Fateful Choices in the Intensive-Care Nursery.* Berkeley: University of California Press.

Arluck, A., and J. Peterson

1981   Accidental Medicalization of Old Age and Its Social Control Implications. In *Dimensions: Aging, Culture, and Health,* edited by C. Fry. New York: Praeger.

Baba, M.

1986   *Business and Industrial Anthropology: An Overview.* Washington, D.C.: American Anthropological Association.

REFERENCES

Bachelard, G.
1994   *The Poetics of Space.* 1964. Reprint, Boston: Beacon Press.

Ball, D. W.
1970   An Abortion Clinic Ethnography. In *Social Psychology through Symbolic Interaction,* edited by G. P. Stone and H. A. Farberman, pp. 196–206. Waltham, Mass.: Ginn Blaisdell.

Becker, G., and S. Kaufman
1995   Managing an Uncertain Illness Trajectory in Old Age: Patients' and Physicians' Views of Stroke. *Medical Anthropology Quarterly* 9:165–187.

Becker, H. S.
1982   *Artworlds.* Berkeley: University of California Press.

Beckett, S.
1970   *Malone Dies.* 1956. Reprint, New York: Grove Press.

Begley, C. E.
1993   Cost Containment and Conflicts of Interest in the Care of the Elderly. In *Facing Limits: Ethics and Health Care for the Elderly,* edited by G. A. Winslow and J. R. Walters. Boulder, Col.: Westview Press.

Berdes, C.
1987   The Modest Proposal Nursing Home: Dehumanizing Characteristics of Nursing Homes in Memoirs of Nursing Home Residents. *Journal of Applied Gerontology* 6 (4):372–388.

Berry, W.
1990   *What Are People For?* San Francisco: North Point.
1999   *The Memory of Old Jack.* 1974. Reprint, Washington, D.C.: Counterpoint.

Besdine, R. W.
1983   Decisions to Withhold Treatment from Nursing Home Residents. *Journal of the American Geriatrics Society* 31:602–606.

Blackman, M.
1994   *Death Comes to the Anthropologist: Reflections on the Haida Mortuary Potlatch.* Presentation to the American Anthropological Association Annual Meeting, Atlanta, Ga.

Blumer, H.
1969   *Symbolic Interactionism: Perspective and Method.* Englewood Cliffs, N.J.: Prentice-Hall.

Boon, J. A.
2001   Kenneth Burke's "True Irony": A Model for Ethnography, Still. In *Irony in Action,* edited by J. W. Fernandez and M. T. Huber. Chicago: University of Chicago Press.

Bowers, B. J.

1988   Family Perceptions of Care in a Nursing Home. *The Gerontologist* 28 (3):361–368.

Bowers, B., and M. Becker

1992   Nurse's Aides in Nursing Homes: The Relationship between Organization and Quality. *The Gerontologist* 32 (3):360–366.

Bowker, L.

1982   *Humanizing Institutions for the Aged.* Lexington, Mass.: Lexington Books.

Brody, E.

1985   The Social Aspects of Nursing Home Care. In *The Teaching Nursing Home,* edited by E. L. Schneider, C. J. Wendland, A. W. Zimmer, N. List, and M. Ory. New York: Raven Press.

1986   The Role of the Family in Nursing Homes. In *Mental Illness in Nursing Homes: Agenda for Research,* edited by M. S. Harper and B. D. Lebowitz. Washington, D.C.: US Government Printing Office.

Brody, E., N. Dempsey, and R. Pruchno

1990   Mental Health of Sons and Daughters of the Institutionalized Aged. *The Gerontologist* 30:212–219.

Buckwalter, K. C., and G. R. Hall

1987   Families of the Institutionalized Older Adult: A Neglected Resource. In *Aging, Health, and Family: Long-Term Care,* edited by T. H. Brubaker. Newbury Park, Cal.: Sage Publications.

Burger, S. G., and C. C. Williams

1996   Individualized Care. Guest editorial in a special March issue of *Journal of Gerontological Nursing* 22 (3):5.

Burke, K.

1969   *A Grammar of Motives.* Berkeley: University of California Press.

1973   *The Philosophy of Literary Form.* Berkeley: University of California Press.

Burner, S. T., D. R. Waldo, and D. R. McKusick

1992   National Health Expenditures Projections through 2030. *Health Care Financing Review* 14:1–29.

Burnside, R. N.

1996   Life Review and Reminiscence in Nursing Practice. In *Aging and Biography: Explorations in Adult Development,* edited by J. E. Birren, G. M. Kenyon, J. Ruth, J. J. F. Schroots, and T. Svensson. New York: Springer Publishing Company.

Burton, J. R.

1994   The Evolution of Nursing Homes into Comprehensive Geriatrics Centers: A Perspective. *Journal of the American Geriatric Society* 42:794–796.

REFERENCES

Butler, R. N.
1975   *Why Survive? Being Old in America.* San Francisco: Harper and Row.

Cairl, R., J. Kosberg, N. Henderson, and E. Pfeiffer
1991   *Special Care for Alzheimer's Disease Patients: An Exploratory Study of Dementia-Specific Care Units.* Tampa: University of South Florida, Suncoast Gerontology Center.

Callahan, D.
1987   *Setting Limits: Medical Goals in an Aging Society.* New York: Simon and Schuster.

1993   Intolerable Necessity: Limiting Health Care for the Elderly. In *Facing Limits: Ethics and Health Care for the Elderly,* edited by G. A. Winslow and J. R. Walters. Boulder, Col.: Westview Press.

Cannon, W.
1939   *The Wisdom of the Body.* New York: W. W. Norton.

Carder, P. C.
1999   The Value of Independence in Old Age. Ph.D. diss., College of Urban and Public Affairs, Portland State University.

Charrow, R. P.
1991   Controlling Health-Care Costs: A Major Problem in Need of an Enlightened Solution. *The Journal of NIH Research* 3 (3):74–77.

Clark, L. W., and K. Witte
1991   Nature and Efficacy of Communication Management in Alzheimer's Disease. In *Dementia and Communication,* edited by R. Lubinski. Philadelphia: Decker.

Clarke, A. E.
1997   A Social Worlds Research Adventure: The Case of Reproductive Science. In *Grounded Theory in Practice,* edited by A. Strauss and J. Corbin, pp. 63–94. Thousand Oaks, Cal.: Sage Publications.

Clifford, J.
1986   On Ethnographic Allegory. In *Writing Culture: The Poetics and Politics of Ethnography,* edited by J. Clifford and G. E. Marcus. Berkeley: University of California Press.

Clifford, J., and G. E. Marcus, eds.
1986   *Writing Culture: The Poetics and Politics of Ethnography.* Berkeley: University of California Press.

Cohen, G. D.
1994   Forward: Toward New Models of Care. *Alzheimer's Disease and Associated Disorders* 8 (Supplement 1):S2–S4.

Cohn, M. D.

1988   Consultation Strategies with Families. In *Mental Health Consultation in Nursing Homes,* edited by M. A. Smyer, M. D. Cohn, and D. Brannon. New York: New York University Press.

Cohn, M. D., and G. M. Jay

1988   Families in Long-Term Care Settings. In *Mental Health Consultation in Nursing Homes,* edited by M. A. Smyer, M. D. Cohn, and D. Brannon. New York: New York University Press.

Cole, T. R.

1992   *The Journey of Life: A Cultural History of Aging in America.* New York: Cambridge University Press.

Coleman, M., S. Looney, J. O'Brien, C. Pastorino, and C. Turner

2002   The Eden Alternative: Findings after 1 Year of Implementation. *Journal of Gerontology: Medical Sciences* 57A:M422–427.

Cook, J. B.

1984   Reminiscing: How It Can Help Confused Nursing Home Residents. Social Case Work. *The Journal of Contemporary Social Work* (February):90–93.

Coons, D., ed.

1991   *Specialized Dementia Care Units.* Baltimore, Md.: Johns Hopkins University Press.

Cranford, R. E.

1988   The Persistent Vegetative State: The Medical Reality (Getting the Facts Straight). *Hastings Center Report* 18:27–32.

Davidson, B., R. Laan, M. Hirschfield, A. Norberg, E. Pitman, L. J. Ying

1990   Ethical Reasoning Associated with the Feeding of Terminally Ill Elderly Cancer Patients. *Cancer Nursing* 13 (5):286–292.

Dempsey, N., and R. Pruchno

1993   The Family's Role in the Nursing Home: Predictors of Technical and Non-technical Assistance. *Journal of Gerontological Social Work* 21:127–145.

Diamond, T.

1988   Social Policy and Everyday Life in Nursing Homes: A Critical Ethnography. In *The Worth of Women's Work: A Qualitative Synthesis,* edited by A. Stratham, E. Miller, and H. Mauksch, pp. 39–55. Albany: State University of New York Press.

1992   *Making Gray Gold: Narratives of Nursing Home Care.* 1986. Reprint, Chicago: University of Chicago Press.

1995   The Culture of Care in a Nursing Home: Effects of a Medicalized Model of Long Term Care. In *The Culture of Long Term Care: Nursing Home Ethnography,* edited by J. N. Henderson and M. D. Vesperi. New York: Bergin and Garvey Publishers, Inc.

REFERENCES

Dorland
1985   *Dorland's Illustrated Medical Dictionary*. 26th edition. Philadelphia: Saunders.

Douglas, M.
1966   *Purity and Danger*. London: Routledge and Kegan Paul.

Dowd, J.
1975   Aging as Exchange: A Preface to Theory. *Journal of Gerontology* 30 (5):584–595.

Duncan, M. J., and D. L. Morgan
1994   Sharing the Caring: Family Caregivers' Views of Their Relationships with Nursing Home Staff. *The Gerontologist* 34 (2):235–244.

Dunlop, B. D.
1979   *The Growth of Nursing Home Care*. Lexington, Mass: Lexington Books.

Eisenberg, L., and A. Kleinman, eds.
1980   *The Relevance of Social Science for Medicine*. Boston: Reid.

Erikson, E. H., J. M. Erikson, and H. Q. Kivnick
1986   *Vital Involvement in Old Age*. New York: W. W. Norton.

Estes, C. L., and E. A. Binney
1989   The Biomedicalization of Aging: Dangers and Dilemmas. *The Gerontologist* 29:587–596.

Everard, K., G. D. Rowles, and D. M. High
1994   Nursing Home Room Changes: Toward a Decision-Making Model. *The Gerontologist* 34 (4):520–527.

Farmer, B. C.
1996   *A Nursing Home and Its Organizational Climate: An Ethnography*. Westport, Conn.: Auburn House.

Fernandez, J. W., and M. T. Huber
2001   Introduction: The Anthropology of Irony. In *Irony in Action,* edited by J. W. Fernandez and M. T. Huber. Chicago: University of Chicago Press.

Fischer, M. M. J.
1986   Ethnicity and the Post-Modern Arts of Memory. In *Writing Culture: The Poetics and Politics of Ethnography*, edited by J. Clifford and G. E. Marcus. Berkeley: University of California Press.

Foner, N.
1994   *The Caregiving Dilemma: Work in an American Nursing Home*. Berkeley: University of California Press.

Foucault, M.
1979   *Discipline and Punish: The Birth of the Prison*. New York: Vintage.

Fujimura, J. H.
1996   *Crafting Science: A Sociohistory of the Quest for the Genetics of Cancer.*
         Cambridge: Harvard University Press.
1997   Cancer Research: Where Social Worlds Meet. In *Grounded Theory in
         Practice,* edited by A. Strauss and J. Corbin, pp. 95–130. Thousand Oaks,
         Cal.: Sage Publications.

Gard, R.
1992   *Beyond the Thin Line: A Personal Journey into the World of Alzheimer's Disease.*
         Madison, Wis.: Prairie Oak Press.

Geertz, C.
1973   Thick Description: Toward an Interpretive Theory of Culture. In *The
         Interpretation of Culture: Selected Essays of Clifford Geertz,* pp. 3–30. New York:
         Basic Books.

Glassie, H.
1995   Home-Making: A Cross-Cultural Perspective on the Conversion of Space
         into Place. A lecture given in the Experience of Place Series, Waldron Arts
         Center, Bloomington, Ind.

Good, B. J.
1994   *Medicine, Rationality and Experience.* Boston: Cambridge University Press.

Goffman, E.
1961   *Asylums: Essays on the Social Situation of Mental Patients and Other Inmates.*
         Garden City, N.J.: Anchor Books.

Green, B. S.
1993   *Gerontology and the Construction of Old Age.* New York: Aldine de Gruyter.

Groger, L.
1994   Decision as Process: A Conceptual Model of Black Elders' Nursing Home
         Placement. *Journal of Aging Studies* 8 (1):77–94.
1995   Health Trajectories and Long-Term Care Choices: What Stories Told by
         Informants Can Tell Us. In *The Culture of Long Term Care: Nursing Home
         Ethnography,* edited by J. N. Henderson and M. D. Vesperi, pp. 55–69.
         Westport, Conn.: Bergin and Garvey Publishers, Inc.

Gubrium, J. F.
1975   *Living and Dying at Murray Manor.* New York: St. Martin's Press.
1986   *Oldtimers and Alzheimer's: The Descriptive Organization of Senility.* Greenwich,
         Conn.: JAI Press.
1991   *The Mosaic of Care: Frail Elderly and Their Families in the Real World.* New
         York: Springer.
1993   *Speaking of Life: Horizons of Meaning for Nursing Home Residents.* New York:
         Aldine de Gruyter.

1995   Perspective and Story in Nursing Home Ethnography. In *The Culture of Long Term Care: Nursing Home Ethnography*, edited by J. N. Henderson and M. D. Vesperi. New York: Bergin and Garvey Publishers, Inc.

Gubrium, J. F., and J. A. Holstein
1990   *What Is Family?* Mountain View, Cal.: Mayfield Publishing Company.

Haber, C.
1983   *Beyond Sixty-Five: The Dilemma of Old Age in America's Past.* Cambridge: Cambridge University Press.

Haight, B. K., Y. Michel, and S. Hendrix
1998   Life Review: Preventing Despair in Newly Relocated Nursing Home Residents: Short- and Long-Term Effects. *International Journal of Aging and Human Development* 47 (2):119–142.

Hall, G., and K. Buckwalter
1986   *Professionally Lowered Stress Threshold.* Iowa City: University of Iowa Hospitals and Clinics.

Harrington, C.
1984   Public Policy and the Nursing Home Industry. In *Readings in the Political Economy of Aging*, edited by M. Minkler and C. E. Estes. New York: Baywood Publishing Company.
1990   Wages and Benefits of Nursing Personnel in Nursing Homes: Correcting the Inequities. *Nursing Economic$.* (6):378–385.
1995   The Nursing Home Industry: Public Policy in the 1990's. In *Perspectives in Medical Sociology*, 2nd edition, edited by P. Brown. Prospect Heights, Ill.: Waveland Press Inc.

Hasselkus, B. R.
1992   The Family Caregiver as Interpreter in the Geriatric Medical Interview. *Medical Anthropology Quarterly* 6 (3):288–304.

Havens, B.
1995   Long-Term Care Diversity within the Care Continuum. *Canadian Journal on Aging* Summer 14 (2):245–262.

Hazan, H.
1980   *The Limbo People: A Study of the Constitution of the Time Universe among the Aged.* London: Routledge and Kegan Paul.
1992   *Managing Change in Old Age: The Control of Meaning in an Institutional Setting.* Albany: State University of New York Press.

Heidegger, M.
1971   *Poetry, Language, Thought.* New York: Harper and Row.

Heiselman, T., and L. S. Noelker
1991   Enhancing Mutual Respect among Nursing Assistants, Residents, and Residents' Families. *The Gerontologist* 31 (4):552–555.

Henderson, J. N.

1981   Nursing Home Housekeepers: Indigenous Agents of Psychosocial Support. *Human Organization* 40:300–305.

1987a   Dementia-Specific Care Units in Nursing Homes: What's So Special? Do They Work? In *The Family Caregiver: Lifeline to the Frail Patient,* edited by J. N. Henderson and E. Pfeiffer. Tampa: University of South Florida, Suncoast Gerontology Center.

1987b   Mental Disorders in the Elderly: Dementia and Its Sociocultural Correlates. In *The Elderly as Modern Pioneers,* edited by P. Silverman. Bloomington: Indiana University Press.

1987c   Suncoast Gerontology Center Studies Alzheimer's Dementia–Specific Survey. *Pulse* 6:10.

1994a   Care of the Elderly in Dementia-Specific Care Units. In *International Perspectives on Healthcare for the Elderly,* edited by G. Stopp, Jr. New York: Peter Lang.

1994b   The Culture of Special Care Units: An Anthropological Perspective on Ethnographic Research in Nursing Home Settings. *Alzheimer's Disease and Associated Disorders* 8 (Supplement 1):S410–S416.

1994c   Bed, Body, and Soul: The Job of the Nursing Home Aide. *Generations* 18:20–22.

1994d   Protecting the Frustrated Eloper. *The Journal of Long-Term Care Administration* 21:13–14.

1995   The Culture of Care in a Nursing Home: Effects of a Medicalized Model of Long Term Care. In *The Culture of Long Term Care: Nursing Home Ethnography,* edited by J. N. Henderson and M. D. Vesperi, pp. 37–54. Westport, Conn.: Bergin and Garvey Publishers, Inc.

Henderson, J. N., and L. C. Henderson

2002   Cultural Construction of Disease: A "Supernormal" Construct of Dementia in an American Indian Tribe. *Journal of Cross-Cultural Gerontology* 17:197–212.

Henderson, J. N., and M. D. Vesperi, eds.

1995   *The Culture of Nursing Home Care: Nursing Home Ethnography.* Westport, Conn.: Bergin and Garvey Publishers, Inc.

Henderson, J. N., and M. Whaley

1997   Cultural Factors in Geriatric Rehabilitation: Ethnic-Specific and Generational Cultures. *Journal of Geriatric Rehabilitation* 12 (3):1–9.

Henry, J.

1963   *Culture Against Man.* New York: Random House.

Herskovits, E.

1995   Struggling over Subjectivity: Debates about the "Self" and Alzheimer's Disease. *Medical Anthropology Quarterly* 9:146–164.

Hertz, R.

1960   A Contribution to the Study of the Collective Representation of Death. In *Death and the Right Hand*. 1928. Reprint, Glencoe, Ill.: Free Press.

High, D. M., and G. D. Rowles

1994   Who Makes Decisions for Nursing Home Residents When They Can't: Understanding Progressive Surrogacy. Paper presented at the 47th Annual National Meeting of the Gerontological Society of America. Atlanta, Ga.

1995   Nursing Home Residents, Families, and Decision Making: Toward an Understanding of Progressive Surrogacy. *Journal of Aging Studies* 9 (2):101–117.

Hirschfeld, M., and L. Ziv

1989   When a Demented Patient Refuses Food: Ethical Arguments of Nurses in Israel. *Palliative Medicine* 4 (1):25–30.

Hiss, T.

1990   *The Experience of Place*. New York: Random House.

Hochschild, A. R.

1973   *The Unexpected Community: Portrait of an Old Age Subculture*. Berkeley: University of California Press.

Hoffman, S., and C. Platt

2000   *Comforting the Confused*. New York: Springer.

Holmes, D., D. Lindemann, M. Ory, and J. Teresi

1994   Measurement of Service Units and Costs of Care for Persons with Dementia in Special Care Units. *Alzheimer's Disease and Associated Disorders* 8 (Supplement 1):S328–S340.

Holstein, J. A., and J. F. Gubrium

1995   *The Active Interview*. Thousand Oaks, Cal.: Sage Publications.

Hornum, B.

1995   Assessing Types of Residential Accommodations for the Elderly: Liminality and Communitas. In *The Culture of Long Term Care: Nursing Home Ethnography*, edited by J. N. Henderson and M. D. Vesperi, pp. 151–164. Westport, Conn.: Bergin and Garvey Publishers, Inc.

Illich, I.

1978   *Toward a History of Needs*. New York: Pantheon.

Institute of Medicine

1986   *Improving the Quality of Care in Nursing Homes*. Washington, D.C.: National Academy Press.

Jackson, M.

1995   *At Home in the World*. Durham, N.C.: Duke University Press.

Johnson, C. L., and L. A. Grant
1985   *The Nursing Home in American Society.* Baltimore, Md.: Johns Hopkins
        University Press.

Jones, A.
2002   The National Nursing Home Survey: 1999 Summary. National Center for
        Health Statistics. *Vital Health Stat* 13 (152).

Jorm, A. F.
1990   *The Epidemiology of Alzheimer's Disease and Related Disorders.* New York:
        Chapman and Hall.

Kahana, E.
1982   A Congruence Model of Person-Environment Interaction. In *Aging and the
        Environment: Theoretical Approaches,* edited by M. P. Lawton, P. G. Windley,
        and T. O. Byerts. New York: Springer-Verlag.

Kane, R. A.
1988   Assessing Quality in Nursing Homes. *Clinics in Geriatric Medicine* 4:655–666.

**Kane, R. A., A. L. Kaplan, E. K. Urv-Wong, I. C. Freeman, M. A. Aroskar,
and M. Fitch**
1997   Everyday Matters in the Lives of Nursing Home Residents: Wish for and
        Perception of Choice and Control. *Journal of the American Geriatrics Society*
        45:1086–1093.

Kane, R. L., and R. A. Kane
1978   Care of the Aged: Old Problems in Need of New Solutions. *Science* 200
        (May 26):913–19.

Kane, R. A., R. L. Kane, and R. C. Ladd
1998   *The Heart of Long-Term Care.* New York: Oxford University Press.

Kane, R. A., and K. B. Wilson
1993   *Assisted Living in the United States: A New Paradigm for Residential Care for
        Frail Older Persons?* Washington, D.C.: American Association of Retired
        Persons.

Kapp, M. B., ed.
1994   *Patient Self-Determination in Long-Term Care: Implementing the PSDA in Medical
        Decisions.* New York: Springer Publishing Company.

Kapp, M. B., and K. B. Wilson
1995   Assisted Living and Negotiated Risk. *Journal of Ethics Law and Aging* 1
        (1):5–13.

Kari, N., and P. Michels
1991   The Lazarus Project: A Politics of Empowerment. *American Journal of
        Occupational Therapy* 45 (8):719–725.

Karr, K.
1991   *Promises to Keep: The Family's Role in Nursing Home Care.* Buffalo, N.Y.:
        Prometheus Books.

Katz, S.

1996   *Disciplining Old Age: The Formation of Gerontological Knowledge.*
Charlottesville: University Press of Virginia.

Katz, S., A. B. Ford, B. W. Moskowitz, B. A. Jackson, and M. W. Jaffee

1963   Studies of Illness in the Aged—The Index of ADL: A Standardized
Measure of Biological and Psychosocial Function. *Journal of the American
Medical Association* 185:914–919.

Kayser-Jones, J. S.

1981   *Old, Alone, and Neglected: Care of the Aged in Scotland and the United States.*
Berkeley: University of California Press.

1986   Distributive Justice and the Treatment of Acute Illness in Nursing Homes.
Social Science and Medicine 23:1279–1286.

1990a   The Use of Nasogastric Feeding Tubes in Nursing Homes: Patient, Family
and Health Care Provider Perspectives. *The Gerontologist* 30, 469–479.

1990b   *Old, Alone, and Neglected: Care of the Aged in the United States and Scotland*
(with a new epilogue). Berkeley: University of California Press.

1991   The Impact of the Environment on the Quality of Care in Nursing Homes:
A Social-Psychological Perspective. *Holistic Nursing Practice* 5:29–38.

1992   Culture, Environment, and Restraints: A Conceptual Model for Research
and Practice. *Journal of Gerontological Nursing* 18 (11):13–20.

1993   The Cultural Context of Eating in Nursing Homes. In *Recent Advances in
Aging Science: Proceedings of the XVth Congress of the International Association
of Gerontology,* edited by E. Beregi, I. A. Gergely, and K. Rajczi,
pp. 2205–2208. Bologna: Monduzzi Editore.

1993   Influence of the Environment on Falls in Nursing Homes: A Conceptual
Model. In *Advances in Long-Term Care, Volume II,* edited by R. Kane,
M. Mezey, and P. Katz. New York: Springer Publishing.

1994   Health Promotion and Disease Prevention: Eating and Nutritional
Support in Nursing Homes. *Proceedings of the Conference on Health Promotion
and Disease Prevention with Older Adults,* May 5–6, pp. 75-85. Oakland:
University of California at Berkeley.

1995   Decision Making in the Treatment of Acute Illness in Nursing Homes:
Framing the Decision Problem, Treatment Plan, and Outcome. *Medical
Anthropology Quarterly* 9:236–256.

Kayser-Jones, J. S., and M. Kapp

1989   Advocacy for the Mentally Impaired Elderly: A Case Study Analysis.
American Journal of Law and Medicine 14:353–376.

Kayser-Jones, J. S., C. L. Wiener, and J. C. Barbaccia

1989   Factors Contributing to the Hospitalization of Nursing Home Residents.
The Gerontologist. 29:502-510.

Korosec-Serfaty, P.

1985　Experience and Use of the Dwelling. In *Home Environments,* edited by I. Altman and C. M. Werner. New York: Plenum Press.

Koury, L. N., and R. Lubinski

1991　Effective In-Service Training for Staff Working with Communication-Impaired Patients. In *Dementia and Communication,* edited by R. Lubinski. Philadelphia: Decker.

Krech, D., R. C. Crutchfield, and E. L. Ballachey

1962　*Individual in Society: A Textbook of Social Psychology.* New York: Harper and Row.

Krupat, A.

1992　*Ethnocriticism: Ethnography, History, Literature.* Berkeley: University of California Press.

Kuhn, T. S.

1962　*The Structure of Scientific Revolutions.* Chicago: University of Chicago Press.

1970　*The Structure of Scientific Revolutions.* 2nd ed. Chicago: University of Chicago Press.

Laird, C.

1979　*Limbo: A Memoir about Life in a Nursing Home by a Survivor.* Novato, Cal.: Chandler and Sharp.

Lakoff, G., and M. Johnson

1980　*Metaphors We Live By.* Chicago: University of Chicago Press.

Lawton, M. P.

1975　Competence, Environmental Press, and Adaption. In *Theory Development in Environment and Aging,* edited by P. G. Windley, T. O. Byerts, and G. Ernst. Washington, D.C.: Gerontological Society.

Lawton, M. P.

1980　Psychosocial and Environmental Approaches to the Care of Senile Dementia Patients. In *Psychopathology in the Aged,* edited by J. O. Cole and J. E. Barrett. New York: Raven.

Lawton M. P., and L. Nahemow

1973　Ecology and the Aging Process. In *The Psychology of Adult Development and Aging,* edited by C. Eisdorfer and M. P. Lawton. Washington, D.C.: American Psychological Association.

Leach, E.

1976　*Culture and Communication.* Cambridge: Cambridge University Press.

Least-Heat Moon, W.

1991　*PrairyErth.* Boston: Houghton Mifflin.

LeCompte, M. D., and J. P. Goetz
1982   Problems of Reliability and Validity in Ethnographic Research. *Review of Educational Research* 52:31–60.

Lepper, M. H.
1983   The Role of Anthropology in Health Care: An Imperative at the Research and Practice Level. In *Clinical Anthropology,* edited by D. B. Shimkin and P. Gold. New York: University Press of America.

Lidz, C. W., L. Fischer, and R. M. Arnold
1992   *The Erosion of Autonomy in Long-Term Care.* New York: Oxford University Press.

Liebowitz, B. M., M. P. Lawton, and A. Waldman
1979   Evaluation: Designing for Confused Elderly People. *AL4 Journal* (February):59–61.

Linsk, N. L., et al.
1988   Families, Alzheimer's Disease and Nursing Homes. *Journal of Applied Gerontology* 7 (3):331–349.

Litwak, E.
1985   *Helping the Elderly: The Complementary Roles of Informal Networks and Formal Systems.* New York: The Guilford Press.

Lofland, J.
1996   *Social Movement Organizations.* New York: Aldine de Gruyter.

Luborsky, M.
1987   Analysis of Multiple Life Histories. *Ethos* 15:366–381.

Lyman, K. A.
1989   Bringing the Social Back In: A Critique of the Biomedicalization of Dementia. *The Gerontologist* 29: 597–605.

1993   *Day In, Day Out with Alzheimer's: Stress in Caregiving Relationships.* Philadelphia: Temple University Press.

Malmberg, B., and S. H. Zarit
1993   Group Homes for People with Dementia: A Swedish Example. *The Gerontologist* 33:682–686.

Mann, A. H., R. Jenkins, P. S. Cross, and B. J. Gurland
1984   Comparison of the Prescriptions Received by the Elderly in Long-Term Care in New York and London. *Psychological Medicine* 14:891–897.

Marcus, G. E.
1986   Contemporary Problems of Ethnography in the Modern World System. In *Writing Culture: The Poetics and Politics of Ethnography,* edited by J. Clifford and G. E. Marcus. Berkeley: University of California Press.

Maslow, K.

1994a   Current Knowledge about Special Care Units: Findings of a Study by the US Office of Technology Assessment. *Alzheimer's Disease and Associated Disorders* 8 (Supplement 1):S14–S40.

1994b   Current Education, Research, Regulatory, and Reimbursement Issues in Special Care Units. *Alzheimer's Disease and Associated Disorders* 8 (Supplement 1):S424–433.

McCullough, L. B.

1984   Medical Care for Elderly Patients with Diminished Competence: An Ethical Analysis. *Journal of the American Geriatrics Society* 32:150–153.

McFall, S., and B. H. Miller

1992   Caregiver Burden and Nursing Home Admission of Frail Elderly Persons. *Journal of Gerontology: Social Sciences* 47 (2):S73–79.

Mendelson, M. A.

1974   *Tender Loving Greed.* New York: Alfred A. Knopf.

Miller, J. A., and K. B. Wilson

1991   Concepts in Community Living: Assisted Living Program in Portland, Oregon. In *Community-Based Long-Term Care: Innovative Models,* edited by J. A. Miller, pp. 189–201. Newbury Park, Cal.: Sage Publications.

Mitchell, J. B., and H. T. Hewes

1986   Why Won't Physicians Make Nursing Home Visits? *The Gerontologist* 26:650–654.

Mitchell, J. M., and B. J. Kemp

2000   Quality of Life in Assisted Living Homes: A Multidimensional Analysis. *Journal of Gerontology: Psychological Sciences* 55B:P117–P127.

Moller, V.

1995   Research as a Tool for Empowerment. In *Empowering Older People: An International Approach,* edited by D. Thursz, C. Nusberg, and J. Prather. Wesport, Conn.: Auburn House.

Mollica, R. L., K. B. Wilson, B. S. Ryther, and H. J. Lamarche

1995   *Guide to Assisted Living and State Policy.* Minneapolis: University of Minnesota, National Long-Term Care Resource Center.

Monohan, D. J.

1993   Utilization of Dementia-Specific Respite Day Care for Clients and Their Caregivers in a Social Model Program. *Journal of Gerontological Social Work* 20:57–70.

Montgomery, R.

1982   Impact of Institutional Care Policies on Family Integration. *The Gerontologist* 22 (1):54–58.

Moody, Harry R.

1988   Toward a Critical Gerontology: The Contribution of the Humanities to Theories of Aging. In *Emergent Theories of Aging,* edited by J. E. Birren and V. L. Bengtson. New York: Springer Publishing Company.

Moos, R. H.

1980   Specialized Living Environments for Older People: A Conceptual Framework for Evaluation. *Journal of Social Issues* 36 (2):75–96.

Moos, R. H., and S. Lemke

1985   Assessing and Improving Social Ecological Settings. In *Handbook of Social Intervention,* edited by E. Seidman. Beverly Hills, Cal.: Sage Publications.

Morley, J., and J. Flaherty

2002   Putting the "Home" Back in "Nursing Home." *Journal of Gerontology: Medical Sciences* 57A:M419–421.

Morse, J. M.

1989   Strategies for Sampling. In *Qualitative Nursing Research: A Contemporary Dialogue,* edited by J. M. Morse. Rockville, Md.: Aspen.

Morycz, R.

1985   Caregiving Strain and the Desire to Institutionalize Family Members with Alzheimer's Disease. *Research in Aging* 7:329–361.

Moss, F., and V. J. Halamandaris

1977   *Too Old, Too Sick, Too Bad: Nursing Homes in America.* Germantown, Md.: Aspen.

Moss, M., and P. Kurland

1979   Family Visiting with Institutionalized Mentally Impaired Aged. *Journal of Gerontological Social Work* 1:271–278.

Naleppa, M.

1996   Families and Institutionalized Elderly: A Review. *Journal of Gerontological Social Work* 27:87–111.

O'Brien, M. E.

1989   *Anatomy of a Nursing Home: A New View of Residential Life.* Owings Mills, Md.: National Health Publishing.

Office of Technology Assessment

1987   *Losing a Million Minds.* US Government Printing Office.

Ohta, R., and B. Ohta

1988   Special Units for Alzheimer's Disease: A Critical Look. *The Gerontologist* 28 (6):803–808.

Olson, E.

1993   Ethical Issues in the Nursing Home. *The Mount Sinai Journal of Medicine* 60 (6):555–559.

O'Malley, N. C.

1991   Age-Based Rationing of Health Care: A Descriptive Study of Professional Attitudes. *Health Care Management Review* 16 (1):83–93.

Palmer, R. M.

1990   "Failure to Thrive" in the Elderly: Diagnosis and Management. *Geriatrics* 45 (9):47–55.

Pellegrino, E. D.

1993   A Philosophy of Finitude: Ethics and the Humanities in the Allocation of Resources. In *Facing Limits: Ethics and Health Care for the Elderly,* edited by G. A. Winslow and J. R. Walters. Boulder, Col.: Westview Press.

Pelto, P. J.

1970   *Anthropological Research: The Structure of Inquiry.* New York: Harper and Row.

Perkinson, M. A.

1992   Maximizing Personal Efficacy in Older Adults: The Empowerment of Volunteers in a Multipurpose Senior Center. *Physical and Occupational Therapy in Geriatrics* 10 (3):57–72.

1995   Socialization to the Family Caregiving Role within a Continuing Care Retirement Community. *Medical Anthropology* 16 (3):249–268.

1998   Family Roles in Nursing Homes. Final report to the AARP Andrus Foundation.

Peterson-Veach, E., ed.

1995   *Experiencing Place: The Evergreen Project Journal.* Bloomington, Ind.: Bloomington Hospital.

Pillemer, K., C. Hegeman, B. Albright, and C. Henderson

1998   Building Bridges between Families and Nursing Home Staff: The Partners in Care Program. *The Gerontologist* 38 (4):499–503.

Post, S. G.

1993.   Alzheimer's Disease and Physician-Assisted Suicide. *Associated Disorders* 7:65–68.

Pratt, C., et al.

1987   The Forgotten Client: Family Caregivers to Institutionalized Dementia Patients. In *Aging, Health, and Family: Long-Term Care,* edited by T. Brubaker. Newbury Park, Cal.: Sage Publications.

Pratt, G.

1982   The House as an Expression of Social Worlds. In *Housing and Identity,* edited by J. S. Duncan, pp. 135–180. New York: Holmes and Meier Publishers.

Press, I.

1969   Ambiguity and Innovation: Implications for the Genesis of the Culture Broker. *American Anthropologist* 7 (2):205–217.

Randall, P., S. Burkhardt, and J. Kutcher

1990   Exterior Space for Patients with Alzheimer's Disease and Related
        Disorders. *The American Journal of Alzheimer's Care and Related Disorders and
        Research* 5 (July/August):31–37.

Rappaport, J.

1981   In Praise of Paradox: A Social Policy of Empowerment over Prevention.
        American Journal of Community Psychology 9 (1):1–25.

1983   Studies in Empowerment: Steps toward Understanding and Action.
        Prevention in Human Services 3 (213):3.

Ray, R. E.

1996   A Postmodern Perspective on Feminist Gerontology. *The Gerontologist* 36
        (5):674–680.

Regnier, V. A.

1994   *Assisted Living Housing for the Elderly: Design Innovations from the United States
        and Europe.* New York: Van Nostrand Reinhold.

Regnier, V. A., J. Hamilton, and S. Yatabe

1991   *Best Practices in Assisted Living.* Los Angeles: UCLA, Long-Term Care
        National Resource Center.

Retsinas, J.

1986   *It's OK, Mom: The Nursing Home from a Sociological Perspective.* New York: The
        Tiresias Press.

Rodin, J.

1986   Aging and Health: Effects of the Sense of Control. *Science* 233
        (4770):1271–1276.

Ross, J. K.

1977   *Old People, New Lives: Community Creation in a Retirement Residence.* Chicago:
        The University of Chicago Press.

Roth, D., A. Stevens, L. Burgio, and K. Burgio

2002   Timed-Event Sequential Analysis of Agitation in Nursing Home Residents
        during Personal Care Interactions with Nursing Assistants. *Journal of
        Gerontology: Psychological Sciences,* 57B:P461–P468.

Rowles, G. D.

1978   *Prisoners of Space? Exploring the Geographical Experience of Older People.*
        Boulder, Col.: Westview Press.

Rowles, G. D., J. Concotelli, and D. M. High

1996   Community Integration of a Rural Nursing Home. *Journal of Applied
        Gerontology* 15 (2):188–201.

Rowles, G. D., and D. M. High

1996   Individualizing Care: Family Roles in Nursing Home Decision Making.
        Journal of Gerontological Nursing 22 (3):20–25.

Rowles, G. D., and S. Reinharz

1988   Qualitative Gerontology: Themes and Challenges. In *Qualitative Gerontology,* edited by S. Reinharz and G. D. Rowles, pp. 3–33. New York: Springer.

Rubin, A., and G. E. Shuttlesworth

1983   Engaging Families as Support Resources in Nursing Home Care: Ambiguity in the Subdivision of Tasks. *The Gerontologist* 23 (6):632–636.

Rubinstein, R. L., J. C. Kilbride, and S. Nagy

1992   *Elders Living Alone: Frailty and the Perception of Choice.* New York: Aldine de Gruyter.

Ryan, A. A., and H. F. Scullion

2000   Family and Staff Perceptions of the Role of Families in Nursing Homes. *Journal of Advanced Nursing* 32 (3):626–634.

Sand, B., R. Yeaworth, and B. McCabe

1992   Alzheimer's Disease: Special Care Units in Long-Term Care Facilities. *Journal of Gerontological Nursing* (March):28–34.

Sanders, S. R.

1993   *Staying Put: Making a Home in a Restless World.* Boston: Beacon Press.

Sanjek, R.

1990   On Ethnographic Validity. In *Fieldnotes: The Makings of Anthropology,* edited by R. Sanjek. Ithaca, N.Y.: Cornell University Press.

Savishinsky, J. S.

1991   *The Ends of Time: Life and Work in a Nursing Home.* New York: Bergin and Garvey Publishers, Inc.

1995   In and Out of Bounds: The Ethics of Respect in Studying Nursing Homes. In *The Culture of Long Term Care: Nursing Home Ethnography,* edited by J. N. Henderson and M. D. Vesperi, pp. 93–109. Westport, Conn.: Bergin and Garvey Publishers, Inc.

Schatzman, L., and A. Strauss

1973   *Field Research: Strategies for a Natural Sociology.* Englewood Cliffs, N.J.: Prentice-Hall.

Schein, E. H.

1987   *The Clinical Perspective in Fieldwork.* Beverly Hills, Cal.: Sage Publications.

Schneider, E. L., and J. M. Guralnik

1990   The Aging of America: Impact on Health Care Costs. *Journal of the American Medical Association* 263:2335–2340.

Schwab, B., R. E. Drake, and E. M. Burghardt

1988   Health Care of the Chronically Mentally Ill: The Culture Broker Model. *Community Mental Health Journal* 24 (3):174–184.

Schwab, G.

1986   *The Intermediate Area between Life and Death: On Samuel Beckett's* "The Unnamable. Memory and Desire," edited by K. Woodward and M. M. Schwartz. Bloomington: Indiana University Press.

Schwartz, A. N., and M. E. Vogel

1990   Nursing Home Staff and Residents' Families' Role Expectations. *The Gerontologist* 30 (1):49–53.

Senior and Disabled Service Division (SDSD)

1989   *Assisted Living: A Social Model Approach to Services.* Salem: Oregon Senior and Disabled Services Division, Department of Health and Human Services.

Shawler, C., G. D. Rowles, and D. M. High

2001   Analysis of Key Incidents in the Life of a Nursing Home Resident. *The Gerontologist* 41 (5):612–622.

Shibutani, T

1955   Reference Groups as Perspectives. *American Journal of Sociology* 60:562–569.

Shield, R. R.

1988   *Uneasy Endings: Daily Life in an American Nursing Home.* Ithaca, N.Y.: Cornell University Press.

1995   Ethics in the Nursing Home: Cases, Choices, and Issues. In *The Culture of Long Term Care: Nursing Home Ethnography,* edited by. J. N. Henderson and M. D. Vesperi, pp. 111–126. Westport, Conn.: Bergin and Garvey Publishers, Inc.

1996   Managing the Care of Nursing Home Patients: The Challenge of Integration. In *Annual Review of Gerontology and Geriatrics, Vol. 16, 1996. Focus on Managed Care and Quality Assurance: Integrating Acute and Chronic Care,* edited by R. J. Nowcomer and A. M. Wilkinson. New York: Springer Publishing Company.

Silverman, M., and C. McAllister

1995   Continuities and Discontinuities in the Life Course: Experiences of Demented Persons in a Residential Alzheimer's Facility. In *The Culture of Long Term Care: Nursing Home Ethnography,* edited by. J. N. Henderson and M. D. Vesperi, pp. 197–220. Westport, Conn.: Bergin and Garvey Publishers, Inc.

Sloane, P. D., and L. J. Mathew, eds.

1991   *Dementia Units in Long-Term Care.* Baltimore, Md.: Johns Hopkins University Press.

Smith, K. L., and V. Bengtson

1979   Positive Consequences of Institutionalization: Solidarity between Elderly Parents and Their Middle-Aged Children. *The Gerontologist* 19 (5):438–447.

Smith, V. K., and R. Eggleston

1991   Medical versus the Social Model. *Caring* 10:34–37.

Snyder, G.

1990   *The Practice of the Wild.* New York: North Point Press.

Solomon, R.

1983   Serving Families of Institutionalized Aged: The Four Crises. In
        Gerontological Social Work Practice in Long-Term Care, edited by S. Getzel and
        M. Mellor. New York: Hayworth Press.

Stafford, P. B.

1991   The Social Construction of Alzheimer's Disease. In *Biosemiotics: The Semiotic
        Web,* edited by T. A. Sebeok and J. Umiker-Sebeok. Berlin: Mouton de
        Gruyter.

Stein, H. F.

n.d.   Uncomfortable Knowledge: An Ethnographic Clinical Training Model.
        Family Systems Medicine 6:117–128.

1990   *American Medicine as Culture.* Boulder, Col.: Westview Press.

Stephens, M., J. Kinney, and P. Ogrocki

1991   Stressors and Well-Being among Caregivers to Older Adults with
        Dementia: The In-Home versus Nursing Home Experience. *The
        Gerontologist* 31 (21):217–223.

Strahan, B., and B. J. Burns

1991   *Mental Illness in Nursing Homes.* Hyattsville, Md.: National Center for
        Health Statistics.

Strauss, A. L.

1982   Social Worlds and Legitimation Processes. In *Studies in Symbolic Interaction,*
        edited by N. K. Denzin, pp. 171–190. Greenwich, Conn.: JAI Press.

1987   *Qualitative Analysis for Social Scientists.* Cambridge: Cambridge University
        Press.

Strauss, A. L., S. Fagerhaugh, B. Seuzek, and C. Wiener

1985   *The Social Organization of Medical Work.* Chicago: University of Chicago
        Press.

Streim, J. E., and I. R. Katz

1994   Federal Regulations and the Care of Patients with Dementia in the
        Nursing Home. *Medical Clinics of North America* 78:895–909.

Stull, D., J. Cosbey, K. Bowman, and M. McNutt

1997   Institutionalization: A Continuation of Family Care. *The Journal of Applied
        Gerontology* 16:379–402.

Taft, L. B., and M. F. Nehrke

1990   Reminiscence, Life Review, and Ego Integrity in Nursing Home Residents.
        International Journal of Aging and Human Development 30 (3):189–196.

Taira, E. D., ed.

1986   *Therapeutic Interventions for the Person with Dementia.* New York: Haworth.

Thomas, W. H.

1994   *The Eden Alternative: Nature, Hope and Nursing Homes.* Sherburne, N.Y.: Eden Alternative Foundation.

1996   *Life Worth Living: How Someone You Love Can Still Enjoy Life in a Nursing Home.* Acton, Mass.: VanderWyk and Burnham.

Tilse, C.

1997   She Wouldn't Dump Me: The Purpose and Meaning of Visiting a Spouse in Residential Care. *Journal of Family Studies* 3:196–208.

Tobin, S., and R. Kulys

1981   The Family in the Institutionalization of the Elderly. *Journal of Social Issues* 37 (3):145–157.

Tobin, S., and M. Lieberman

1976   *Last Home for the Aged.* San Francisco: Jossey-Bass.

Townsend, A. L.

1990   Nursing Home Care and Family Caregivers' Stress. In *Stress and Coping in Later-Life Families,* edited by M. Parris Stephens, J. Crowther, S. Hobfall, and D. Tennenbaum, pp.267–285. New York: Hemisphere Publishing Corporation.

Tuan, Y.

1977   *Space and Place: The Perspective of Experience.* Minneapolis: University of Minnesota Press.

Tylor, E.

1904   *Anthropology: An Introduction to the Study of Man and Civilization.* New York: Appleton and Co.

US Department of Commerce, Bureau of the Census

1987   An Aging World. In *International Population Reports.* Washington, D.C.: US Government Printing Office.

US Department of Health and Human Services (USDHHS)

1994   *Caring for Frail Elderly People: Policies in Evolution.* Waashington, D. C.: US Government Printing Office.

Van Willigen, J.

1986   Cultural Brokerage. In *Applied Anthropology: An Introduction,* edited by J. Van Willigen. Boston: Bergin and Garvey Publishers, Inc.

Vesperi, M. D.

1983   The Reluctant Consumer: Nursing Home Residents in the Post-Bergman Era. In *Growing Old in Different Societies: Cross-Cultural Perspectives,* edited by J. Sokolovsky, pp. 225–237. Belmont, Cal.: Wadsworth Publishing Co.

1987   The Reluctant Consumer: Nursing Home Reform in the Post-Bergman
           Era. In *Growing Old in Different Societies: Cross-Cultural Perspectives,* edited by
           J. Sokolovsky. Reprint, Littleton, Mass.: Copley.
1995   Nursing Home Research Comes of Age: Toward an Ethnological
           Perspective on Long Term Care. In *The Culture of Long Term Care: Nursing
           Home Ethnography,* edited by J. N. Henderson and M. D. Vesperi. New York:
           Bergin and Garvey Publishers, Inc.

Vladeck, B.
1980   *Unloving Care: The Nursing Home Tragedy.* New York: Basic Books.

Wallace, A. F. C.
1961   The Psychic Unity of Human Groups. In *Theory in Anthropology,* edited by
           R. A. Manners and D. Kaplan. Chicago: Aldine-Atherton.

Wang, F. T. Y.
2002   Contesting Identity of Taiwanese Home-Care Workers: Worker, Daughter,
           and Do-Gooder? *Journal of Aging Studies* 16:37–55.

Weisman, G., U. Cohen, and K. Day
1991   Architectural Planning and Design for Dementia Care Units. In *Specialized
           Dementia Care Units,* edited by D. Coons. Baltimore, Md.: Johns Hopkins
           University Press.

Weschler, R.
1986   Empowering Elderly as Community Leaders: From Dependence to
           Dignity. Paper presented at the annual meeting of the American Society
           on Aging, San Francisco.

Weschler, R., and M. Minkler
1986   A Community-Oriented Approach to Health Promotion: The Tenderloin
           Senior Outreach Project. In *Wellness and Health Promotion for the Elderly,*
           edited by K. Dychtwald and J. MacLean. Rockville, Md.: Aspen Publishers.

Whyte, W. H.
1988   *City: Rediscovering the Center.* New York: Doubleday.

Wiener, C. L., and J. S. Kayser-Jones
1989   Defensive Work in Nursing Homes: Accountability Gone Amok. *Social
           Science and Medicine* 28:37–44.
1990   The Uneasy Fate of Nursing Home Residents: An Organizational-
           Interaction Perspective. *Sociology of Health and Illness* 12 (1):84–104.

Williams, C. C.
1990   Long-Term Care and the Human Spirit. *Generations* (fall):25–28.

Williams, M., G. Doyle, E. Feeney, P. Lenihan, and S. Salisbury
1991   Alzheimer's Unit by Design. *Geriatric Nursing* (January/February):34–36.

REFERENCES

Wilson, K. B.

1990   Assisted Living: The Merger of Housing and Long-Term Care Services. In *Long Term Care Advances* 1:1–8. Durham, N.C.: Duke University Center for the Study of Aging and Human Development.

1991   Concepts in Community Living: Assisted Living Program in Portland, Oregon. In *Community-Based Long-Term Care: Innovative Models*, edited by J. A. Miller. Newbury Park, Cal.: Sage Publications.

1996   *Assisted Living: Reconceptualizing Regulations to Meet Consumers' Needs and Preferences*. Washington, D.C.: American Association of Retired Persons.

Wilson, T. P.

1970   Normative and Interpretive Paradigms in Sociology. In *Understanding Everyday Life*, edited by J. C. Douglas. Chicago: Aldine.

Woodward, K.

1991   *Aging and Its Discontents: Freud and Other Fictions*. Bloomington: Indiana University Press.

Yamamoto-Mitani, N., C. S. Aneshensel, and L. Levy-Storms

2002   Patterns of Family Visiting with Institutionalized Elders: The Case of Dementia. *Journal of Gerontology: Social Sciences* 57B (4):S234–S246.

York, J., and R. J. Calsyn

1977   Family Involvement in Nursing Homes. *The Gerontologist* 17:500–505.

Zarit, S. H., and C. J. Whitlatch

1992   Institutional Placement: Phases of the Transition. *The Gerontologist* 32:665–672.

Zedlewski, S. R., and T. D. McBride

1992   The Changing Profile of the Elderly: Effects on Future Long-Term Care Needs and Financing. *The Millbank Quarterly* 70:247–275.

Zimmerman, S. I., P. Sloane, and J. K. Eckert

2002   *Assisted Living: Needs Practices and Policies in Residential Care for the Elderly*. Baltimore, Md.: Johns Hopkins University Press.

Index

School of American Research
Advanced Seminar Series

PUBLISHED BY SAR PRESS

CHACO & HOHOKAM: PREHISTORIC
REGIONAL SYSTEMS IN THE AMERICAN
SOUTHWEST
  Patricia L. Crown &
  W. James Judge, eds.

RECAPTURING ANTHROPOLOGY:
WORKING IN THE PRESENT
  Richard G. Fox, ed.

WAR IN THE TRIBAL ZONE: EXPANDING
STATES AND INDIGENOUS WARFARE
  R. Brian Ferguson &
  Neil L. Whitehead, eds.

IDEOLOGY AND PRE-COLUMBIAN
CIVILIZATIONS
  Arthur A. Demarest &
  Geoffrey W. Conrad, eds.

DREAMING: ANTHROPOLOGICAL AND
PSYCHOLOGICAL INTERPRETATIONS
  Barbara Tedlock, ed.

HISTORICAL ECOLOGY: CULTURAL
KNOWLEDGE AND CHANGING
LANDSCAPES
  Carole L. Crumley, ed.

THEMES IN SOUTHWEST PREHISTORY
  George J. Gumerman, ed.

MEMORY, HISTORY, AND OPPOSITION
UNDER STATE SOCIALISM
  Rubie S. Watson, ed.

OTHER INTENTIONS: CULTURAL
CONTEXTS AND THE ATTRIBUTION
OF INNER STATES
  Lawrence Rosen, ed.

LAST HUNTERS–FIRST FARMERS: NEW
PERSPECTIVES ON THE PREHISTORIC
TRANSITION TO AGRICULTURE
  T. Douglas Price &
  Anne Birgitte Gebauer, eds.

MAKING ALTERNATIVE HISTORIES:
THE PRACTICE OF ARCHAEOLOGY AND
HISTORY IN NON-WESTERN SETTINGS
  Peter R. Schmidt &
  Thomas C. Patterson, eds.

SENSES OF PLACE
  Steven Feld & Keith H. Basso, eds.

CYBORGS & CITADELS:
ANTHROPOLOGICAL INTERVENTIONS IN
EMERGING SCIENCES AND TECHNOLOGIES
  Gary Lee Downey & Joseph Dumit, eds.

ARCHAIC STATES
  Gary M. Feinman & Joyce Marcus, eds.

CRITICAL ANTHROPOLOGY NOW:
UNEXPECTED CONTEXTS, SHIFTING
CONSTITUENCIES, CHANGING AGENDAS
  George E. Marcus, ed.

THE ORIGINS OF LANGUAGE: WHAT
NONHUMAN PRIMATES CAN TELL US
  Barbara J. King, ed.

REGIMES OF LANGUAGE: IDEOLOGIES,
POLITIES, AND IDENTITIES
  Paul V. Kroskrity, ed.

BIOLOGY, BRAINS, AND BEHAVIOR: THE
EVOLUTION OF HUMAN DEVELOPMENT
  Sue Taylor Parker, Jonas Langer, &
  Michael L. McKinney, eds.

WOMEN & MEN IN THE PREHISPANIC
SOUTHWEST: LABOR, POWER, & PRESTIGE
  Patricia L. Crown, ed.

HISTORY IN PERSON: ENDURING
STRUGGLES, CONTENTIOUS PRACTICE,
INTIMATE IDENTITIES
  Dorothy Holland & Jean Lave, eds.

THE EMPIRE OF THINGS: REGIMES OF
VALUE AND MATERIAL CULTURE
  Fred R. Myers, ed.

PUBLISHED BY UNIVERSITY OF NEW MEXICO PRESS

Participants in the School of American Research advanced seminar "Nursing Home Ethnography," Santa Fe, New Mexico, November 1995. Front row standing: Philip Stafford, Joel Savishinsky, J. Neil Henderson, Haim Hazan, Maria Vesperi, and Renee Shields. Seated from left: Jeanie Kayser-Jones and Margaret Perkinson. Upper back row from left: Graham Rowles and Jaber Gubrium.